Engels, Manchester, and the Working Class

Engels, Manchester, and the Working Class

STEVEN MARCUS

VINTAGE BOOKS
A DIVISION OF RANDOM HOUSE, NEW YORK

FIRST VINTAGE BOOKS EDITION, MARCH 1975

Copyright © 1974 by Steven Marcus

All rights reserved under International and Pan-American
Copyright Conventions. Published in the United States by
Random House, Inc., New York, and simultaneously in Canada
by Random House of Canada Limited, Toronto. Originally
published by Random House, Inc., in 1974.
Jacket photo used by permission of The Mansell Collection,
London.

Library of Congress Cataloging in Publication Data

Marcus, Steven.
  Engels, Manchester, and the working class.

  Bibliography: p.
  1. Engels, Friedrich, 1820–1895. Die Lage der
Arbeitenden Klasse in England. I. Title.
[HD8389.E534 1975]   301.44′42′0942   74–22048
ISBN 0–394–71406–7

Manufactured in the United States of America

To
Lionel Trilling

Acknowledgments

A PART of this study, in different form, has appeared as a chapter in *The Victorian City: Images and Realities* (London, 1973), 2 vols., edited by H. J. Dyos and Michael Wolff. I want to thank both editors for their kindness and cooperation. H. J. Dyos in particular merits a special note of gratitude for tireless encouragement and cajolery.

The last draft of this work was completed at the Center for Advanced Study in the Behavioral Sciences, at Stanford, California. The administration and staff of that institution were most helpful. My thanks go especially to Miriam Gallaher.

Devra Rosenberg has helped me with bibliography and proofs.

A number of friends and colleagues read the manuscript at different stages and offered critical suggestions on a variety of topics. I want to express my thanks to Lillian Hellman, Eugene Genovese, F. W. Dupee and Lionel Trilling for their generosity in this connection. J. P. Bauke read through the manuscript critically with the question of translation in mind and helped me considerably with the rendering of certain passages. My wife, Gertrud Lenzer, made her stalwart energies and intelligence continually available to me, for which as she knows she has my unfailing gratitude.

Preface

THE FOLLOWING STUDY tries to consider a number of things together. First, there is a place: Manchester, the site and center of the first Industrial Revolution, a new kind of city in which the formation of a new kind of human world seemed to be occurring. Second, a relatively brief moment in time, roughly the fifteen years from 1835 to 1850, during which Britain—and Manchester—underwent the first grand crisis of the newly emerging system of social existence, the system known to us historically as industrialism or industrial capitalism. Third, there is a young man, Friedrich Engels, whose fortunes in life had brought him to this place at this time. Engels was in his early twenties when he first arrived in Manchester; he was the son of a prosperous German textile mill-owner, and the purpose of his protracted visit—it lasted twenty months—was to complete his business training in the Manchester cotton mills and offices owned in partnership by his father. In addition, this young foreign businessman was an intellectual (although the term did not yet exist), and a self-taught one to boot; he had not been a university student and had not even completed the course of study in the *Gymnasium* of his native Rhineland town. Such disadvantages, however, did not deter him from holding definite views on a far-flung variety of recondite subjects; and he had already begun to publish essays, articles and journalistic pieces in certain organs of the liberal, democratic, radical and left-wing German-language movements.

The combination of these three elements resulted some two and a half years later in a book, *The Condition of the Working Class in England in 1844.* This effort, Engels' first major publication in a distinguished career that was to continue without interruption for the next half-century, is also the best and most original work that he ever wrote, and the final purpose of the study that follows is its critical examination.

The purpose and terms of the study having been framed, it may be fitting at the outset to direct attention to a number of difficulties. In particular there are the obvious dangers attaching to the fact that the following essay trespasses on certain specialist disciplines and fields of study in which I can claim no professional competence. It touches unavoidably upon such matters as the history of socialism, of Marxist thought and Marxism, and of social theory in general. It fishes perforce in the troubled, not to say polluted, waters of the history and theory of the Industrial Revolution. In the nature of the case, it is compelled to deal with questions that involve the lively interests of urban studies and urban sociology. Finally, it deals with certain problems of nineteenth-century English literature and cultural life and history. It is only in the last of these that I feel qualified to fix critical judgments and render them in their (necessarily) argumentative form. I think it therefore useful to admit at once that this study almost certainly offends on a number of counts, and that historians, social scientists and others will find errors, innocences and crudities of thought that are probably, in the nature of the undertaking, inevitable, apart from whatever mistakes and awkwardnesses might have been avoided. To this it must be added that I was able to find no acceptable alternative in which the first class of error might be automatically eliminated.

At the same time, it would be less than candid of me to deny that the taking up of such difficulties was not, in part, the result of deliberate intention. In this sense the present work may be regarded as part of a continuing experiment; some of its purposes may be described as follows: to ascertain how far literary criticism can help us understand history and society; to see how far the intellectual discipline that begins with the work of close textual analysis can help us understand certain social, historical or theoretical documents. In a previous study (*The Other Victorians*) most of the material I dealt with analytically could be appraised as "bad text," in the sense that its complexities and contradictions were largely unconscious and revealed themselves in the prose as unintended ambiguities, lapses, *non sequiturs* and other less than logical formations. In the present study I have taken a "good text," most of whose complexity is a result of conscious intention, and whose ambiguities, paradoxes and contradictions attach as much to its object as to itself.

If this work succeeds in some measure, it may, perhaps, have some salutary effect on literary criticism or study in its present uneasy state as well. If literary criticism is not to decline further than it already has into aesthetic or political fashionability on the one side and academic stupor on the other, it must—in my judgment—now that its heroic modern period is past, begin to draw with increasing deliberation upon the other cognitive disciplines. For literature and literary criticism are very little if they cannot sustain the claim to cognitive status. Either we take literature seriously in this sense or we don't. If we don't, then we can study and discuss it in a formal or formalistic way—as the arranging of patterns and designs, as a superior form of organized amusement, as a series of language games (all of which have their due place in a full account of the process). If we do, however, then we have to regard literature in ways that are comparable to the ways we regard any of the essential and fundamental human activities, such as language, sexuality or economics, although literature itself may not be ultimately irreducible as these three seem to be. And by the same token we have to regard the study of literature with the same seriousness that we regard the disciplines of study appropriate to those other activities.

This, of course, is no place to argue theoretically the case for literature and the study of literature as modes of knowledge. This

much may be said, however, in brief and in passing. According to
Max Weber's way of thinking, that which is distinctively and
constitutively significant about human activity is that it produces
meaning.[1] Literary criticism, the study of literature, is nothing if
it is not the study of meaning and meanings as they appear
essentially in the forms of literature. It is, in addition, and by
means of its own activity, the creation of further meaning. In
these attributes literature and literary criticism are no different
from other essential human activities and the branches of study
that have grown up around them—both the activity and the
discourse appropriate to it are cognitive and produce meaning.
What is in this context singular and distinctive about literature is
its all-inclusiveness: it draws no abstract line about itself. It
confines itself to no single mode of discourse, but can include as
part of its dramatic discursiveness all other modes of discourse. It
rises to no one series of generalities, uniquely represents experience from that point of view which is inaccessible to final abstract
definition, and yet communicates generalities about that which
cannot be abstractly stated or generally defined. It prototypically
envisages human existence in the concrete, in those individual
instances that cannot be quantified and yet are representative.

It is for such reasons (though not for such reasons alone) that
literary criticism must take note within itself of other cognitive
disciplines and modes of discourse. And it must do so, I suggest,
not in the spirit of the superannuated or extinct "man of letters,"
who was an all-around amateur authority on everything, but in
the spirit and tradition of the critical intellectual, a less immediately attractive, though equally problematical, professional role,
but the only one, in my view, that is currently accessible and
defensible. The standards and expectations thus set for literary
criticism may appear impossible to approximate, let alone attain.

---

[1] This assertion in no way contradicts the theoretical tradition in which Marx and
Engels are to be located. It may indeed be regarded as part of that tradition and as a
latterly developed branch of it which is still subsumed within its major directional
tendencies.

That has nothing to do with the standards themselves—with their truth or relevance or usefulness.

Finally, there is one further difficulty that I should mention. Engels' book was written in German, which is not my native language. On this score, the literary critic has to be an altogether scrupulous witness: his vocation itself is in question. And he is required to acknowledge that no matter how hard he works and how well he knows this second language, he can never achieve the deep, unconscious inwardness with it, can never taste the pith or living vividness or nerve of it as he can with his mother tongue and its literature. Something is bound to be lost, something will get by, some meanings hinted at askance and on the wing will not be taken. Accordingly literary criticism is obliged to call attention to this limitation and to caution the reader of the loss, although it is in the nature of things that what has been lost cannot, at this point, be disclosed.

These perplexities are compounded if the text (or texts) in question happen to be fairly difficult ones—as in this instance they are. And the perplexities are further compounded if the history of their translations has been as uninspiring as the history of the translations of Marx's and Engels' works has generally proved to be. *The Condition of the Working Class in England in 1844* is certainly no exception to this rule. The troubles began almost as soon as Engels learned that the American socialist and reformer Florence Kelley Wischnewetzky was at work on a translation. Following his regular practice with other texts, Engels undertook to prepare a "new preface to the English translation," in which he would "refer as fully as space will permit to the change in the condition of the British working class that has taken place in the interval" of forty years, "to the improved position of a more or less privileged minority, to the certainly not alleviated misery of the great body, and especially to the impending change for worse which must necessarily follow the breakdown of the industrial monopoly of England in consequence of the increasing competition, in the markets of the world, of Continental Europe and especially of America." He

would also make certain additions and add a number of notes that
"link the book with the present day." And he undertook to go
through Mrs. Wischnewetzky's rendering and to revise it where
revision was required. The manuscript of the translation arrived
in London at the beginning of 1886, and shortly thereafter Engels
wrote to a trusted friend that he had in his possession this
manuscript "for revision," and that "some passages . . . will take
some time." Indeed, he goes on, with his habitual personal
modesty, "I can't understand what this person now finds in the
old thing."

In his correspondence with Mrs. Wischnewetzky, Engels
continued to insist upon the historical character of the work, upon
its datedness and specificity. Mrs. Wischnewetzky evidently
wanted to "universalize" the book by changing its title and
dropping the "in 1844." Engels refused to allow the revision: "As
to the title: I cannot omit the 1844, because the omission would
give an entirely false idea of what the reader has to expect. And as
I, by the preface and appendix, take certain responsibility, I
cannot consent to its being left out." There was, however, one
omission that he was willing to urge. The original "dedication to
the English Workingmen should be left out. It has no meaning
today." He is apparently still smarting about how the English
proletariat regularly "disgraced itself" by voting and behaving
against its own best interests.

Engels spent something like a month going over the manuscript of the translation. At first, he noted that Mrs. Wischnewetzky had had as much trouble getting acquainted with "my
peculiar old-fashioned German" as he was having with her
American English. A year later, after many troubles, bitter and
protracted squabbles among the members of the movement in
America (factional shenanigans which at this date seem pointless
to unravel), and frustrating delays in publication, he was less
generous—although he confined his remarks to the ear of a third
party. Mrs. Wischnewetzky, he pertinently snorted, "translates
like a factory"; moreover, he added, she has left "all the real work
to me." On the one hand he is laying claim to and, as it were,

"authorizing" the translation; on the other he is disavowing it.
Anyone who consults that first translation will have no difficulty
in understanding Engels' divided feelings. It is generally lame and
graceless and preserves few of the characteristic vigors and
earthinesses of Engels' prose. But something else is involved in
this matter, which Engels reveals at the end of the letter in which
he returned the revised translation to Mrs. Wischnewetzky.
"The semi-Hegelian language of a good many passages of my old
book," he wrote, "is not only untranslatable but has lost the
greater part of its meaning even in German. I have therefore
modernized it as much as possible." That is certainly one form of
revisionism; and it is just as certainly one way of dealing with
textual difficulties. The reasons that moved Engels to such
considerable, and dubious, editorial measures are extremely
complex and I won't go into them here; the result, however, was
that the translation that has come down to us is additionally
defective in exactly the sense indicated by Engels' "modernizing"
remarks. And when some seventy years later a second translation
in English was published, the outcome was still worse.

For part of the interest today in *The Condition of the Working
Class in England*—I adopt the shorter title purely as a matter of
convenience—lies precisely in the semi-Hegelianisms of "a good
many passages" of that old book. In it we see Engels, and the
idiom of conceptualization he had acquired by cultural inheritance, in a state of passage or transition; the transformation
undergone is, of course, analogous to that wrought and experienced by Marx in his own writings of the same period. In what
follows I have tried to do justice to that which the later Engels
regarded as "untranslatable," and have tried to recover some of
the meaning that, forty years after having written it, he felt had
been lost.[2]

[2] The two major editions are as follows: Karl Marx and Friedrich Engels, *Werke* (Berlin,
1961ff.), hereafter referred to as *Werke*; Karl Marx and Friedrich Engels, *Historisch-
kritische Gesamtausgabe*, ed. D. Rjazanov and V. Adoratskij (Berlin, 1927ff.), hereafter
referred to as *MEGA*. For the letters referred to in this introduction, see *Letters to
Americans*, ed. A. Trachtenberg (New York, 1953), pp. 245, 133, 148, 150, 167, 152,
149, 182, 151.

Contents

Engels, Manchester, and the Working Class

Historical Prologue[*]

All other things being equal, the government under which,
without external aids like naturalization and immigration,
the citizens increase and multiply most, is infallibly the best
government. That under which the people diminishes and
wastes away is the worst. Statisticians, this is your problem:
count, measure, compare.
—Jean-Jacques Rousseau, *The Social Contract*,
Book III, Chapter 9

MANCHESTER, the virtual if not the nominal capital city of the
county of Lancashire, is located some two hundred miles to
the northwest of London. It is about thirty miles from Liverpool,
the chief port on the western coast of Britain. During the first
half—and perhaps more—of the nineteenth century it was, after
London, the most important city in England in almost every
sense; it was certainly the most sensational. Manchester could be,
and was, pointed to as the living embodiment of what was
happening in and to the modern world. It was the principal site of
what was rapidly coming to be thought of as the Industrial
Revolution, and was widely regarded as the ur-scene, concentrated specimen, and paradigm of what such a revolution was
portending both for good and bad.

*Professional historians will recognize at once the sources from which this account is
drawn. They are the unavoidable ones.

Although there is no one place designated as a starting point for an account of how things had gotten to where they were, historians nowadays tend to begin by calling attention to the schedules, rates, and indices of demography. In this as in so much else Manchester has to be regarded as undergoing a development that was typical for many other centers of change in England, and for England as a whole. Sometime in the middle of the eighteenth century, an unprecedented growth in population began to occur; the reasons for this sudden surge remain complex and obscure, but what had been an almost static or stagnant population in England and Wales, estimated at between 5.8 and 6 million people for the years 1700–1740, suddenly began to increase, and at increasing rates. By 1780 the population was about 7.5 million; by 1801, the year of the first census, it had grown to about 9 million; fifty years later the population had doubled to 18 million. The rates of increase followed a similar course, rising from an estimated 3.5 percent for the decade 1741–1751, to about 7 percent for 1751–1771, to 10–11 percent for the following twenty years, and continuing their rise to a peak of 16 percent for the decade 1811–1821.

Much of this phenomenal growth was concentrated in the towns, and Manchester was a representative instance. In 1773 the township was estimated to contain 24,000 people; the first census in 1801 listed a figure of 70,000. By 1831 this had doubled to 142,000; 1841 posted a figure of 217,000; and in 1851 the population stood at 250,409. The highest rate of growth was reached in the decade 1821–1831, when Manchester's population increased by almost 45 percent; and the rate in its twin community, Salford, on the other side of the Irwell, was for that same ten-year period even higher, 55.9 percent. By the middle of the 1840's, if one took the conurbation of Manchester-Salford and the built-up areas contiguous to it, one had an essentially unbroken urban space containing upwards of 400,000 people. The dates are significant as well, for what was additionally revealed in the census of 1851 was that slightly more than 50 percent of the population of Great Britain was now constituted of city dwellers, the passage of a historic and, for the foreseeable future, probably irreversible point of development.

This population was stratified in a number of ways. The chief of these was economic. Of all the towns in its district, Manchester had the largest middle class, since it was a commercial and financial as well as an industrial center. One estimate for the mid-1830's judged that 64 percent of Manchester's population were working-class wage earners; Salford was estimated to have 74 percent; and outlying industrial towns went up to 90 percent. Another line of demarcation had to do with the national origins of part of that working-class population; in 1840 about 20 percent of Manchester's working class were Irish, typically employed at the bottom of the heap, or underemployed, or unemployed—and living in circumstances that corresponded to their place in the economic scale of things. A third distinction had to do with industrial occupation. The cotton industry dominated Manchester, and one estimate held that about 30 percent of the town was directly engaged in the production of cottons.

This phenomenal development had been as unforeseen, unplanned and unregulated as it was unexampled and apparently unaccountable. As a result of a number of those peculiarities out of which social history is made, Manchester had almost no local government to speak of, and what little there was had almost no pertinence or meaning to the modern world. For more than five hundred years Manchester had remained as a manor, and was in one part of its legal existence "governed" more or less as a feudal estate, or personal holding—which meant in effect that it did not go through a legal evolution, into a municipality with municipal institutions, which corresponded in any real sense to its actual evolution, into an unmistakable super-modern urban center. It was neither a corporate town nor a town returning burgesses to Parliament—neither, that is to say, a municipal borough nor a parliamentary borough. Its judicial-administrative structure was utterly archaic: the Court Leet or heritable manorial court—with

its officers of boroughreeve, Constables, etc.—remained essentially intact and in the hands of a traditional, compact Anglican
Tory oligarchy until the middle of the nineteenth century.
Although local government was supplemented in the late eighteenth century by the institution of a number of Police Commissioners, there was no adequate police or policing (in the extended
sense of the term), and there was little machinery for providing
the expanding town with what it most needed, modern forms of
administrative organization. Not until the reforms of the 1830's
did things begin substantially to change; yet by then Manchester
had long since become one of the most famous and wealthy places
in the world, even though it did not have the right to run itself as
a city. As a result of the Reform Act of 1832, Manchester for the
first time became a borough returning two members to Parliament, Salford also returning one member of its own. In 1835 the
Municipal Corporations Act permitted the beginnings of substantive urban administrative reorganization, and in 1838 Manchester
was at last incorporated. The first Borough Council—of Mayor,
Alderman and Councillors—met in that year, and during the
1840's large-scale local reforms of police, sanitation, and other
administrative institutions began. Finally, in 1845, the town itself
bought up the manorial rights from the Mosley family for the sum
of £200,000, emancipating itself yet further into the ardors of
self-government.[1] Such symbolic status was additionally en-
hanced in 1847 when Manchester was granted a bishopric, and
this led in turn to its becoming at last in 1853 a city, a legal term
reserved in England for incorporated towns that are or have been
a bishop's see.

[1] £200,000 is the figure traditionally if not altogether precisely given. Under the terms
of the agreement, £5,000 was paid down as a deposit. The balance was subject to a yearly
interest at the rate of 3¾ percent and was to be liquidated in annual payments varying
from £4,000 to £6,000 at the option of the Corporation. If we calculate that the sinking
fund was diminished at the highest possible rate, in thirty-two and one half years the
principal of £200,000 would have been paid off along with £122,484 in interest. The
lowest possible rate would have taken forty-eight and three quarters years, and the interest
payments would have amounted to almost £182,000, in effect almost doubling the
purchase price.

Paradoxically, it was these absurd and archaic institutional structures that had permitted, at least in part, the development in Manchester of the newest, most free and most modern kind of industrial economy. For it was precisely the absence of the monopoly privileges and prescriptive rights exercised by the more "advanced" medieval city corporations and their associated burgesses that allowed or stimulated the growth of new commercial and industrial communities in areas beyond the confines of the traditional "city economy." There, and elsewhere in England, a series of interlocking and mutually enhancing changes and developments, beginning at various points in the past, but noticeably accelerating after 1780, produced that Industrial Revolution which seems to be the only really permanent revolution. The process is too well known to need and too complex to allow anything but the most summary of glances. Changes in colonial holdings and trade fed into a rapidly opening and expanding market economy, which fed back in turn into the system of foreign trade. Both of these were connected with changes in agriculture: with the beginnings of a new agricultural technology, with changes in land tenure such as enclosures and consolidation of holdings, and with the increasing capitalization of a farming economy in which, for the first time in European history, the peasant had disappeared. Such developments naturally had their resonance in the demographic upheaval already mentioned: everything was beginning to move toward lift-off. There were also coinciding and reinforcing developments in commerce and finance, and in the systems of transportation, that were by no means negligible. Yet the place in which the entire process broke loose into open visibility, the locus of revolutionary change, accelerated growth and ever increasing direct and subsidiary demand, as a world market for the mass production of goods for mass consumption was first brought into being, was one industry —cotton. And cotton meant Manchester.

Cotton also meant overseas trade, since in contrast to the older dominant textile industry of wool, the raw material could not be grown at home. At first cotton was imported from India in two forms: as raw yarn to be combined with flax to make fustian, the preindustrial predecessor of modern cheap cotton goods; and as woven calicoes which were also to be replaced by machine-made cloth. It meant overseas trade as well, in the sense that at the next stage of the process it was inseparably connected with the African slave trade and the slave plantations of the West Indies; these plantations became for a while the chief suppliers of the raw material, and after 1790 it was the slave states of the American South that became the major producers for Lancashire's mills. They were important consumers as well, as were the other "underdeveloped" parts of the world. Indeed, the market for a time seemed limitless—particularly since for part of the period England had a virtual monopoly not only on the means of production but over trade in large areas of the world. Under such conditions, and with the additional circumstance that the new technologies in cotton were relatively inexpensive and thus did not require heavy outlay in original capital investment, the rates of profit were astronomical and were only equaled by the rates of growth in production. By the middle of the century billions of yards of cotton cloth were being produced each year. As a final historical irony, India, the original supplier and manufacturer of the material, was methodically de-industrialized and became in turn one of the great overseas markets for Lancashire's "new" cloths.[2]

The new inventions that pushed the cotton industry into revolution were relatively simple; a number of them were contrived in the vicinity of Manchester itself. The two major

[2] In 1853, for example, cotton goods to the value of £5,680,069 were exported to India. Other comparable figures are £4,182,901 to the United States, almost £3,500,000 to various German-speaking territories on the Continent, £1,288,366 to Brazil, and over £1,000,000 each to China and Australia. The total figures for cotton during that year were estimated at £54,000,000 of which £21,000,000 were consumed in Great Britain and Ireland and about £33,000,000 were exported. The combined figure represents approximately half the cotton industry of the world.

operations into which the manufacture of cotton can be divided
are spinning and weaving (for the sake of simplicity, two others,
carding and printing, are overlooked here). In the middle of the
eighteenth century handloom weaving was more efficient than
hand spinning—and the adoption of the flying shuttle kept it so
for some years longer. The first great innovations occurred in
spinning, and their homely names—the spinning jenny and the
mule, for instance—suggest the modesty of their origins. The
mechanization of spinning increased the production of yarn
stupendously, and as a result toward the end of the eighteenth
century there was a large demand for handloom weavers.
Handloom weaving still largely went on under the domestic or
putting-out system of production; it could be pursued at home, at
the workingman's own pace, within the rhythms of the traditional
organization of domestic economy, and it paid well besides. The
fate of the handloom weavers in the decades that followed 1815,
when power looms came inevitably to displace them, is one of the
most famous, as well as one of the earliest, of technological horror
stories. Before that, however, it was in spinning that the drama
was to be observed. With the increased mechanization of the
spinning processes, the work of spinning was further rationalized
by having the machines driven by mechanical rather than human
power. Water power was first utilized, but with the invention of
the steam engine, everything was lifted up in scale again.
Although James Watt took out his patent in 1769, it was in 1784
that he perfected the first rotary steam engine, and so gave to the
modern world its most important single invention—a mechanical
and thus controllable source of what was for practical purposes
limitless power. This power, a central source of mechanical
energy, brought men together around it, ran machines attached to
it at a uniform speed, integrated the activities of the spinners who
tended the machines, and made them into part of the larger
complex machine itself. These immense cotton spinning factories
or mills of the late eighteenth century were something new in the
world. After 1815 weaving was increasingly brought into

factories as well, and within a short time cotton became the first industry in which production was wholly mechanized. The next step was to adapt the men, women and children who worked at the machines to the unvarying requirements of those instruments; and this too was achieved, although the adaptors ran into some resistance on the part of the adaptees. By the mid-1830's it was estimated that about a million and a half people were directly and indirectly dependent on employment in the production of cotton. Out of those at work in the factories themselves, almost half were women and nearly 15 percent were children under fourteen. The census of 1851 revealed that the number of men and women who worked as domestic servants was twice as large as the number of those who worked directly in cotton. Yet it was cotton that, along with agriculture, dominated the national economy.[3] That domination was expressed in various other figures, one of them, for example, showing that by the 1830's the cotton industry was producing nearly one half of all British exports.

The historical experience of industrialization is not to be separated from that of urbanization. The two tended to occur together and reinforce one another, the reciprocating effects of each upon the other being further intensified by the demographic escalation that continued throughout the period. All three were riding the same exponential curve. The industrial disciplines, the conditions of work, terms of employment, continual insecurity and continual competition are not to be segregated, in their effects as formative experiences, from the conditions of living in the new industrial towns, from the housing, sanitary provisions— or lack of them—institutions of relief or welfare—or lack of them—from all the new densities and stresses of existence in these unparalleled circumstances. The working men and women who came out at the other end of this process were the first to go

---

[3] The 1851 figures for Great Britain revealed that about 1,800,000 males and females were engaged in agriculture and over 1,000,000 were employed as domestic servants. About 525,000 were employed in working cotton and another half-million in other textiles such as wool, silk and linen.

through what we now understand as a world-historical experience. As a group they bore the marks of survivors; they bear
those marks to this very day.

It is not to be imagined that all this was taking place in some
remote urban-industrial Lancashire vacuum. It was, to say the
least, a period of lively activity. The first half of it comes to an
end in 1815 and is overshadowed by the French Revolution and
the Napoleonic Wars. The second half, which closes somewhere
around 1848 or shortly thereafter is a period of unprecedented
social change and social crisis in modern British history. Unrest
was widespread and was thought by many to be nearing
revolutionary proportions. It rose from many sources, manifested
itself in a variety of movements and activities and was dealt with,
or not, in a multitude of responses and adaptations. I can only
touch most briefly on a few of these.

One of the chief preconditions for all such movements was the
state of the national economy itself. After a period of rigorous
deflationary "readjustment" following the cessation of international hostilities, the economy entered upon a series of what were
later to be understood as general cyclical movements occurring
with what appeared to be periodic regularity: throes of boom
were followed by convulsions of bust. The intervals of deepest
depression and economic crisis were 1825–1826, 1836–1837,
1839–1842, 1846–1848. The question of whether these murderous yo-yo-like ups and downs were either aberrancies of a
self-acting, self-regulating system, or altogether alien to it and
caused by outside and accidental influences, or whether they
were integral to the workings of such an economy at this stage in
its development, began, as the period moved on, to surface as a
subject for argument.

Although the attention of the nation as a whole—by which one
must essentially mean those in command of power—was before
1815 chiefly directed upon international events and war, this does
not mean that all internal agitation and protest disappeared. The

character of such activity, however, was continually shifting, as the example of turbulent Manchester readily demonstrates. At the beginning of the French Revolution, radicalism in Manchester was most prominently associated with a group of middle-class Dissenting manufacturers who led an agitation for repeal of the Test and Corporation Acts, which discriminated against them on religious grounds, and for parliamentary reform. They also formed the Manchester Constitutional Society, which supported the Paris Jacobins—by sending greetings to them. Chief among these reformers was Thomas Walker (radical, manufacturer, but Churchman rather than Dissenter) who brought out Part I of Thomas Paine's *Rights of Man* in 1791. All this was too much for the ruling Anglican Tories, who formed a rival Church and King Club and in December 1792 raised a "loyal" Manchester mob to stone the offices of the *Manchester Herald,* the reformers' newspaper, and to attack the house of Walker himself. The point to be noticed here is that at this juncture popular sentiment was on the side of the traditional ruling group and could be enlisted to act in traditional ways in its behalf. When war was declared against France in 1793, popular support for it was spontaneous and enthusiastic. By 1795, however, the dislocating effects of the war upon economic conditions began to be felt in rising prices, selectively falling wages, and hunger. Food riots broke out in 1797 and 1799, and from this time forward there was a steady stream of industrial protest from among the distressed working people and a gradual shifting of popular opinion toward political reform.

On the other side, government and the upper and middle classes in general were intensely fearful of English Jacobinism in any form and had more or less declared a moratorium on reform for the duration (which endured in the event for forty years). In 1799 and 1800 Combination Acts were passed prohibiting trade unions in any form in all industries (earlier in the eighteenth century particular industries had been singled out for prohibition). Although the working people of Britain, including the then relatively small group of factory workers, were certainly not yet organized as a class and even more certainly did not consciously think of themselves as a class—with everything that such an identification implies—the statutes themselves were a significant straw in the wind. Moreover, many working people tended not to get the message, and both illegal combinations and various subterfuges were resorted to.[4] In 1810 in Manchester the first great strike of factory workers took place; several thousand cotton spinners walked out in a concerted effort, and organized their activities on remarkably modern lines—weekly strike pay, for example, was raised and distributed. And from 1811 to 1813— and in minor outbursts for three or four more years—framework knitters in the midlands, woolen croppers in the West Riding of Yorkshire, and handloom weavers in Lancashire rose up in riot to break the new machines that were being installed by forward-looking masters to produce cheaper cloths more efficiently. This epidemic of violence against property was responded to with due savagery by legally constituted authority, and, their criminal phase of existence having come to an end, the Luddite Riots, as they were called, passed into history where they persisted as a cardinal illustration of useless and purely expressive irrationality on the part of men who were unable to understand the superior rationality by which, for example, they were to be replaced by machines. Recent research, however, has suggested quite persuasively that they were much more than this: that their irrationality was irrational only on certain assumptions; that they were connected with a native radical tradition (which had largely gone underground after the 1790's) as much as they were with the older communal economy that was rapidly going into extinction; that they were consciously organized movements of protest with filiations both with an old tradition of machine-breaking and riot

---

[4] Under such circumstances of proscription, these primitive trade unions would disguise themselves as sick clubs and benefit societies and would use public houses as fronts for their meetings.

and with the still-to-be-born and as yet prohibited trade unions.

With the war over in 1815, social problems and economic distress came to the forefront of consciousness, and reform was put back on the national agenda. Parliamentary reform, in fact, was widely held to be the one answer to all problems, and a great agitation of propaganda, action, meetings, petitions, clubs and societies broke out in all parts of the country. The leaders of the movement for reform tended to be middle class; the muscle was supplied by working people, rural weavers as well as urban factory hands or artisans in workshops. Manchester, the capital of industry, was also a capital of dissent, dissidence and disturbance —though unlike Birmingham, its radicalism tended to be separated into distinct working-class and middle-class groups. Two incidents from those years may be touched upon. In March 1817, a large body of men—most of them weavers—set off to walk from Manchester to London; each man carried a blanket and a petition (the petition concerned other grievances than Reform). Word got to London that the entire laboring population of Lancashire and Yorkshire were erupting southward, bent on general and bloody insurrection. The marchers were quickly dispersed by dragoons, their leaders jailed. In 1819, after a bad harvest the year before, the campaign for reform came to one of its many climaxes. On August 16, a mass meeting was held in St. Peter's Fields in Manchester. Henry Hunt, leader of the campaign for reform, began to address a gathering of some sixty thousand people. The local magistrates ordered the local mounted yeomanry in to arrest Hunt; regular mounted troops were sent in to extricate the yeomen. The foreseeable promptly took place: panic set in, accompanied by violence and brutality, and when the dust cleared eleven of the crowd were dead and hundreds injured. The massacre was at once known as Peterloo. It would be forever associated with Manchester, with the growth of working-class consciousness, as one of the great dramatic renderings of class hatred.[5] It provoked an immense uproar of protest

---

[5] An imperishable moment. An officer of the Hussars called out to the yeomanry—i.e.,

and outraged indignation—which in itself came to very little, yet was never to be forgotten. It is about as close to unadorned class warfare as England was to get, and polarized Manchester was the appropriate place for it to have occurred.

And so it went. We cannot recount the expanding and contracting yearly course of the enormous campaign which finally led in 1832, amid commotions of nearly revolutionary intensity, to the passage of the Reform Act.[6] Perhaps a generalization may be hazarded. The great drawn-out movement may be regarded as in its own very English way a partial analogue of the first phases of the French Revolution. The middle class (in France, the Third Estate or bourgeoisie) speaking out for the nation and regarding and representing its peculiar interests as the interest of the universal whole managed to call out large enough masses of the disenfranchised "lower orders" to demonstrate on its behalf. What such a demonstration, providing it is large and continuous enough, always provokes is the threat of a crisis of legitimacy. The crisis was averted, the Constitution reformed, and the middle classes began to be enfranchised. Began to be, not were. Political power remained in the hands of the traditional aristocratic and landowning interests, who also retained for quite some time their monopoly of high political offices, posts and influence. But the middle classes had been let in in good time. As for the lower groups who had worked for a wider suffrage and who had looked forward to reform with expectations or fantasies of social redemption, their elation soon turned to disappointment, to apathy, to despair, and finally to other forms of social action.

On any account, the 1830's are a decade of critical importance. The decade began, symbolically one might say, with a revolution

---

Manchester owners, shopkeepers, members of the middle classes—who were cutting away with their swords at the people who were wedged tightly together: "For shame, gentlemen; what are you about? The people cannot get away."

[6] In 1829 the Roman Catholic Relief Act was passed, emancipating Roman Catholics from such civil disabilities as exclusion from all government positions and membership in Parliament.

in France and the opening of the first passenger railway, between, naturally, Manchester and Liverpool. In cotton a falling margin of profit created technical problems for the manufacturers (who did not cease to enrich themselves) and further misery for those who were already miserable enough: reduction in wages to sub-subsistence level, increased competition for work, short-time employment, and unemployment. It was, in addition to the Reform Act of 1832, a period of famous and infamous legislation. The chief infamy occurred in 1834 with the passage into law of the Poor Law Reform Act (the New Poor Law), without doubt one of the most despised and hated pieces of lawmaking in the entire history of England. The law was as modern, up-to-date and socially scientific as Jeremy Bentham himself could have wished for (Bentham was not around to savor this first fine fruit of his lifelong labors, having passed to his just reward in 1832). It provided England with a new model of administrative machinery —centralized decision-making on substantive issues of policy, professionalized civil servants, bureaucratic rationality. Its theoretical foundation was equally unimpeachable, being nothing other than a natural law in the Malthusian subsystem of Political Economy. Thus armed with science, Edwin Chadwick, James Kay (later Kay-Shuttleworth), and their associates went forth to set the poor in order—i.e., to deal with, if not to "solve," the problem of poverty. In essence, what they did was to create the first recognizably modern welfare system. The most rational and efficient policy would have been simply to abolish the poor, who were "redundant" anyway. Since taboos rendered this course impracticable, the reformers resorted to Bentham's binaries— maximization of pleasure and minimization of pain—whereupon the print-out delivered to them the principle of "less eligibility." It was now necessary to enter the workhouse to be eligible for relief, and conditions there were to be made so miserable, so repellent, so harsh, so unpleasant, so punitive that the destitute poor would be likely to choose any kind of existence on the outside rather than seek relief within. If there seems today to be a touch of insanity in such proceedings it is to be ascribed not to the individual persons who were involved but in the way they had chosen to conceive of the questions at stake. Putting to one side the native ruffian brutality that had not yet been "Victorianized" out of these middle-class reformers, we can see that the structure imposed by them upon this immense problem—and hence the structure of their "solution" to it—was purely that of formal, economic rationality: the English poor were to have the privilege of being the first group whose humanity was cost-accounted. The response to this scheme among the industrial working class, particularly in the industrial North, was anger of epic intensity and a concerted movement of resistance. It brought forth *Oliver Twist* as well,[7] and there were other critics and sympathizers among the middle and upper classes. But on the whole this piece of class legislation was responded to along class lines.

Not all the new laws were so tainted. In 1833, coming after years of mass agitation, endless ideological skirmishes and parliamentary maneuvering, a Factory Act was passed. Minimal as its provisions were, it was the first *effective* step taken to limit and regulate conditions of work in the textile industry.[8] In 1835, the Municipal Corporations Act, mentioned earlier, provided for modernization of urban government. Other activities which did not issue in legislation may also be mentioned. In 1789, a young Welshman named Robert Owen borrowed £100 and went into the cotton manufacturing business in Manchester. In 1800, he moved to New Lanark near Glasgow to take over the running of

---

[7] It was both characteristic of Bentham and exemplary of some of the things he stood for that he should have expended a great deal of ingenuity in trying to estimate the net value of children, or the "non-aged," as a group. His way of framing what was for him a conundrum is itself informing: What was the value of an average child; was he worth more or less than nothing?

[8] Earlier Factory Acts in 1802, 1819, 1825 and 1831 had been entered in the statute books, but these were very limited in scope and so ineffective in operation (largely because they failed to make workable provisions for inspection and enforcement) as to be dead letters.

a cotton mill there. Within ten years he had made himself a fortune, and while he was doing so, created and conducted a utopian experiment in his industrial village. Owen had what he called "a new view of society," which was also "a new moral world." Instead of being controlled by competition and the rules of the market, the new society would be informed by the principles of community and cooperation. Paternalistic himself, Owen was nonetheless the first important socialist figure in Britain. By the 1820's the vision that Owen broadcast with such tireless confidence had begun to have results, at least among the working people; pamphlets, papers and other publications began to see the light of day; classes for debate, disputation and propaganda were widely held; small clubs, organizations and societies sprang up. There were even attempts at setting up communities and cooperatives. Although each of these activities might have been minuscule in size and abortive in immediate effect, it was out of such undertakings that the English working class continued to form its consciousness.

Much of the energy from these activities fed into the nascent trade unions, which after the repeal in the mid-1820's of the Combination Acts were legally free to continue operations in the open. The movement was further charged with the anger and disillusionment that followed the realization that the reform of 1832 was not going to lead to anything like working-class enfranchisement, let alone minimum wages or relief of economic distress. Most of the early unions were very small and very weak; they were mostly local and often badly led. They were the object of unremitting execration on the part of the largest majority of owners, who organized their strongest efforts against the new organizers. In the early years these efforts were more successful than not, but the resilience of the organizers after every defeat was a genuine portent. There were also by the early 1830's several large-scale industrial organizations in Lancashire and Yorkshire particularly, and matters took fire when Robert Owen proposed that all the workingmen in England be organized into a single union under socialist leadership. On a day to be decided upon, a general strike would be called, the means of production would be peacefully taken over, and the new world would begin. The Grand National Consolidated Trades Union under Owen's leadership flourished during the early months of 1834 and then suddenly collapsed. The government prosecuted and transported to Australia for seven years six Dorsetshire laborers for trying to organize a union; the crime they were found guilty of was administering illegal oaths. The Tolpuddle martyrs, as they were called, made it clear that it wasn't the industrial owners alone who were resolute upon the repression of working-class organization. By June of 1834 the Grand National had passed into oblivion.

Yet the irrepressible human need for action and for justice soon asserted itself again. All the movements and agitations touched upon in the foregoing discussion—the resistance to the New Poor Law, the campaign for factory reform and a shorter working day, the cooperative and trades union associations—were all brought together and caught up in the first great historical movement of the British working class, the phenomenon known as Chartism. One of its major centers was Manchester. But before turning to Chartist activities as they were exemplified in Manchester, I want to mention very briefly another large-scale political agitation that shared the scene with Chartism during the 1830's and 1840's. This was the industrial middle class's equivalent to Chartism; its exclusive center was Manchester; and it ended in a dramatic success. I am referring to the Anti-Corn Law League.

The first Corn Law was passed in 1815 and was a protectionist measure in the interest of landowners and farmers. It was designed so that foreign grains (particularly wheat) could enter the British market only when the domestic price of grain had risen above a certain level. In other words, it seemed, theoretically, to ensure an artificially high cost of living imposed by the politically dominant landed interests on the urban and industrial middle classes and the masses of working people. The law was modified in 1822 and again in 1828, this time providing sliding

scales but still retaining the principle of protection. Although
these laws were never exactly popular, intensive resistance did
not begin until the late 1830's when depression and bad harvests
pressed upon middle and working classes alike. A group of
middle-class radicals formed the Manchester Anti-Corn Law
Association in 1838; in 1839 this became the Anti-Corn Law
League, whose aim was repeal of the laws in the name of free
trade and prosperity. The campaign, once launched, soon became
a national issue, and remained identified with Manchester and its
mystique even after League headquarters was moved to London.
Immense campaign funds were raised (in the beginning almost
entirely from Manchester), an enormous work of printing
propaganda was organized (including, inevitably, a newspaper),
great meetings were held throughout the country addressed by
League speakers, who referred to the movement in impassioned
religious terms. (Manchester was a center of Nonconformity;
"Free trade is Jesus Christ" is an actual slogan of the time.)[9]
Manchester's business leaders, with their rough and ready sense
of class interest, did not scruple to make the issue of class conflict
work for them in their opposition to aristocracy; some even flirted
with the idea of a shutdown of their factories to move the
working classes into outright rebellion. This did not prove
necessary, and the great crusade ended in tumultuous scenes of
triumph with the passage of repeal in 1846 by a government
headed by Robert Peel. At least two of the leaders of the
Anti-Corn Law campaign, Richard Cobden and John Bright,
were catapulted onto the stage of national celebrity as a result of
their efforts. The outcome was understood on all sides to be a
famous victory.

No such success was to accompany Chartism at any phase of its
existence, nor can it be so succinctly described. Apart from its

[9] To go along with another famous epigram from the Manchester of the period:
"Adulteration of food was only a form of competition." The two were combined in yet a
third vintage Mancunianism. At one vestry meeting, John Edward Taylor, Unitarian,
manufacturer, and first editor of the *Manchester Guardian*, argued that religion ought to be
a "marketable commodity."

importance, the one thing that most historians are agreed upon is its diverse and contradictory character and a complexity of composition that makes it very difficult to describe with both conciseness and precision. To begin with, it was not a single movement but a series of varying working-class protests whose aims were often exclusive of one another. Its leadership was equally diverse, and indeed Chartist activities tended to be locally specific and directed toward local ends. Yet it was also a national mass movement, the first of its kind anywhere. At the same time its official ideological program was taken from the movements for parliamentary reform of the late eighteenth century, and were, overtly, purely political in aim. "The People's Charter" had "Six Points": universal manhood suffrage, payment of members of Parliament, secret ballot, annual elections, equal electoral districts, abolition of the property qualification for membership in the House of Commons. The exclusively political goals corresponded to the organizational origins of the Charter. In the wake of 1832, radicals who had worked for reform but who had been left disenfranchised by the limited nature of the new electoral arrangements went back to work. In London, William Lovett, a self-educated skilled artisan, began organizing the London Working Men's Association, and sought support in a constituency to be largely composed of craftsmen and artisans from the upper levels of the working class. In Birmingham, Thomas Attwood brought back to life the Birmingham Political Union, which had worked for reform until 1832. The BPU had been an organization whose membership had been mixed—both middle and working class—in accordance with the mixed (rather than polarized) social and economic structure of Birmingham: industry there tended typically to be organized in small workshops rather than in the vast factories of Manchester. The revived BPU still included middle-class members, but from a lower stratum of that class: smaller masters and professional men. When Lovett, with the aid of Francis Place, drew up the Charter in May 1838, Attwood came in and began work upon a plan for a national petition in favor of the Charter, this petition to be brought before Parliament after a "People's Convention" had been convened in London.

The third large part of the Chartists was more heterogeneous in both membership and leadership and was certainly not neatly organized when it was organized at all. Its constituency was essentially the industrial working class both new and old—those who were both employed and unemployed by new industries, those who were both being fed and starved by the new industrial system: spinners and handloom weavers, miners and framework knitters. Its power was largely in the provinces and largely in the North. Its leaders, not nearly so "respectable" as Lovett and Attwood, included such figures as the Tory, Richard Oastler, chief agitator in the North against the New Poor Law; the radical one-time Methodist minister, J. R. Stephen; George Julian Harney, militant leader of the London Democratic Association, which, split off from the London Working Men's Association, sought to organize that part of the working class ignored by Lovett; James Bronterre O'Brien, Jacobin socialist and editor of *The Northern Star,* the Chartist national newspaper and organ of its most aggressive wing. Chief among these was another radical Irishman, Feargus O'Connor, famous orator, tireless agitator, gifted demagogue. He took to the North and to the workers in the industrial districts, becoming the chief spokesman for their deep and terrible discontents—which he expressed not in his speeches alone but through *The Northern Star*, his mouthpiece in print. Such men made up the loosely connected left wing of Chartism that did not hesitate to speak in public of physical force—or the *threat* of physical force—as opposed to those other milder Chartists who spoke of "moral force" (although the radical Chartist slogan, "Peaceably if we may, forcibly if we must," suggests a continuous range of altering opinions rather than strictly defined categories of yes and no).[10] Such distinctions also

---

[10] They were by no means alone in this tactic. Even such a constitutionalist as Daniel O'Connell could not refrain, when he was leading the campaign in Ireland for Catholic

point to differences in class composition and appeal among the various parts of the continually shifting whole.

Thus it seems clear that ordinary workingmen became Chartists for any number of reasons and that it meant different things to different groups among them. Specific local or sectional social and economic grievances ran into a pervasive and generalized consciousness of injustice. Although the leaders of the movement were involved from the outset in struggles for power and squabbles over principle and precedent, they did manage to remain in essential agreement on the Charter itself, and the external history of the movement is the campaign, renewed three times, to collect masses of signatures for a series of National Petitions which were addressed to the House of Commons. The first Petition was presented to the House in the summer of 1839; it contained almost 1,300,000 signatures and was promptly rejected by 237 votes to 48, a majority of 189. The contingency plan in the event of such failure was to have been, again, a general strike, "the sacred month," as it was called. This program had to be abandoned when the Chartists realized that sufficiently widespread support in the country was not forthcoming. Many of the leaders were nonetheless put in jail. Again in 1842, and again in concurrence with a cyclical depression in trade, the Charter was gotten out. This time more than 3,317,000 signatures were procured; the Petition was presented and inevitably rejected. The leaders were more divided than ever and remained so even when the movement came alive again in 1848, under the dual stimulus this time of economic distress and the goings-on in France. On this final occasion, it was alleged that 6,000,000 signatures had been collected (the claim was disputed), and a great rally scheduled to meet at Kennington Common to send off the Petition to Parliament came to nothing. The troops and police far outnumbered the Chartist gathering (there were 200,000 special

---

Emancipation, from holding out the threat of physical violence. In some measure it was part of the boisterous and full-blooded tradition of political rhetoric that the period had inherited.

constables alone), and the procession to Westminster was interdicted. O'Connor urged the crowd to comply, they did, and Chartism vanished from London. It survived feebly here and there in the fifties and then became a memory.

Yet Chartism was more than just another failed series of petitions. For in the way of such movements it gathered to itself most of the grievances, protests, disturbances and hostilities—the strikes, insurrections, riots and turbulent demonstrations—that regularly punctuated the period if they did not positively characterize it. Manchester with its long history of riot and protest led the way for Chartism in Lancashire. Starting in 1837 an extended period of chronic economic distress set in; the crisis further exacerbated the already intense feelings of class division in the city and surrounding towns, particularly since the cotton masters, following the doctrines of political economy, generally refused to do anything to help the out-of-work and sometimes starving operatives, among whom as usual the weavers were suffering most terribly. In such a situation, Chartism originally appealed as "a knife-and-fork question, a bread and cheese question"—that is to say, political reform was understood as being a translation for economic relief or improvement. It was also seen in terms of class conflict, and the opposition of the masters to the recently raised agitation for trades unions, against the New Poor Law, and for the ten-hour working day was put to use again as these movements became part of Chartism. When the masters in 1838 formed the Anti-Corn Law League, the Chartists quickly regarded it with hostility and undertook to disrupt the League's meetings. (The League responded in character, hiring groups of Irishmen to disrupt, with due violence, the disrupters.) The masters themselves saw in Chartism a threat to property, and their conduct expressed that primary assumption. All the ingredients of a proto-revolutionary situation seemed to be in the making.

Preliminary activities began in 1837 with meetings, speeches, formation of ad hoc associations, resolutions, petitions, manifestoes. They continued into 1838, and during the summer a series of large outdoor meetings and demonstrations were held. These came to a climax in September with a giant meeting at Kersal Moor, near Manchester. Upwards of 50,000 people attended; it was the largest gathering in the district since Peterloo, and Peterloo was bitterly present in everyone's mind—the very banners that were carried on the day of the massacre were carried again to this meeting almost twenty years later. As if this were not alarming enough, the Chartists continued to hold massive outdoor meetings (their organization was largely taken over from the Primitive Methodists), many of them by torchlight. The rhetoric at these occasions steadily escalated, even as support in the rank and file seemed to slip away. Dissension among the leadership soon broke out. The more militant wing advocating the threat of physical force won organizational control—raising the anxiety level among the middle classes to new heights—but the extremists were unable to command popular support. A second meeting at Kersal Moor in the spring of 1839 drew 20,000 fewer people than had the gathering the previous autumn, and the crowd itself was visibly unagitational. In the summer of 1839, after the rejection of the first Petition and the collapse of the idea of a general strike, arrests of leaders on a large scale began, and soon there were very few leaders at liberty. In any case there were few enough of their following left to lead; only the most economically desperate among them, the handloom weavers, hung on in any numbers. In a sense they had nowhere else to go.

On November 5, 1839, an actual if minuscule insurrectionary rising occurred at Newport on the border of Wales. It was easily put down (and its leaders transported), but the government and the middle classes were convinced that the rising was planned by the extremists as a signal for general and bloody revolution in the North. Whether there was such a conspiracy or not has never been determined; in any event, the rising was not contagious, and when in the spring of 1840 most of the Chartist leaders were arrested and imprisoned, the movement went into a prolonged eclipse. It began to revive once more in late 1841 under the impact of further severe economic distress—bad harvests and thus high cost of bread plus falling wages.[11] By this time most of the leaders were out of jail again. Yet even as the movement came back to life it split into factions, especially among the Irish—a radical wing following O'Connor in opposing any cooperation with the middle-class Anti-Corn Law League, a moderate faction led by Daniel O'Connell supporting the League. Nonetheless, organization for the second Petition went rapidly ahead, with the North—Lancashire, Cheshire and Yorkshire—now the center of the movement; 100,000 signatures came from Manchester alone. The second National Convention met in London in the spring of 1842 on the occasion of the presentation to Parliament of the great National Petition, which was promptly thrown out. The Convention dissolved and the movement went once more into rapid disintegration. As summer waxed, so did privation, suffering and distress. The manufacturing districts had become a scene of horrors. In Stockport, about eight miles from Manchester, so many families had been evicted from their homes for failure to pay rent, that someone in a spasm of desperate wit had chalked upon a door "Stockport to Let"—it was to become a grim national joke. At this extreme juncture the workingmen turned to direct action.

Amid high prices for bread, some textile manufacturers announced an intention to reduce the wages of weavers and spinners. Operatives met in large numbers to protest, and on August 5 in Ashton-under-Lyne, the men spontaneously ceased work. Shortly thereafter they marched into Manchester, where the same thing occurred. From Manchester the strike rapidly spread in all directions. The working people spontaneously turned out, and stopped work by pulling out the plugs from the

[11] In the spring of 1842, the Home Secretary reported that almost 1,500,000 people in England and Wales were paupers and receiving poor relief. The total population then was about 16 million.

factory boilers; hence the name given to the episode—the Plug Plot riots (there was no plot and few riots). In Manchester itself over 50,000 hands were on strike and some 200 places of work closed down. There was little violence on the part of the strikers. The sudden uprising was economic and industrial in origin and aim rather than political. Chartism itself was not at first involved, but as the strike-riots spread, the Chartist leaders tried to take advantage of them. They were, however, divided among themselves over whether to support the action, and by the time they decided to affirm it, the moment for decisive action had passed, as had another early opportunity to create an alliance in the working class that would bring together action directed toward economic and social ends with action that had political aims. The striking operatives were defeated within a couple of months; they returned to their mills having exacted no concessions from their masters. Yet in a number of senses, the great strike was a portent of the future: it suggested unmistakably (if only through hindsight) that an industrial movement among working people was taking shape in ways that were spontaneous and unpredictable but by no means gratuitous or meaningless. It also suggested that such a movement had to have a political arm. If Chartism demonstrated that it was incapable of being such an arm, it had at least supplied large numbers of industrial working people with a more or less coherent political vision, which, however skewed it may have been to their actual condition, was of enormous value in the formation of their consciousness of themselves as a class.

Chartism effectively ends here, and it is convenient as well to end this account at this moment of a social crisis that has briefly subsided but has by no means been resolved. For it is at just this moment too that Friedrich Engels comes to England and to Lancashire.

The Town

Here about I passed over Medlock River, and so within less than a mile to Manchester. Manchester on the south side of the Irwel standith in Salfordshire, and is the fairest, best buildid, quikkest, and most populous toune of all Lancastreshire . . . There be divers stone bridges in the toune, but the best of iii arches is over Irwel. This bridge divideth Manchester from Salford, the which is a large suburb to Manchester. On this bridge is a praty little chapel . . . On Hirk River are divers fair milles that serve the toune. . . . The toune of Manchester standith on a hard rocke of stone else Irwel as well apperith in the west ripe [bank] had been noiful [harmful] to the toune.

—John Leland

THE CONDITION OF THE WORKING CLASS IN ENGLAND IN 1844 is generally agreed to be a "classic." If it did little else, the new translation and edition by W. O. Henderson and W. H. Chaloner, published more than a decade ago, made that much abundantly clear.[1] Yet the grounds on which that "classical"

[1] The extraordinary deficiencies of both the editors' attitudes and proceedings have been expertly dealt with by Asa Briggs, *New Statesman* (March 22, 1958), pp. 379–380, and E. J. Hobsbawm, "History and the 'Dark Satanic Mills,' " *Labouring Men* (London, 1964), pp. 105–119. In consequence there is no need for me to rehearse these inadequacies in any detail—with a single exception. The new translation, though it is vigorous and pithy—and thus does capture certain qualities of Engels' prose—is extremely loose,

28

standing rests remain largely unexamined. If we put to one side
the library of printed gestures made out of piety and in the course
of ritual observances, we have left a scattering of comments. In
the main these assent to Engels' claim that his work was the first
"to deal with *all* the various types of English workers" (4); to
remarks about the surprising accuracy of his report and upon the
vigor of his attack; and to a few general statements about the
importance of this work to the history of the study of urbanism.
Almost nothing has been done to demonstrate concretely what
kind of book *The Condition of the Working Class in England* is,
what makes it outstanding among works of its kind and of its
time, or to elucidate those qualities of mind that render it after
such a considerable interval of history so readable, so moving, so
vividly living a document. In other words, why is it still a classic?

The first thing to observe is that such a question is extremely
complex. And the first requirement in setting about to answer it
is to recognize that complexity. The second is to locate the work
in certain relevant contexts. Since its central and most important
sections have to do with Manchester, and with Engels' experience
of it, the first of these contexts is supplied by contemporary
observations of that place—by visitors and travelers both English
and foreign, among whom Engels must of course be numbered, as
well as by native or local inhabitants. My intention in this
undertaking is not to compose an anthology of such observations

---

frequently inaccurate, and on occasion it garbles or reverses Engels' meaning. In what
follows, I have tried wherever possible to cite this widely available edition, and have
invariably cited the page in it (in parentheses) on which the relevant passage occurs.
Often, however, I have been forced to substitute translations of my own. When a passage
from Engels contains some kind of difficulty, density or ambiguity, I have supplied the
German as well.

It would nevertheless be unfair to Henderson and Chaloner to omit an acknowledgment
of gratitude. In tracking down the originals of so many of Engels' sources and in printing
them in their original form, they have performed a genuine service.

In addition, two essentially orthodox rehearsals of the materials should be noted: Horst
Ullrich, *Der Junge Engels*, 2 vols. (Berlin, 1961, 1966); and Auguste Cornu, *Karl Marx et
Friedrich Engels*, 4 vols. (Paris, 1955–1970). Both of these narrative accounts are minimal
in their analysis, and as a result are apt to be misleading.

or to supplement such a useful compilation as that offered—almost, as it were, by the way—by Asa Briggs.[2] The purpose I have in mind is to set out a number of classes of observation and categories of analysis from among those most commonly made. By examining the language of selected passages we can, I think, begin to see how people perceived Manchester, what they thought about it, and what they thought they thought about it. Taken together, such passages establish for us a critical context in which Engels' study may be regarded from a number of different analytic points of view. While this "contextualizing" forces us to delay somewhat the consideration of Engels, I think that his achievement cannot be appreciated adequately until one is acquainted in some detail with the responses of other writers—including some of the period's greatest figures—to the experience of Manchester.

On November 6, 1838, Charles Dickens made his first visit to Manchester. A few days before this he had passed through Birmingham and Wolverhampton, traveling, he wrote, "through miles of cinder-paths and blazing furnaces and roaring steam engines, and such a mass of dirt, gloom and misery as I never before witnessed." As for Manchester itself, his first surviving remarks on the experience occur in a letter written to E. M. Fitzgerald at the end of December. "So far as seeing goes," he stoutly affirmed, "I have seen enough for my purpose, and what I have seen has disgusted and astonished me beyond all measure. I mean to strike the heaviest blow in my power for these unfortunate creatures. . . ." The blow was a long time in getting delivered, about fifteen years, to be exact; it came finally in the publication of *Hard Times*. Yet what, in fact, did Dickens see that was enough for his purpose? We learn this in the opening

---

[2] Asa Briggs, *Victorian Cities* (London, 1963), pp. 83–137 and *passim*. It should be added that Briggs' comments on Engels, though they are very brief, are also very telling.

sentence of this same letter, where Dickens writes: "I went, some weeks ago, to Manchester, and saw the *worst* cotton mill. And then I saw the *best. Ex uno disce omnes.* There was no great difference between them." [3] Whether there was no great difference between the worst and the best is a matter that cannot be decided upon here—at that moment Dickens was certainly in no mind to make such distinctions as may have been pointed out to him or that he may have noticed on his own. What is more important is his use of the Latin tag. Dickens hardly ever resorted to this commonplace device. His Latin was not that extensive, and besides he had no need for it. Much of his genius lay precisely in the primitive power of his relation to the English language—in his ability to transform, articulate and differentiate his immediate perceptions and subsequent reflections by means of its resources. His use of Latin at this juncture suggests several things. It suggests how truly foreign and strange the experience must have been. It suggests as well the need Dickens must have felt to put some psychic space between himself and that experience—the dropping into Latin represents in part a tactic of distancing, in part a tactic of denial. In addition, we should note the genuine inappropriateness of the words from Virgil to the quintessentially modern Manchester. The disjunction between "fact" and "expression" thus disclosed suggests something of the inadequacy of the conceptual field to which Dickens at this time had access. To be sure, he was in no sense alone in reaching out for support from the ancient past. Indeed the literature of commentary on Manchester fairly abounds with quotations from Greek and Latin, allusions to classical mythology, and references to and analogies with ancient history—which is one reason for my having chosen to begin here. As these instances accumulate, it should be added, their incapacity to perform the explanatory

[3] *The Letters of Charles Dickens*, ed. Madeline House and Graham Storey (Oxford, 1965), I, 447, 483–484.

function for which they were ostensibly enlisted also becomes increasingly evident.[4]

In the month that preceded Dickens' first visit, Thomas Carlyle had had his turn. On his way home to Chelsea from a holiday in the North, he stopped off at Manchester to visit a married sister. In bed at night, his chronic insomnia was intensified by the uninterrupted groanings of a dutifully persistent but inarticulate watchman. "Groo-o-o-o," he howled incoherently, "again and again at various distances, dying out and then growing loud again, for an hour or more." These noises were finally brought to an end by angry insistences on the part of Carlyle, who then settled down to wait out the night.

At five in the morning all was still as sleep and darkness. At half-past five all went off like an enormous mill-race or ocean-tide. The Boom-m-m, far and wide. It was the mills that were all starting then, and creishy [greasy] drudges by the million taking post there. I have heard few sounds more impressive to me in the mood I was in.[5]

The points of contrast are quickly apparent. The senseless or unintelligible mutterings of the watchman—perhaps he was drunk, perhaps tongue-tied, perhaps merely representatively "old-fashioned" [6]—give way to the "impressive," intelligible, and

---

[4] Manchester apparently continued to exert a distracting influence on Dickens' mind. In 1843, he spoke to the first Annual Soirée of the Manchester Athenaeum. The address he delivered on this occasion leads one to conclude that he thought he was visiting a Mechanics' Institute. See *The Speeches of Charles Dickens*, ed. K. J. Fielding (Oxford, 1960), pp. 44–51. Perhaps the fact that the Soirée was being held in the Free Trade Hall which was built on the site of Peterloo had somehow gotten into his head.

By 1852 he was referring to Manchester as "that awful machine"—scarcely one of his more inspired or original utterances. *Letters from Charles Dickens to Angela Burdett-Coutts, 1841–1865*, ed. Edgar Johnson (London, 1953), p. 205.

[5] J. A. Froude, *Thomas Carlyle: A History of His Life in London* (New York, 1910), I, 127.

[6] See, for example, "Police of the Metropolis," *Edinburgh Review*, XLVIII (1828), 411–412. What was true of London ten years before, when the New Police had not yet been instituted, still held generally for Manchester in 1838. "The watch is appointed by

widely resonant boom of the mills starting up. Nevertheless, the first terms in which Carlyle expresses this process contain a latent, perhaps not-so-latent, contradiction. The diminutive and human is replaced by the large and natural. That is to say, in seeking to find an equivalent for the sense of massive and irresistible force conveyed to him by the sound of the mills starting up, Carlyle has hit upon the notion of the sound made by the rapid or rushing movement of an immense body of water. In the literature describing Manchester, these metaphors from nature are, not surprisingly, extremely common—this passage from Carlyle, in my opinion, is about as good as they get.[7] Yet whether we read about volcanoes or earthquakes, about storm-clouds, whirlpools or vortexes, about vast hives and swarms of industrious bees, there remains something incoherent and severely defective in the use to which these metaphors are generally and conventionally put.[8] The point is not that nature had ceased to exist at Manchester; it existed indeed, but the form which its existence now took was that of continuous and radical transformation. Metaphor itself, of course, is a species of transformation, but the alterations envisaged in most of these figures from nature

---

the different parishes, which hold no correspondence together: They are assigned to separate beats, and scrupulously adhere to their limits. . . . Persons, too, are selected as watchmen, who will bring the lowest expense on the parish—the labourer, who has worked all day, and must sleep in his box at night, or the aged pauper, whose infirmities would make him an object of relief."

See also A. Redford and I. Russell, *The History of Local Government in Manchester* (London, 1939), I, 87–97, 202f., 342 and *passim*.

[7] There are a number of further associational backings for the figure that Carlyle has used. The mills first did employ water power, and were now using large quantities of water in the generation of steam, as well as in numerous other processes; and the Atlantic tides on which the raw cotton from America was conveyed to England have an oblique, secondary relevance in addition.

[8] That incoherence may be followed back directly into the life of the period. When, for example, the first Robert Peel, the successful cotton spinner of Blackburn, obtained in 1792 the grant of a coat of arms, the arms were decorated with "a bee volant *or*" and "a demi-lion rampant *argent* . . . holding a shuttle *or*." Norman Gash, *Mr. Secretary Peel* (London, 1961), p. 23.

fail to catch up or correspond to the literal and figurative
alternations of form and substance, of nature and humanity, of
which Manchester was then the central scene.

Carlyle does, however, manage to capture some of that. For the
annoying old watchman of the night is himself split up and
transformed. His maddening Groo-o-o-o becomes, as we have
seen, the richly signifying Boom-m-m of the mills. But his
solitary figure posting the rounds of his watch is also divided and
becomes the "creishy drudges by the million taking post" at the
mills. The medieval watcher of the city's nighttime peace is
subdivided and multiplied into those millions who tend and watch
the machines of the modern city's daily activity.[9] This process is
not, however, conceived of by Carlyle as simple or unmodified
progress. Those millions are greasy and drudges; and if the
watchman's senseless noises have become the speaking boom of
the mills, the millions at their posts have been rendered
mute—unless we are indeed to take the resonating sound of the
mills as their collective, wordless voice, which would be a
brilliant, if unconscious, suggestive representation of another side
of the division of labor. (I am not sure that the passage warrants
this interpretation.) In its density and compressed ironic depth,
the passage taken as a whole is among the best of its kind. And it
may be useful in this regard to remind ourselves by anticipation
that there is nothing accidental in the fact that Carlyle, of all the
British writers of the time, exerted the most immediate and

[9] With the laying in of gas light, which began in the factories in 1805, soon after the
successful illumination by gas was first achieved, the proportions of the traditional working
day were dramatically altered, and the watches of the night, particularly for factory
workers, dramatically shortened—although the usual way of putting, or obscuring, the
matter is to say that the day was dramatically extended. See E. J. Hobsbawm, *Industry and
Empire* (New York, 1968), p. 43.

In addition the cost of lighting by gas was less than half of that required by oil and
candles. In the early years many of the large spinning factories in Manchester made their
own gas. The Manchester Police Commissioners, who were in charge of the street-light-
ing for the town, began to make gas in 1807, and by 1829 it was claimed that the "whole
interior of the town is now lighted with gas." For an account of this development, see
Redford and Russell, *The History of Local Government in Manchester*, I, 263ff.

important influence on the young Engels, a topic I shall return to later on.

Engels could not have read this passage, but he did read another version of it. Carlyle's nocturnal adventure was impressive enough for it to recur to him during the next year while he was writing *Chartism*. Chapter VIII of that pamphlet, entitled "New Eras," is cast into the form of reflections uttered by one of Carlyle's personae, Herr Professor Sauerteig. Sauerteig ruminates upon "World-History," and upon the "grand tasks assigned" therein to the English people. The first of these is "the grand Industrial task of conquering some half or more of this Ter-raqueous Planet for the use of man," and in the course of outlining how this lot has fallen to the English, he comes at length back to our subject and to Carlyle's earlier experience.

Manchester, with its cotton-fuzz, its smoke and dust, its tumult and contentious squalor, is hideous to thee? Think not so: A precious substance, beautiful as magic dreams, and yet no dream but a reality, lies hidden in that noisome wrappage;—a wrappage struggling indeed (look at Chartisms and suchlike) to cast itself off, and leave the beauty free and visible there! Hast thou heard, with sound ears, the awakening of a Manchester, on Monday morning, at half-past five by the clock; the rushing-off of its thousand mills, like the boom of an Atlantic tide, ten-thousand times ten-thousand spools and spindles all set humming there,—it is perhaps, if thou knew it well, sublime as a Niagara, or more so. Cotton-spinning is the clothing of the naked in its result; the triumph of man over matter in its means. Soot and despair are not the essence of it; they are divisible from it,—at this hour, are they not crying fiercely to be divided?

Although this passage contains a number of Carlyle's characteris-tic virtues, it seems to me distinctly inferior to the earlier effort. The best part remains the central, reworked memory of Carlyle's night-long auditory experience, which has been compressed and slightly altered: Manchester is now as sublime as Niagara, perhaps "more so"—it is still not different in kind.[10] The memory is given in a series of statements whose logical working out is something less than precise. The hideousness and noisomeness of the early industrial world are here regarded as mere "wrappage"; they are not organic to the good that will emerge either out of them or through them in the future; they are, in a virtually mechanical sense, "divisible" from the undoubted achievement, and are not held together either as historically inseparable functions of one another, or as inseparable means and ends, or even as inseparable concomitant occurrences. There is no need to argue that Carlyle was, at this point in his career, regularly able to reason with greater penetration and complexity than this. Yet even in this imperfect and failed instance, his writing reveals a habit or style of thinking with which Engels, as we shall see, was thoroughly familiar, and which served to make what Carlyle had to offer him so readily accessible.[11]

At that meeting in October 1843 of the Manchester Athenaeum in which Dickens spoke from the chair, one of the other speakers was Disraeli. He and his wife had been visiting the city

[10] I assume that Carlyle's use of the term "sublime" is carrying its full, technical sense.

[11] Carlyle's distinctive importance may be further suggested by a comparison. Entering Belfast "through a most wretched suburb," Keats was struck by "the most disgusting of all noises . . . the sound of the Shuttle." *The Letters of John Keats*, ed. H. B. Forman (London, 1948), p. 174. This was in 1818; Keats was referring to hand-loom weaving, not massed power-driven machinery; and even though they were both born in the same year (1795) Keats died young, while Carlyle was a late developer. All true; in spite of which Keats gives no sign of being open to the kind of experience that Carlyle is able to represent.

By 1850, however, Carlyle himself was no longer open to it. In "Hudson's Statue," one of the *Latter-Day Pamphlets*, he urged: "I do not want cheaper cotton, swifter railways; I want what Novalis calls 'God, Freedom, Immortality': will swift railways, and sacrifices to Hudson, help me towards that?" Maybe not; but the posing of such alternatives, in such terms, was precisely one of the false oppositions that it had been Carlyle's great earlier virtue to expose and counteract.

where they had been, in her words, "much fêted." He had not planned to attend the meeting, much less to speak, but "they sent a deputation of ladies, which, you know, he could not refuse, so he went, and made a fine speech for them—all said by far the finest—literary not political." [12] In one sense, the literary not political would stick. Disraeli turned his days in Manchester to immediate account in *Coningsby*, which he began to write soon after he left, and which was published in the spring of 1844.[13] Since the relevant passages have been often quoted before, I take the liberty of dealing with them in a summary and compressed way. Coningsby's adventures begin "during the heat of a refulgent summer in the green district of some ancient forest" in "one of our midland counties." A rain squall drives the youth into an inn where he makes his first acquaintance with the great Sidonia. Coningsby has been mooning over visions of "a beautiful Ondine," and "a Dryad of sylvan Greece," and confesses to the mysterious stranger his desire to travel. " 'What would I not give to see Athens!' " Sidonia replies that he's seen it all and more. " 'Phantoms and spectres! The age of ruins is past. Have you seen Manchester?' " [14] This is pithy, portentous, and oracular enough to be memorialized, and it has been. It happens also to be true, but the vague if characteristic inflationary tone of the statement—in part paradoxically caused by the deliberate casualness with which the momentous juxtaposition is thrown out—makes it difficult to say just *how* it is true. Disraeli appears to have sensed something of this himself. Although he packs Coningsby off in short order to see Manchester, before his young hero is allowed to enter "the great METROPOLIS OF LABOUR," [15] Disraeli intervenes

[12] W. F. Monypenny and G. E. Buckle, *The Life of Benjamin Disraeli*, rev. ed. in 2 vols. (London, 1929), I, 583 (vol. II, ch. 6, in 6-vol. ed.).

[13] Monypenny and Buckle, I, 595 (vol. II, ch. 7, 6-vol. ed.); Robert Blake, *Disraeli* (New York, 1967), pp. 173*n*, 190.

[14] Bk. III, ch. 1.

[15] Bk. III, ch. 5.

with a short, essayistic chapter. Speaking in his own authorial voice—which is indistinguishable from that of Sidonia—he elaborates upon that pointed utterance.

He begins by locating Manchester among the representative cities of Western history; each of these cities "is the type of some great idea." The typology culminates in Manchester, which embodies in the modern world what Athens did in the ancient, "the distinctive faculty." That faculty is "science," by which he means technology. The preeminent value attaching to this activity is "the useful," which "in the minds of men . . . has succeeded to the beautiful." Thus, instead of Athens we have "a Lancashire village . . . expanded into a mighty region of factories and warehouses. Yet," he goes on, "rightly understood, Manchester is as great a human exploit as Athens." That "rightly," he is aware, may require a considerable quantity of understanding, an ambiguity supported, in these circumstances, by his apt choice of the word "exploit." [16] At the same time, Disraeli continues, the inhabitants of Manchester are not as conscious of who they are or what they have done as the Athenians were. "They do not fully comprehend the position which they occupy. It is the philosopher alone who can conceive of the grandeur of Manchester, and the immensity of its future. There are yet great truths to tell, if we had either the courage to announce or the temper to receive them." [17] The sense of this seems to be that the inhabitants *cannot* fully comprehend how matters stand; the philosopher alone can "conceive" of such things because they have largely to do with the latent and the immanent, with futurity. We are back again with the oracular and with the idea, already touched on by Carlyle, of an emergent process. Nevertheless, the oracular

[16] He might have chosen "achievement" or any other number of varying equivalents. Although the *Oxford English Dictionary* (OED) lists 1847 as the earliest date for the use of the verb "exploit" in the sense of "to utilize for selfish purposes; to make capital out of," the noun "exploitation" in the sense of "turning to account . . . utilizing for selfish purposes" is cited as occurring as early as 1803. The OED, one should add, is often, and not surprisingly, tardy in its datings.

[17] *Coningsby*, Bk. IV, ch. 1.

appears to withhold the great truths it has to tell, presumably
because of some defect of "courage" or "temper" in ourselves—
that "we" is both broad and uncertain in its reference. The
passage ends, therefore, on a note of subdued, if unspecified,
apprehensiveness, and Disraeli seems once again to have picked
up a hint from Carlyle who, the year before, had written that
Manchester was "as wonderful, as fearful, unimaginable, as the
oldest Salem [Jerusalem] or Prophetic City." [18]

With this much clarified, or at least amplified, we rejoin
Coningsby. He has journeyed to Manchester, passing over "the
plains where iron and coal supersede turf and corn, dingy as the
entrance of Hades, and flaming with furnaces. . . ." The
association of the early industrial world with the classical infernal
regions proved in practice to have been virtually irresistible. In
Manchester, Coningsby stops at the Adelphi Hotel, equips
himself with the *Guide*, and looks about him. He notices that
"even his bedroom was lit by gas." He sniffs the summer air and
finds it "sweet, even in this land of smoke and toil." He feels "a
sensation such as in Lisbon or Lima precedes an earthquake. The
house appears to quiver. It is a sympathetic affection occasioned
by a steam-engine in a neighbouring factory." The idea of the
earthquake, one supposes, is legitimized by the notion of a house
being able to feel or suffer a sympathetic affection. In the streets,
Coningsby finds himself "among illumined factories, with more
windows than Italian palaces, and smoking chimneys taller than
Egyptian obelisks." The notion that factories were like palaces
was extremely common; the frequency of its incidence is
approached only by the frequency with which the idea that they
were like medieval or feudal castles occurs. The manifold ways in
which such comparisons were appropriate are outnumbered only
by the manifold ways in which they were not. Yet in almost all
such passages one can make out a similar purpose at work; they
reveal the effort to accommodate a new, strange and disturbing or

[18] *Past and Present*, Bk. III, ch. 15.

distressing experience to a familiar and economical conceptual structure. They represent the effort to "tame," domesticate or control that experience before it gets out of hand and manifests itself as anxiety.[19]

So much for the outside. Coningsby then enters factories in which, as Disraeli says, "He saw all." And what does he see?

He entered chambers vaster than are told of in Arabian fable, and peopled with habitants more wondrous than Afrite or Peri. For there he beheld, in long-continued ranks, those mysterious forms full of existence without life that perform with facility, and in an instant, what man can fulfill only with difficulty and in days.

Well—if beautiful Ondines and Dryads of sylvan Greece in the forests of our midland counties, then why not the *Arabian Nights* in our midland towns? Why not factory owners as Ali Babas (but then who are the forty thieves?); why not machines as genii both evil and good, as "fair ones" endowed with grace and beauty? Once again, the point to be grasped is not that these trivializations are original with or idiosyncratic to Disraeli; they occur widely and with almost predictable regularity. And although very different descriptions of factories were being made at the same time, in a certain sense accounts such as Disraeli's remained for a space unchallenged and unrepudiated in literary or cultural consciousness. They existed, as it were, alongside and isolated from their antithetical counterparts. Not until 1854, when Dickens finally got around to striking that blow of his, were

---

[19] In Disraeli's instance, the effort was consistent. In his speech before the Manchester Athenaeum, he denounced "the prejudice 'which associated with commerce and manufacture an inability to sympathize with the fair inventions of art or the poetic creations of the human intellect,' and held up before the people of Manchester the stimulating examples of the great merchants of Venice, who were the patrons of Titian and Tintoretto; the merchant family of the Medici, who made Florence the home of genius . . . [etc., etc.]." Monypenny and Buckle, I, 582 (vol. II, ch. 6, 6-vol. ed.), citing the *Manchester Guardian*, Oct. 7, 1843.

representations of this kind directly brought to book. In one acrid sentence—in which, I suspect, Dickens had among other things this passage from *Coningsby* in mind—in his description of "a summer day in Coketown," Dickens finishes the whole thing off. "The atmosphere of those Fairy palaces was like the breath of the simoon: and their inhabitants, wasting with heat, toiled languidly in the desert." [20] It was worth waiting for.

The distinction is not that of images *versus* realities—or of literature or language as opposed to the actual, or of "value" as against "fact"—but which images and *which* realities. Which images convey which realities and which fail to convey them or mystify and obscure them? Which realities are susceptible to such images and which are not? Which realities get communicated through the language and which are somehow lost? If much of the reality does not get through in Disraeli, there yet remains that excellent phrase about the machines: "mysterious forms full of existence without life." It is packed with intelligence, and is precisely the kind of idea that Marx makes great and elaborate play with in some of the most powerful sections of volume one of *Capital*. But it is almost as if Disraeli had hit upon that phrase in order to debase the possibilities it extended.[21] There follows a lengthy passage of rococo ratiocination. A machine is an

[20] *Hard Times*, Bk. II, ch. 1. A little earlier Dickens had prepared for this sentence by remarking: "The lights in the great factories, which looked, when they were illuminated, like Fairy palaces—or the travellers by express-train said so . . ." thereby making good to some extent on earlier lapses. Bk. I, ch. 10. One more such delinquency may be noted. In 1851, Dickens collaborated with W. H. Wills on a piece describing the manufacture of plate glass. Although the passages in question were written by Wills, Dickens allowed them to pass; they are qualitatively identical with the kind of thing that by 1854 he was shooting down. See *Charles Dickens' Uncollected Writings from Household Words, 1850–1859*, ed. Harry Stone (Bloomington, 1968), pp. 205–215. A relevant account of part of Dickens' development in this connection is to be found in K. J. Fielding and Anne Smith, "*Hard Times* and the Factory Controversy," *Nineteenth Century Fiction*, XXIV (April 1970), 404–427.

[21] A common enough occurrence at the time. In 1844, for example, the *Manchester Guardian* remarked grandiloquently that "the stranger sees, and wonders at, our almost living machinery, and admires the perseverance and devotion of our people." Quoted in Donald Read, *Press and People, 1790–1850* (London, 1961), p. 147.

undegraded and undegrading slave; it is immensely energetic yet without emotions. Indeed it is a supernatural slave; indeed, he now reverses himself, it is alive. It breathes, "for its breath forms the atmosphere of some towns"; it moves; it has a voice. "Does not the spindle sing like a merry girl at her work, and the steam-engine roar in jolly chorus, like a strong artisan handling his lusty tools and gaining a fair day's wages for a fair day's toil?" What seems plainly to have happened in this passage is that Disraeli has failed to recollect that cotton-spinning and word-spinning are two distinct activities.

His "animation" of the machine has, however, had the effect of reminding Disraeli that the factory contains certain other "habitants," [22] and it is to them that he now turns. "Nor should the weaving-room be forgotten, where a thousand or fifteen hundred girls may be observed in their coral necklaces, working like Penelope in the day-time; some pretty, some pert, some graceful and jocund, some absorbed in their occupation; a little serious some, few sad." By this point the reader may be so surfeited with allusions that the sole recourse left to him is simply to shrug one more of them off. If he is not, it may occur to him to wonder where Disraeli had parked his eyes, or just what he thought he was seeing, as in the course of being "much fêted" he was conducted about a number of mills. It is a question that takes considerable answering, particularly if we recall that Disraeli opened this sub-episode with the conclusive "He saw all." In such a gesture, he resembles no one so much as Dr. Ure, who looked upon children in the mills and was persuaded that he saw "lively elves" whose work "seemed to resemble a sport, in which habit gave them a pleasing dexterity," who were continually "taking pleasure in the light play of their muscles," and who induced in the onlooker the following reflection: "It was delightful to

---

[22] The early technocrat and state socialist Constantin Pecqueur (1801–1887) referred to the new machines as *"associantes, socialisantes, agglomérantes."* Quoted in George Lichtheim, *The Origins of Socialism* (New York, 1969), pp. 77, 250.

observe the nimbleness with which they pieced the broken ends, as the mule-carriage began to recede from the fixed roller beam . . ." [23] As for the fifteen hundred coral-bedecked Penelopes, and the descriptive adjectives with which Disraeli further adorns them, I shall run the risk of anticipating myself and simply juxtapose this from Engels: "I cannot recall having seen a single healthy, tall and well-built girl in the throstle room of the mill in Manchester in which I worked. The girls were all small, poorly developed or stunted [schlecht gewachsen] and their build was poorly compacted or foreshortened [eigentümlich gedrängten Baus]. The general appearance of their figures was decidedly unattractive [hässlich, lit., ugly]" (185).[24] It only remains to be determined whether as between the spinning- and weaving-rooms some sort of sexual selection was being conducted among the female operatives.

Coningsby comes toward the end of the "several days" that he has devoted to "the comprehension of Manchester." He has been in "a new world, pregnant with new ideas and suggestive of new trains of thought and feeling." He has witnessed "this unprecedented partnership between capital and science, working on a

---

[23] Andrew Ure, *The Philosophy of Manufactures,* 2d ed. (London, 1835), p. 301. Engels (189–190) quotes the larger passage in which these phrases occur.

[24] This, it may be useful to recall, comes from the Engels who had already begun his liaison with a factory-girl, Mary Burns, with whom he was to live as man and wife until her death in 1863.

It was not only the appearance of the girls that Disraeli seems to have screened from memory. He has also forgotten that he has Coningsby visit the mills during the summer and what the temperature maintained in them was like even in cold weather. Both of these circumstances are brought together by C. C. F. Greville who visited Manchester in November 1845. "On Thursday I went to Manchester, and saw one of the great cotton and one of the great silk manufactories . . . The heat of the room in the former of them was intense, but the man who showed them to us told us it was caused by the intense friction and the room might be much cooler but the people liked the heat . . . In the hot factory rooms the women look very wan, very dirty, and one should guess very miserable." *The Greville Memoirs, 1814–1860,* eds. Lytton Strachey and Roger Fulford (London, 1938), V, 238–240.

spot which Nature had indicated as the fitting theatre of their exploits." [25] The operative word is "theatre," and all Disraeli's dealings with Manchester here have been gotten up and "staged." The fanciness, the hifalutin literariness, the compulsive and factitious mythologizing all point toward the same considerations. They are means of guarding oneself against the impact of certain experiences, and they are equally means of supplying what experience has not given. In this regard, Disraeli represents an extremely elaborated instance of what we observed in Dickens' Latin tag. Yet the matter is not that simple. For in the following year, in *Sybil*, Disraeli was to write again about the conditions of industrial working-class life, this time to very different effect and from an altered standpoint. Those passages are justly celebrated. In the preface to *Sybil* he wrote that "the descriptions generally were written from his own observation," an affirmation that he repeated in the 1870 General Preface to the Novels: "I had visited and observed with care all the localities introduced." Even his devoted biographers find that a bit too much to let pass without remark. What Disraeli omitted to mention, of course, was that he had been doing his homework in the Blue Books (official reports and records of investigations), particularly those of the Children's Commission, and that the famous scenes in *Sybil* emerge from them as from a direct source. [26] The implications that flow from this circumstance are too complex to enter upon with any adequacy here. It may be that Disraeli was simply ignorant and half-blind in 1843–1844 and that he overcame these deficiencies as he was at work on *Sybil*. In my opinion, something else is pertinent as well. It was in fact easier to read about such things than it was to experience them directly. Articulated, written, and printed language imposed a preformed structure on them; the arrangement of an official report—however laden with

[25] Bk. IV, ch. 2.
[26] Monypenny and Buckle, III, 648f. (vol. II, ch. 6, 6-vol. ed.).

direct testimony its appendices might be—interposed yet another formal structure between the immediate concrete realities of human experience and the reader, and served to create some of the distance that virtually everyone at the time seemed to need. And they needed it with good reason.

What I am suggesting is that in these scenes of early industrial life—as it came to its first great crisis in the 1830's and '40's—something new had happened. In part that newness consisted in the actual conditions that were being created and disclosed; in part it had to do with human consciousness struggling to make, and often to resist, the radical alterations and accommodations within itself that these conditions required. Both of these are different aspects of the same immense series of phenomena; both of these reveal, however, that what had entered the world was the distinctively modern conscious experience of the extreme. Men were abruptly discovering that human existence—that is to say, human social existence—had evolved in such a way that masses of human beings were now constrained to conduct their lives under conditions of unimaginable extremity. It was one of those junctures at which a part of all of us today was first created.[27]

One did not have to have been newly created then in order to appreciate the magnitude of such occurrences.[28] In 1839, at the time of his appointment to command of the northern district, Major-General Sir Charles James Napier was fifty-seven years old. He made no secret of his sympathy with the poor, and was soon told to confine his remarks to military matters. He did not live in Manchester but in a nearby town, and at one point, he writes:

[27] The inception of the modern experience of the extreme in politics had occurred somewhat earlier in the French Revolution. The Irish famine of 1846–1848 was virtually a laboratory in which experiments in early modern extremity were to be observed.

[28] E. P. Thompson, *The Making of the English Working Class* (London, 1963), pp. 190–212, collects a number of earlier instances indicating acute awareness of the significance of what was happening.

I ought to be at Manchester, but unless under positive orders, who can resolve to run up a chimney? Some duties are not to be done voluntarily, and to live in a chimney is one. Manchester is the chimney of the world. Rich rascals, poor rogues, drunken ragamuffins and prostitutes form the moral; soot made into paste by rain the physique, and the only view is a long chimney: what a place! the entrance to hell realized.[29]

The prose is characteristically candid and racy. Napier expresses rather than conceals what it is that is causing him to respond so acutely. The chimneys of Manchester occasioned nearly as much commentary as the factories of which they were a part.[30] Almost inevitably the response to them was articulated in the typically ambivalent pastoral imagery of the period. One reads repeatedly about "forests" of chimneys, or about their belching forth "clouds" of smoke, which are sometimes fancied up into flocks of darkened sheep. Napier's response is not of this order; nor is it of the order of Disraeli's Egyptian obelisks.[31] Manchester itself and as a whole is for him a chimney; and he regards the effort of will

---

[29] Sir William Napier, *The Life and Opinions of General Sir Charles James Napier* (London, 1857), II, 56–57. Both Napiers were, providentially, favorites of Engels, who fancied himself, and was, something of an amateur expert on military affairs and history. Charles, he declared, was "the greatest general England has produced since Marlborough . . . But," he continued, correctly, "Napier was an independent man, too proud to stoop to the reigning oligarchy . . ." *New York Daily Tribune,* February 20, 1858; reprinted in *Karl Marx on Colonialism and Modernization,* ed. Schlomo Avineri (New York, 1969), p. 270. On another occasion he wrote that "old General Charles Napier accomplished feats in India in 1842 that really remind one of Alexander the Great." *Werke,* XXVIII, 581; translated in Marx and Engels, *Letters to Americans, 1848–1895* (New York, 1953), p. 58. William's *History of the War in the Peninsula and the South of France,* Engels declared in 1851, was "by far the best military-historical writing I have read up to now." *Werke,* XXVII, 555; translated in *Letters to Americans,* p. 21.

[30] In certain quarters, Manchester was known as "The City of Long Chimneys." The rate of change in the early Industrial Revolution may be suggested by the fact that in 1786, according to a contemporary observer, "only one chimney, that of Arkwright's spinning mill, was seen to rise above the town. Fifteen years later Manchester had about fifty spinning mills, most of them worked by steam." Paul Mantoux, *The Industrial Revolution in the Eighteenth Century* (New York, 1961 ed.), p. 358.

[31] The following is a representative illustration of contemporary descriptive prose. "Forests of chimneys, clouds of smoke and volumes of vapour, like the seething of some

that is required for him if he is to drive horizontally into the city as equivalent to the vertical exertions of a miserable and harried climbing-boy. But Manchester is more than a great chimney; it is the chimney of the world. In this phrase Napier has captured something of the exemplary significance of Manchester; he registers the radical alterations of concentration or density and of scale that the first Industrial Revolution was bringing about in human, social existence. Now one city can concentrate in itself, both representatively and actually, a global or world function; beneath this there is indistinctly implied the notion of the world—and of existence—as some kind of whole.

At this point Napier tries to develop his figure in another direction. Falling back on memories of schoolroom lessons in rhetoric, he divides things up under two heads, the moral and the physical, and begins a quasi-allegorical enumeration. The moral essence of the city (he has unconsciously shifted to thinking in organismic terms) is made up of a rag-bag of types whom he regards at once both sardonically and sympathetically. Rich rascals = the manufacturers and merchants; poor rogues = workingmen driven to Chartism and violence; drunken raga-

---

stupendous cauldron, occupy the entire landscape; there is no sky, but a dark gray haze, variegated by masses of smoke more dense than the rest, which look like fleeces of black wool, or clouds of sublimated ink." Further on, the writer remarks that if the chimneys were "built of stone instead of brick, when they cease to vomit forth smoke they might pass for triumphant columns," thereby getting the worst of both worlds. Cyrus Redding, *An Illustrated Itinerary of the County of Lancashire* (London, n.d., but pretty clearly ca. 1842).

Early Dickens is rather better. "'On every side, and far as the eye could see into the heavy distance, tall chimneys, crowding on each other, and presenting that endless repetition of the same dull, ugly, form, which is the horror of oppressive dreams, poured out their plague of smoke, obscured the light, and made foul the melancholy air . . . before, behind and to the right and left, was the same interminable perspective of brick towers, never ceasing in their black vomit, blasting all things living or inanimate, shutting out the face of day, and closing in on all these horrors with a dense dark cloud." *The Old Curiosity Shop,* ch. 45. What is better is the hallucinatory intensity with which the aversiveness is registered, and the avoidance, for at least a dozen lines, of language taken from the repertory of pastoral-classical literature. It is not, however, as richly differentiated as the passage from Napier, although Dickens will surpass that in due time as well.

muffins = the Irish; prostitutes = ? The physical essence consists of the soot that rains down from those chimneys being softened into a paste by real rain to form a layer or film of grime that covers everything. What Napier has done here is to substitute the by-product or wastes of the industrial system for the direct objects of production, or for both of them taken together, as the physical essence of the city. He has also chosen to regard the layer of pasty grime that universally covers or films over everything and forms its new outer integument as being the essence of that which lies within it and which it covers. That is to say, in both the bag of types and the sooty paste, Napier's imaginative language beautifully confirms what he has at the outset openly confessed: his determination to remain as exterior as possible to this repellent urban world. That such a resolution was not easy to sustain is demonstrated in Napier's next statement, "and the only view is a long chimney," in which specific location is dissolved. This verbal dislocation communicates something of the anxiety and conflict that Napier also acknowledges feeling. In his final utterance, however, he regains that more secure external point of vantage: "what a place! the entrance to hell realized!" Napier's hell, however, is not Disraeli's conventional Hades; although he probably had in mind recollections of Dante's Dis and the motto written over its gates, the form in which he puts his exclamation allows us to take it differently. He may mean that hell had heretofore only been imagined by men; now it has been realized in actuality—it is, in other words, a human creation or invention, although its status today is different from what it was in the past. If this reading is plausible, then we begin, with Napier, to approach a mythologizing of the modern industrial city which takes place at a different pitch of self-consciousness than that revealed in the passages from Disraeli.

So much for the notable personages.[32] When we turn to lesser

---

[32] One such figure is missing—the Mrs. Gaskell of *Mary Barton*, *North and South* and the letters. My omission of her may be justified on two counts. First, an adequate analytic

lights the problem of selectivity becomes even more acute. The quantity of comment is enormous, the varieties of form and range of opinion only slightly less so. If we were to begin by placing at one extreme of the scale this kind of visitor's remark, "At Manchester there was nothing to be seen; but we spent two hours in ascertaining this fact," [33] and to end by placing, say, Engels' at the other extreme, we would never have done beginning. Out of the mass of material I have chosen a group of passages that seem to me both pertinent and symptomatic. The first of these is taken from W. Cooke Taylor's *Notes of a Tour in the Manufacturing Districts of Lancashire* (1842). Cooke Taylor opens his account by recalling his earliest view of Manchester, which expectably enough was of "the forest of chimneys pouring forth volumes of steam and smoke, forming an inky canopy which seemed to embrace and involve the entire place. I felt that I was in the presence of those two mighty and mysterious agencies, fire and water, proverbially the best of servants and the worst of masters." Since then, however, whatever apprehensions and unfavorable opinions he might have entertained of the factory system if not of Manchester, have been dispelled, and he writes as an advocate of the former, although he is sympathetic to the sufferings of the Lancashire operatives. In his advocacy he stresses, as others had done before him, the astonishing newness of this system.

The steam-engine had no precedent, the spinning-jenny is without ancestry, the mule and the power-loom entered on no prepared heritage: they sprang into sudden existence like Minerva from the brain

---

account of what she has to say on this score would occupy far too many pages in such a study as this. Second, and more to the point, what Mrs. Gaskell does have to say in large measure and at almost every critical juncture confirms what Engels had said before her—as I hope in several instances to be able to demonstrate.

[33] Catherine Sinclair, *Hill and Valley: or, Hours in England and Wales* (New York, 1838). This anti-observation brings to mind a remark published at a later date. In chapter XVII, "How the Change Came," in *News from Nowhere* (1890), William Morris has old Hammond refer to "a place called Manchester, which has now disappeared."

of Jupiter, passing so rapidly through their stage of infancy that they had taken their position in the world and firmly established themselves before there was time to prepare a place for their reception . . . A giant forcing his way into a densely-wedged crowd extends pain and disturbance to its remotest extremity: the individuals he pushes aside push others in their turn, though none know the cause of pressure save those with whom the intruder is immediately in contact; and thus also the Factory system causes its presence to be felt.[34]

The tumbling profusion of associated but not quite compatible metaphors suggests a sort of apprehensiveness. Manchester itself still troubles Cooke Taylor, yet he describes it in commonplace terms. "It is essentially a place of business, where pleasure is unknown as a pursuit and amusements scarcely rank as secondary consideration. Every person who passes you in the streets has the look of thought and the step of haste." The anxiety implicit in these remarks is nevertheless modulated in his description of the manufacturers on the Exchange.

It is the parliament of the lords of cotton—their legislative assembly— which enacts laws as immutable as those of the Medes and Persians, but, unlike every other parliament in the world, very much is done and very little is said . . . Transactions of immense extent are conducted by nods, winks, shrugs, or brief phrases, compared to which the laconisms of the ancient Spartans were specimens of tediousness and verbosity. . . . A stranger would imagine that he had got into one of those communities of dancing dervishes whose rule inculcates silence and perpetual motion.[35]

It may be enough to characterize the odd shrillness of such a passage as Disraeli without the talent.

Cooke Taylor is, interestingly, concerned to confute the notion that Manchester was typical or representative of almost anything. "Contrary to general belief," he contends, "experience

[34] Cooke Taylor, pp. 2–4.
[35] Cooke Taylor, pp. 7–10.

has shown me that Manchester does not afford a fair specimen of the factory population in *any* [italics added] of the conditions of its existence, and that the outward aspect of the place affords a very imperfect test of the state of trade in South Lancashire"—he was writing during the depression in cotton. Several different lines of argument are being huddled together in this sentence, and Cooke Taylor's subsequent statements fail to clarify his meaning or demonstrate his assertion. Manchester is atypical, he writes, because of its large population of "untrained labour." This mass of unskilled and largely immigrant workers, Cooke Taylor then states, is to be connected with "the commerce of cotton" as distinct from the manufacture of it. Yet he cannot support this contention for more than a sentence, and his very next statement constitutes a reversal. "In consequence of the rapidity of the growth of manufactures in Manchester," he writes, "the increase of population very rapidly outstripped the means of accommodation." And once started along this line, he finds himself carried away:

even the factory operatives are badly lodged, and the dwellings of the class below them are the most wretched that can be conceived. This is particularly the case in the township of Manchester: its narrow streets, its courts and cellars, have been abandoned to the poorest grade of all. There they live, hidden from the view of the higher ranks by piles of stores, mills, warehouses, and manufacturing establishments, less known to their wealthy neighbours,—who reside chiefly in the open spaces on Cheetham, Broughton, and Chorlton,—than the inhabitants of New Zealand or Kamtschatka.

However recurrently such observations might be voiced and such comparisons instituted during the period, they remain a moving testimony to the extremities of both actual social conditions and the social attitudes that were being formed about them—in this regard, Cooke Taylor's use of the word "abandoned" is telling and precise. And the kind of observation he offers here is in part an anticipation of Engels. But only in part, for it is exactly the implications that issue from such an observation that he is resolutely unwilling to pursue. The conclusion of his discussion of Manchester represents an extreme formulation of this refusal. Having given much thought to the matter, he writes, "I am persuaded that Manchester must long continue to present an appearance of great destitution and delinquency which does not belong to the town itself, but arises from a class of immigrants and passengers." [36] The disjunctions, isolations and wish-fulfillments are now positively obtrusive. The immense misery becomes merely an "appearance," not a reality; and even as an appearance it does not "belong" to that complex human-social entity called Manchester. It does not even finally "belong" to the class of the poor to whom he seems to be attributing it; it "arises from" them detachably, like some kind of visible effluvium. Still, in the face of such misery, and in the face of the impotence most men felt about doing anything immediate to alleviate it—much less abolish it—it cannot come as a surprise that such mental escapes and avoidances were a regular resort, and were taken by men of good will as well.[37]

Finally, there is a further moment in Cooke Taylor which I should like to mention, since it gives us a larger sense of his notion of the society about him. In a later section of his account he devotes himself to that popular pastime then as now, a discussion of "the state of Crime." He has "obtained very accurate statistical details" on the subject, and sets them forth in tabular form.[38] One

[36] Cooke Taylor, pp. 11–14.

[37] I am putting to one side, though not overlooking, the strong likelihood that Cooke Taylor was also influenced in such remarks by ideological considerations. I also reserve for another place the corollary argument that the statements of hopeless impotence about human and social misery were at precisely this moment in history losing whatever moral legitimacy was still left to them.

[38] The first paper read before the Manchester Statistical Society was by W. R. Greg and was entitled "A Brief Memoir on the Present State of Criminal Statistics." T. S. Ashton, *Economic and Social Investigators in Manchester, 1833–1933* (London, 1934), p.

of these tables, "Miscellaneous Statistics for the year 1841," contains figures for Manchester on such topics as the number of pawnbrokers, public houses and brothels of various descriptions there were to be found in the Borough, on thieves, full- and part-time, on houses "for the reception of Stolen Property," and for "the Resort of Thieves," on lodging houses "where the Sexes indiscriminately Sleep together," and on lodging houses for the mendicant. Among all these unsavory details there is only one that moves Cooke Taylor to overt indignation. It occurs in a line which numbers the "Warehouses and Houses found Open by the Police in 1841"—there were 713 of them. This is a return, Cooke Taylor says, "which I think very disgraceful to Manchester . . . those who offer such temptation by their culpable negligence, should be made to bear some share of the punishment." [39] Such a comment inevitably recalls the celebrated paragraphs in which Thomas Hobbes imagined a state of nature by describing the circumstances of civilized society.[40] The bearing of this conception of society upon the minds of men at this time is a subject to which we shall return.

Cooke Taylor was present at the 1841 Manchester meeting of the Statistical Section of the British Association, and the extreme form in which he cast his unconscious separations and denials was only a telling variant of assertions that were being made all the time. Their range of variation was extensive. They might take the shape of a simple distinction, as, for example, when Cooke

---

14. On the problems connected with the use of criminal statistics, see J. J. Tobias, *Crime and Industrial Society in the Nineteenth Century* (London, 1967), pp. 14–21, 256–267.

[39] Cooke Taylor, pp. 250–255.

[40] *Leviathan*, Pt. I, ch. 13. "Let him therefore consider with himself, when taking a journey, he arms himself, and seeks to go well accompanied; when going to sleep, he locks his doors; when even in his house he locks his chests; and this when he knows there be laws, and public officers, armed, to revenge all injuries done him; what opinion he has of his fellow-subjects, when he rides armed; of his fellow-citizens, when he locks his doors; and of his children, and servants, when he locks his chests." See also C. B. Macpherson, *The Political Theory of Possessive Individualism* (Oxford, 1962), pp. 19ff.

Taylor reports that during the discussion of a paper by James P. Kay-Shuttleworth someone said that "the high rate of mortality in Manchester was owing to the want of drainage, ventilation, etc., and not to the factory system." [41] Kay-Shuttleworth himself was capable of wider sweeps than this, and his famous essay is full of passages such as the following:

we have exposed, with a faithful, though a friendly hand, the condition of the lower orders connected with the manufactures of this town, because we conceive that the evils affecting them result from *foreign and accidental causes*. A system, which promotes the advance of civilization, and diffuses it all over the world—which promises to maintain the peace of nations, by establishing a permanent international law, founded on the benefits of commercial association, cannot be inconsistent with the happiness of the *great mass of the people*.[42]

It all depends, to be sure, on what you mean by "system" and how you define it. What is most striking about this extract, however, is the uncertainty and insecurity concealed within its assertiveness. It begins with an unresolved ambiguity. The lower orders are somehow "connected"—how? loosely? organically? by juxtaposition? causally? casually? spatially? dependently?—with the distinguishing activities of the city. Yet the doubtful, loose syntax allows us to read that their "condition" may also be in some sort connected with those activities. But that connection, nonspecific as it may be, is established only to be immediately disavowed. The disavowal begins with semi-circularity, since "the evils" may be taken as a restatement of "the condition." Whatever they may be, they are brought about by causes that are "foreign"—to both the activities and the system of which they are a part. (One suspects a quasi-conscious allusion to the Irish

[41] Cooke Taylor, p. 262.
[42] James P. Kay-Shuttleworth, *The Moral and Physical Condition of the Working Classes Employed in the Cotton Manufacture in Manchester* (London, 1832), p. 47.

again.) Moreover, such causes are also "accidental"—to the
activities, to the system, and apparently to everything else. They
may be said virtually to have no meaning, which is not quite what
Kay-Shuttleworth set about to say. He goes on to his ringing
conclusion, and we can see how he arrives at it by following the
verbal changes he introduces. He begins with the simple present:
the "system . . . promotes . . . and diffuses" what is good; it
does it and is doing it right now. Such claims are at once qualified
by another form in the present: the system now "promises"; we
are back once again in the future. Those future promises give
way in turn to the participial "establishing": the future is thus
transformed into an indefinite and endless recession; it gets
further away. How then, amid this growing doubt and contingency, is Kay-Shuttleworth to reach the affirmation he seeks? He
does so by reaching out for what is unequivocally certain to him,
"the benefits of commercial association"; the certainty of this is
suggested and reinforced by the definiteness of "founded," the
uninflected past, closed off, conclusive, transparent, the strongest
verbal usage in the sentence. By means of this intervention of the
certain—both conceptually and syntactically—he can now go on
to the incontestable finality of "cannot," and complete his
triumphant demonstration. We can observe, however, that the
demonstration is largely assertion; and we can observe as well
how substantial an area of doubt there is within that triumph, how
many evidences of unconscious ambivalence such statements
disclose. Statements of this kind, it should be added, might be
used in the service of reform or as apologetics. They might also
be used as both simultaneously, and they were.[43]

The writings of the early researchers and reformers in
Manchester and elsewhere merit independent study. It has to be

[43] For a modernized but essentially unimproved version of the argument epitomized
here in the passages from Cooke Taylor and Kay-Shuttleworth, see Neil J. Smelser, *Social
Change in the Industrial Revolution* (London, 1959). For an acute critical appraisal of
Smelser from within his own professional specialization, see Robert A. Nisbet, *Social
Change and History* (New York, 1969), pp. 259ff.

enough to say here that these writings are never "neutral" in any
sense of that term, and are always highly charged with meanings
of all kinds and significances that extend in every direction. This
should not be surprising if we keep in mind the explosive nature
of most of the subjects with which these studies dealt, let alone
the explosive character of the times. The extract discussed above
is simply a single instance out of thousands. One opens Chadwick
at random, for example, and comes across this:

almost all [the extracts to be quoted] will be found to point to one
particular, namely, atmospheric impurity . . . as the main cause of the
ravages of epidemic, endemic, and contagious diseases . . . and as
aggravating most other diseases. The subsequent extracts . . . will show
that the impurity and its evil consequences are greater or less in different
places, according as there is more or less sufficient drainage of houses,
streets, roads, and land, combined with more or less sufficient means of
cleansing and removing solid refuse and impurities, by available supplies
of water for the purpose.[44]

We are in one of those "psycho-historical" moments in which
acute social circumstances intersect with and echo the deepest
unconscious processes and conflicts of individual men and of
groups of men. This confluence and reverberation give to the
ordinary actions of men a density of meaning that they would not
in less severe circumstances manifest; for they were, whether
they knew it or not—and many of them certainly knew
it—acting and living in the midst of a grand historical crisis. One
of the nodes of this crisis, one of the foci of the "psycho-historical" process, was Manchester.

Lastly, let us cast a brief glance at the foreigners. They too
come in all shapes and sizes, and the same constraints on space
will have to be observed in the discussion of them—I limit myself
to two instances, exclusive of course of Engels.

[44] Edwin Chadwick, *Report on the Sanitary Condition of the Labouring Population of
Great Britain* (1842), ed. M. W. Flinn (Edinburgh, 1965), p. 79.

In July 1843, Léon Faucher, a French economist with political ambitions, paid a visit to Lancashire. His experiences there and elsewhere in England shortly appeared in a number of articles published in 1843 and 1844 in the *Revue des Deux Mondes*. These were in turn reprinted, some of them in revised form, in two volumes, as *Études sur l'Angleterre* in 1845. The sections on Manchester were previously translated into English and German and published separately. Engels read the articles as they appeared in French and said that they formed "a better account than any hitherto given either by an English or a German author." (224)[45] Like almost everyone else, Faucher understands Manchester as possessing a central significance in *"la revolution industrielle,"* and after a short historical introduction he turns to it.

Nothing is more curious than the industrial topography of Lancashire. Manchester, like an industrious spider, is placed at the center of the web [*comme une araignée diligente, est posté au centre de la toile*], and sends forth roads and railways towards its auxiliaries, formerly villages, but now towns, which serve as outposts to the grand center of industry.[46]

At the confluence of three rivers, acting as a center from which a series of roads, canals and railroads radiated outward, Manchester represented in its very shape the armature or skeleton—some might say the substructure—of the new form of social organization. Faucher is of course getting all the mileage he can out of the various pertinent meanings of *toile,* but he shifts slightly away from this by the added elaboration of the more "poetic" spider.

It should also be remarked that the notion of the web is not merely a lucky hit by Faucher but is central to the general imagination of society in the middle of the nineteenth century. It

[45] To which Asa Briggs, *Victorian Cities,* pp. 113–114, adds his praise, leaving no need for any addition to this distinguished chorus of approval.

[46] The "member of the Manchester Athenaeum" who translated Faucher's essay mistook the French *"diligente"* for its cognate in English and so mistranslated it.

is to be found almost everywhere. It is prominently there in the later Dickens, it is all over the place in George Eliot, particularly in *Middlemarch,* and it figures centrally for Darwin in the *Origin of Species.* It forms as it were the underlying structural conception of sociology, which regards society as a web of relations. It turns up in the most remote, exotic and least expected places, as, for example, in the radically skeptical and repelling Thoreau:

However, our fates at least are social. Our courses do not diverge; but as the web of destiny is woven it is fulled, and we are cast more and more into the centre. Men naturally, though feebly, seek this alliance, and their actions faintly foretell it.

Such a passage may be regarded as the linguistic equivalent of getting blood out of a stone. Society therein is now representatively and consciously apprehended as our inescapable common fate, if not our doom. Moreover, within the prose itself one can observe the transformation of the classical weaving fates into the technological processes of production, the mediated reflex in consciousness of the actualities of social development.[47] In part the extensible power of this figure of the web had to do with the reality that the industry of "take-off" in the Industrial Revolution was textiles. In part, however, the power of this figure also has something to do with the circumstance that it can be thought of qualitatively as either organic (spun out from the body of a spider) or mechanical (woven by a machine or filiated like a grid)—or as a third thing which partakes of both and yet is neither and something else: that is, the human and social. As we shall see, it is this third quality or category that Engels will focus upon when he comes to write about Manchester.

[47] On top of all this, while Thoreau is pulling himself along the Concord and Merrimack and musing in this ironic vein, he is in fact passing by Lowell, "the city of spindles, and Manchester of America," and later on by Manchester itself, which was to become, bewilderingly, "another Lowell," in whose directory, Thoreau remarks, he read of a "Manchester Athenaeum and Gallery of the Fine Arts." *A Week on the Concord and Merrimack Rivers* [1849] (New York, 1961), pp. 329f., 98, 306f.

In using the spider, Faucher tips the balance toward the organic, a practice that he follows throughout his account and that often lapses into cliché. Doubtless he makes this turn because of the sinister associations that the spider also carries with it, and in his mind it is the sinister and the appalling impressions made by Manchester that tend to remain uppermost.[48] It is "an agglomeration the most extraordinary, the most interesting, and in some respects, the most monstrous, which the progress of society has improvised." There follow some representative "shocked" descriptive comments, and we get to the city itself. "All the houses, all the streets, resemble each other; and yet this uniformity is in the midst of confusion. On closer examination, however, a certain approximation to order is apparent." That looks promising, but the only order that Faucher discovers as he conducts the reader on a guidebook tour about the central section of the city, along the main streets, is that it had been constructed for the convenience of commerce and manufactures and not for human beings, which was true enough. Moreover, he duly notes, in other industrial towns, "industry has been grafted upon a pre-existing state of society," (note the organic again) while at Manchester "industry has found no previous occupant, and knows nothing but itself. Everything is alike, and everything is new; there is nothing but masters and operatives . . . The town realizes in some measure the Utopia of Bentham." That last is a nice twist on a received idea, since it is overwhelmingly evident that the utopia of utility is an anti-utopia for the multitudes who have been building it. He also takes notice, as had many others, of the demographic evacuation of the better-off classes from the center of the city to its periphery. *"La couche supérieure de la société se replie sur les campagnes,"* is his quaint way of phrasing it.[49] As for

[48] And no wonder. In the same year Carlyle found it necessary to remind his English audience that the Manchester operative was still a man and not a "two-legged Cotton-Spider." *Past and Present,* Bk. III, ch. 15.

[49] The earliest notation of this important structural change that I have come across dates from 1816. (In *Victorian Cities,* p. 103, Asa Briggs alludes to an observation that dates from

the rest, Faucher contents himself with this: "Manchester, according to the expression of another practitioner, Mr. Roberton, is nothing but a monstrous village, constructed without any kind of plan." [50] That is all right as far as it goes, which isn't very far. The web and all that it implies have vanished, and we are back amid the horrors, to which Faucher devotes a proportionate number of pages and about which he asks a series of pertinent questions.[51]

The greatest of these visitors was Alexis de Tocqueville, who stopped off in 1835. He too traveled by way of Birmingham, and in all his immediate reflections, Manchester appears at a radical

---

1795.) See W. Farrer and J. Brownbill, eds., *The Victoria History of Manchester* (London, 1911), IV, 182, quoting Joseph Aston, *Picture of Manchester* (Manchester, 1816).

In 1832, Richard Cobden wrote to his brother:

> I have given such a start to Mosley Street, that all the world will be at my heels soon. My next door neighbour, Brooks, of the firm of Cunliffe and Brooks, bankers, has sold his house to be converted into a warehouse. The owner of the house on the other side has given his tenant notice for the same purpose. The house immediately opposite to me has been announced for sale, and my architect is commissioned by George Hole, the calico-printer, to bid 6000 guineas for it; but they want 8000 for what they paid 4500 only five years ago. The architect assures me if I were to put up my house tomorrow, I might have 6000 guineas for it. So as I gave but 3000, and all the world is talking of the bargain here, and there being but one opinion or criterion of man's ability—*the making of money*—I am already thought a clever fellow. John Morley, *The Life of Richard Cobden* [1879] (London, 1903), p. 22.

[50] Léon Faucher, *Études sur L'Angleterre* (Paris, 1845), I, 251–265, 299; the translation of the essay on Manchester was published as *Manchester in 1844* (Manchester, 1844); the corresponding citations appear on pp. 15–26, 67–68; the translations have been slightly corrected.

The Mr. Roberton mentioned in the final quotation was a prominent member of the Manchester Statistical Society. He was actively involved in revealing the goings-on during the construction of the Woodhead tunnel. His work is touched on in Ashton, pp. 38–42; Terry Coleman, *The Railway Navvies* (Penguin, 1968), pp. 115–150, provides a substantial account of this scandal.

[51] Faucher surfaces again within the present context of attention as a result of his activities in the Paris of 1848–1851. He is to be found in *Class Struggles in France, 1848–1850* and *The 18th Brumaire of Louis Bonaparte,* where he comes in for some of Marx's bracing ministrations.

disadvantage.[52] He notes rapidly the absence of government and the prevalence of the Irish, the crowded and dreadful housing, the unclean and unpaved streets, the absence of sanitary conveniences, the disastrous separation of classes, the enormous factories, the bad and unhealthy appearance of the working people. In his few compressed pages of notes, we see a distinguished mind struggling to find terms that will render this assault of horrors coherent. As for the factories, he can do no better than "palaces" or "the huge palaces of industry." These are "scattered" about the landscape, and the wretched dwellings of the poor are in turn "scattered haphazard around them." The roads, which like all else show "every sign of hurried and unfinished work," connect, or barely connect, "the still-disjointed limbs of the great city"— which is here depicted as an unassembled Leviathan, a Frankenstein's monster yet to be put together.

Everything in the exterior appearance of the city attests the individual powers of man; nothing the directing powers of society. At every turn human liberty shows its capricious creative force. There is no trace of the slow continuous action of government.

Tocqueville is making the same statement twice; society in the first set of contrasted pairs is the same as government in the second—and what he really means in both is government. For all their pointedness and illumination there is something inadequate about these oppositions. Horror is not chaos, and a haphazard arrangement is not necessarily an arrangement without form and meaning.[53]

---

[52] As it does for different reasons in the pages of the contemporary urban theorist, Jane Jacobs. See *The Economy of Cities* (New York, 1969), pp. 86ff.

[53] Tocqueville may be unconsciously and ironically remembering a conversation he had with John Bowring during his earlier visit to England. Bowring told him that in England "each county, each town, each parish looks after its own interests. Industry is left to itself; so you will not see an unfinished undertaking in England, for since everything is done with a view to private profit, nothing is undertaken without the necessary capital, and while the project is unfinished, capital is idle."

The entire outward appearance of the town, he goes on, seems to him "the incidental activity of a population bent on gain, which seeks to amass gold so as to have everything else all at once, and in the interval, mistrusts the niceties of life." Is this the principle of coherence that he is looking for? The aristocratic Tocqueville had already written that "the respect paid to wealth in England is enough to make one despair." Everything he saw, he observed, led him to the conclusion that

the whole of English society is based on privileges of money. . . . There is not a country in the world where justice, that first need of peoples, is more the privilege of the rich. . . . Intelligence, even virtue, seem of little account without money. Everything worthwhile is somehow tied up with money. It fills all the gaps that one finds between men, but nothing will take its place.

At Birmingham he saw people working "as if they must get rich by the evening and die the next day." They were generally very intelligent, he adds, "but intelligent in the American way." When he asked whether "a class of unoccupied people" existed in Birmingham, he got back the answer: "No. Everybody works to make a fortune. The fortune made, everyone goes somewhere else to enjoy it." It was a veritable "cult of money . . . the hallmark not of wealth alone, but of power, reputation and glory." It even went beyond all these and minted itself upon the substance of the language. "So where the Frenchman says, 'He has 100,000 francs of income,' the Englishman says, 'He is worth £5,000 a year.'" This is precisely the kind of insight one expects an intelligent foreigner to hit upon, and it is interesting that Engels arrived independently at the same awareness.

The miserable slavery in which money keeps the individual member of the middle classes is by means of the domination of the middle classes as a whole impressed even upon the language itself. Money makes up the worth of a man; this man is worth ten thousand pounds—*"he is worth ten thousand pounds,"* i.e., he owns that sum (312).

[Die elende Sklaverei, in der das Geld den Bourgeois hält, ist durch die Bourgeoisieherrschaft selbst der Sprache aufgedrückt. Das Geld macht den Wert des Mannes aus; dieser Mann is zehntausend Pfund wert—he is worth ten thousand pounds, d.h., er besitzt sie.] [54]

It only remains to be added that this particular question was brought back consciously to its historical origins and thus, in the Hegelian sense, fulfilled and superseded in the single quotation that Marx saw fit to pick up out of Hobbes and drop without comment into a footnote: "The value, or worth of a man, is as of all other things, his price; that is to say, so much as would be given for the use of his power." [55]

---

[54] Engels, like Tocqueville before him, is lumping the aristocracy in as part of the middle classes. "When I speak of the 'bourgeoisie' in this chapter I am referring not only to the middle classes proper but also to the so-called aristocracy." (311) And they do so for similar reasons.

In the *Manifesto* of 1848, Marx and Engels went so far as to assert that the middle classes had achieved "exclusive political sway" over the state; but they later came to realize that in England actual political power had been largely retained by the landed aristocracy which governed nonetheless in the interest of the economically more powerful middle classes.

Henderson and Chaloner have gummed up part of Engels' meaning, and I have had to supply a translation.

[55] *Capital,* Vol. I, pt. ii, ch. 6. There is, of course, a tradition for this that moves in several languages. Tocqueville would have read in Rousseau's first *Discourse* about the modern politicians who, unlike the ancients, "talk only of business and money. One will tell you that in a given country a man is worth the price he would fetch in Algiers; another, following this calculation, will discover some countries where a man is worth nothing and others where he is worth less than nothing. They evaluate men like herds of cattle." Rousseau in turn is alluding to a passage in Montesquieu's *Spirit of the Laws,* XXIII, xvii, which refers to Sir William Petty, who "supposed in his calculations, that a man in England is worth what he could be sold for in Algiers. That can only be true for England; there are countries where a man is worth nothing; there are some where he is worth less than nothing." Jean-Jacques Rousseau, *The First and Second Discourses,* ed. Roger D. Masters (New York, 1964), pp. 51, 71. And Sir William Petty was both the founder of classical English political economy and friend of Hobbes—which brings us at length back to Marx, who was a great admirer of Petty's intellect, if not his character. See his remarks on Petty in the *Critique of Political Economy* and in *Anti-Dühring,* Pt. II, ch. 10 (written by Marx).

It may be useful to recall that English writers were in no way behindhand in their critical recognition. See, for example, *Sense and Sensibility,* ch. 2, which is constructed out

Yet Tocqueville seems unsatisfied that this single abstract principle accounts for the conerete realities by which he has been bombarded. Standing amid this urban debris and rubble, on settled ground that reveals "no trace of surveyor's rod or spirit-level," he slowly begins to make out certain structures. He now conceives of himself as being in a "noisome labyrinth"; later on it is a "damp, dark labyrinth"; this is further particularized into a "great, sombre stretch of brickwork," now and then astonishingly interrupted by "fine stone buildings with Corinthian columns." It might, he continues to try, "be a medieval town with the marvels of the nineteenth century in the middle of it." [56] But this collocation is of no avail, since he immediately finds himself unable to describe, to put into words, the interiors of the workers' dwellings, "these quarters set apart, home of vice and poverty," which at the same time "surround" the huge palaces of industry "and clasp them in their hideous folds." It was almost inevitable that sooner or later those palaces would have led him to Paris, a historical recollection of which flits momentarily through his mind. Some kind of relation, however, seems to be emerging. With this he mentally steps back and reconstructs his vision of one of the districts situated along one of the rivers. It consists largely of ground that is actually "below the level of the river," marshy land, undrained and uncleansed. Behind and above, the area is "overshadowed on every side by immense workshops," and "narrow twisting roads lead down to it." These are "lined with one-story houses," whose outward condition reveals them "even from a distance, as the last refuge a man might find between poverty and death." Nevertheless, "the wretched people

---

of such an awareness and in which one character or another is continually letting off such remarks as: " 'Fifteen years! my dear Fanny; her life cannot be worth half that purchase.' "

[56] Cf. Faucher, p. 16. "It is distinguished neither by those contrasting features which mark the cities of the middle ages, nor by that regularity which characterizes the capitals of recent formation."

reduced to living in them" are not the final reduction. "Below some of their miserable dwellings is a row of cellars to which a sunken corridor leads." Into each of "these damp, repulsive holes," from "twelve to fifteen human beings are crowded pell-mell." He has perceived a simple but terrible configuration. It is down, down, down; it is below, and below the below. Tocqueville has grasped here what Carlyle was to grasp with perhaps even fuller power. Contemplating these same Irish immigrants, Carlyle wrote: "Whosoever struggles, swimming with difficulty, may now find an example how the human being can exist not swimming but sunk." [57] But sunk in what? That is a consideration we must for a moment postpone.[58]

Tocqueville is still not finished, but he is weary. The river seems to him "the Styx of this new Hades." He looks around himself once again and tries still another time to bring what he has seen to intelligible generality, but all he can make out are irreducible polarities: here and there, masters and slaves, wealth

[57] *Chartism,* ch. 4.

[58] "Oh," replied Mr. Pickwick, looking down a dark and filthy staircase, which appeared to lead to a range of damp and gloomy stone vaults, beneath the ground, "and those, I suppose, are the little cellars where the prisoners keep their small quantities of coals. Unpleasant places to have to go down to; but very convenient, I dare say."

"Yes, I shouldn't wonder if they was convenient," replied the gentleman, "seeing that a few people live there, pretty snug. That's the Fair, that is."

"My friend," said Mr. Pickwick, "you don't really mean to say that human beings live down in those wretched dungeons?"

"Don't I?" replied Mr. Roker, with indignant astonishment: "why shouldn't I?"

"Live! Live down there!" exclaimed Mr. Pickwick.

"Live down there! Yes, and die down there, too, wery often!" replied Mr. Roker; "and what of that? Who's got to say anything agin it? Live down there! Yes, and a wery good place it is to live in, ain't it?" *Pickwick Papers,* ch. 41.

The connection between the prison dungeons and the urban cellar dwellings was to be further raised into consciousness in a few years by Edwin Chadwick, who wrote: "More filth, worse physical suffering and moral disorder than Howard describes as affecting the prisoners, are to be found amongst the cellar population of the working people of Liverpool, Manchester, or Leeds, and in large portions of the metropolis." *Report on the Sanitary Condition of the Labouring Population of Great Britain* (1842; 1965 ed.), p. 277.

and poverty, the efforts of thousands and the profit of one. "Here the weakness of the individual seems more feeble and helpless even than in the middle of the wilderness." [59] And he closes this series feebly and distractedly with "here the effects, there the causes." He then turns back to the concrete and notices, as others had done, the thousand noises of this new city, which "are not at all the ordinary sounds one hears in great cities." He is obscurely aware not merely of differences in sounds, but that the level of sound was changing and along with it the structures of auditory experience—in particular those processes having to do with thresholds, filtering and closure. But he can do little more than list further items and details. Finally, he pulls himself together for one last effort.

From this foul drain the greatest stream of human industry flows out to fertilize the whole world. From this filthy sewer pure gold flows. Here humanity attains its most complete development and its most brutish; here civilization works its miracles, and civilized man is turned back almost into a savage.[60]

That is the real thing. The mind, reaching out in its perplexity, has at last discovered the means by which it can appropriate these unbearable extremities and actualities. It does so by reproducing in itself the processes that are occurring out there. The processes are conceived of as a series of enormous transformations; these transformations are composed of contradictions; but the contradictions consist not simply in opposites but in opposites that are at the same time inseparable unifications. The world-transforming achievement is indivisibly bound up with the monstrous human cost and sacrifice.

It is within this rich and varied context of writings that we shall have to regard Engels' work.

[59] Earlier he had noted, "Inability of the poor to act in isolation."
[60] Alexis de Tocqueville, *Journeys to England and Ireland*, ed. J. P. Mayer (New York, 1968), pp. xvii, 45f., 77f., 82f., 93–96.

Friedrich Engels
from 1820 to 1845

It is remarkable how alien and incomprehensible the stuff I had to handle was to me. I was put first into the Manchester department, and there I found fixtures of wrappered blocks labelled incomprehensibly Hard Book or Turkey Twill or the like, rolls of grey and black silesia, flannels with a variety of names, a perplexing range of longcloths and calicoes, endless packages of diaper table-cloths, serviettes, and so forth, and rolls of crash, house cloth, ticking and the like. All that stuff . . . seemed to have been created to make my life burthensome. There were also in this Manchester department cotton dress materials, prints, ginghams and sateens, cretonne and kindred fabrics for covering furniture; stuffs that were rather more understandable but equally irksome to handle.
—H. G. Wells, *Experiment in Autobiography*

FRIEDRICH ENGELS was born in the Rhineland town of Barmen in 1820. He was the eldest son of a prosperous textile manufacturer, who was himself the son and grandson of mill-owners. Although at this time Germany as a whole had hardly been touched by the Industrial Revolution, Barmen had been the site of a developing textile industry since the sixteenth century and was in fact one of

the first areas in Germany to undergo thorough industrialization.[1]
At the time of Engels' birth, the town had a population of about
20,000; it was, however, part of a larger and growing conurbation
of textile centers in the valley of the Wupper river—the
Wuppertal—and surrounding regions. And if we can detect some
understandable hyperbole in the local claim that it was *das
deutsche Manchester,* still it is essential to note that industrial life
was not something that was ever foreign or unfamiliar to
Engels—it lay about him in his infancy. A second major
formative circumstance is to be found in the religion practiced in
the family, in particular by the father. The Calvinist Pietism of
the Reformed Churches of the Lower Rhine was even then
famous. Ascetic, practical, methodical, worldly, industrious and
successful, they almost seem—as one reads about them today—to
have been invented for the convenience of Max Weber.[2] It is
fitting, then, that in the one story from Engels' early childhood
that has come down to us, all these, as well as other influences and
portents, should be inseparably fused. Family records emphasize
the early date at which his kindly and charitable nature expressed
itself—he often gave all his little savings to the poor.[3] What have
we here? the mill-owner's oldest son, anticipating in a small,
lordly way his future social duties; the young Pietist, counting his
blessings as he dispenses them; or do we have a hint of the grown
man who is going to spend the larger part of his adult life
working without complaint to support another man, his family
and his work, again in the cause of the oppressed? It is of course
impossible to say; nevertheless, not every child who has "willingly"—which often means under the pressure of coercive

[1] Gustav Mayer, *Friedrich Engels: Eine Biographie* (The Hague, 1934) I, 4–6; also
W. Koellmann, "The Population of Barmen before and during the period of Industrialization," in D. Glass and D. E. C. Eversley, eds., *Population in History* (London, 1965), pp.
588–607.
[2] See Ernst Troeltsch, *The Social Teaching of the Christian Churches* [1911] (New York,
1960), pp. 656–691; also *Aufsätze zur Geistesgeschichte und Religionssoziologie* (Tübingen,
1925), pp. 488–531.
[3] Mayer, I, 9.

persuasion—given up his pennies continues to give without stint in his later life. In a general sense, then, these predisposing tendencies in Engels' early experience were the personal and psychic counterparts of the two influences which, as John Stuart Mill wrote, "have chiefly shaped the British character since the days of the Stuarts: commercial money-getting business, and religious Puritanism." [4] Or as Mr. Pancks, the harassed rent-collector in *Little Dorrit,* suggests with a certain measure of asperity: " 'Keep me always at it, and I'll keep you always at it, you keep somebody else always at it. There you are with the Whole Duty of Man in a commercial country.' " [5]

Until he was fourteen, Engels attended the Pietist-run *Realschule* in Barmen.[6] He then transferred to the *Gymnasium* in neighboring Elberfeld, a much superior institution. He was not, however, destined to complete his course of work there, and he left a year before his final examinations—which brings us to a first interpretative crux. Engels' biographer, Gustav Mayer, informs us that according to family tradition Friedrich had originally intended to study law and pursue the career of a civil servant. Two versions exist of how this intention came to no account. According to one, Engels' father was opposed to a university education for his son and exercised his full paternal authority in determining that his son should enter commerce, a career for which the latter had no inclination. The other holds that Friedrich himself had renounced the idea of going on to a university course in law, because he already entertained liberal views and did not wish to become a Prussian official. Mayer

---

[4] Inaugural Address" [1867], reprinted in *Mill's Essays on Literature and Society*, ed. J. B. Schneewind (New York, 1965), pp. 403f.

[5] *Little Dorrit*, ch. 13.

[6] In his first published pseudonymous essay, "Letters from the Wuppertal," Engels recalls that on one occasion when a third-form boy asked who Goethe was, one of the teachers replied, *"ein gottloser Mann."* For a modern, satirical version of this, see Kurt Tucholsky, "Hitler und Goethe: Ein Schulaufsatz," *Panter, Tiger & Co.* (Hamburg, 1954), pp. 144–146.

believes that neither of these versions is wholly reliable and cites
in evidence some phrases from the leaving report written by
Engels' headmaster, who was a friend of the family and in whose
house young Engels had lived *en pension*. He wrote that "instead
of his earlier plans for going to the University," young Engels
"believed himself inclined to adopt as his external career" a
business life. At seventeen, Mayer continues, Engels believed that
his "inner and real" career was literature, and although it was
impossible in view of family tradition and the opinions of his
father to pursue such a career openly, it might be possible to
pursue a business life during the day and dwell upon Helicon in
the evenings. Mayer thus effectively discounts the two versions
that come from the family.

This episode bears every sign of being overdetermined, as the
multiplicity of interpretations in the original sources themselves
almost unmistakably suggests. The episode is prototypical. In a
number of the most important decisions in Engels' life it is
impossible to separate out cleanly and unambiguously the roles
played by him and his father, a circumstance which suggests a
depth and complexity in that relation which commentators on
Engels have avoided.[7] Deeply opposed as father and son came to
be, they contrived at the same time never finally to let go of each
other. Without ascribing priority to any of the three accounts of
the decision, we can see that each of them contains truth and
plausibility and that they complement one another. It would be
characteristic of the elder Engels to enforce such a course on his

[7] Henderson and Chaloner argue that Engels wrote *The Condition of the Working Class
in England* essentially to take it out on his father, thereby revealing themselves as
vulgarizers of psychoanalysis, along with their other numerous qualifications. Such
mindless triviality does not, however, license the truly surprising remark of Hobsbawm,
who in the course of vigorously reproving Henderson and Chaloner on just this score,
goes on to state: "We need not waste our time psychoanalysing the young Engels,
because the motives which may or may not have urged him to become a Communist
are totally irrelevant." Which leads one to reflect that it isn't literary
critics alone who have lessons to learn about the nature and meaning of historical
relevance.

son; the father's behavior toward his eldest son was alternately generous and punitive; his concern over the hygiene of his son's spiritual state had authorized him, as he himself confessed, to expose the young boy to "severe punishment"; it also gave him an alibi for snooping among his son's belongings and to be duly horrified by what he had found there before Friedrich was yet fifteen—a "dirty book," a romance set in the thirteenth century that his son had borrowed from a circulating library. Moreover, in the circumstances of the times there was nothing exceptionable about such a decision: the sons of manufacturers, even wealthy ones, often did not go on to the university.[8] At the same time, significant weight must be attached to the statement of the headmaster, in which he appears to be reporting what young Engels had said to him. In that phrase "external career," along with its implied counterpart of an internal career, we can make out that when he was not yet seventeen Engels was prepared to enter, quite openly, upon a style of life whose informing quality was its doubleness. And in fact, Engels did live something like a double life throughout a major part of his career—although again he did so with that curiously disarming openness that constitutes so much of his charm as a person. Furthermore, in choosing these two concurrent careers, the young man seems to have been

---

[8] This practice was followed in England as much as in Germany.

> Mr. Hale met with several pupils. . . . They were mostly of the age when many boys would be still at school, but, according to the prevalent, and apparently well-founded notions of Milton, to make a lad into a good tradesman he must be caught young, and acclimated to the life of the mill, or office, or warehouse. If he were sent to even the Scotch Universities, he came back unsettled for commercial pursuits: how much more so if he went to Oxford or Cambridge, where he could not be entered till he was eighteen? So most of the manufacturers placed their sons in sucking situations at fourteen or fifteen years of age, unsparingly cutting away all off-shoots in the direction of literature or high mental cultivation, in hopes of throwing the whole strength and vigour of the plant into commerce. *North and South*, ch. 8. Milton is of course Manchester.

The later breaking-down of such class-bound or directed conventions of behavior has been discussed by Raymond Williams as a failure of nerve on the part of the English middle class as a whole. *The Long Revolution* (London, 1961), pp. 319ff.

trying to strike a balance between paternal and maternal
identifications, since we know that his interest in literature—
along with his extraordinarily sanguine and flexible temperament
—came in large measure from his mother. We may also note in
the phrase "believed himself inclined [*veranlasst sehe*]" more than
a touch of the tentative and temporary; and it may be conjectured
that young Engels was taking this way as a moratorium and that,
like young people today, he was apprehensive that proceeding
onward and upward without interruption into the university
pipeline would act as a premature foreclosure on possibilities and
capacities that were only now beginning to develop in him. Yet
there is contradiction here as well. Going on to the university
does not now and did not then necessarily imply foreclosure; even
the study of the law did not necessarily imply the Prussian civil
service. And so we are entitled to see something of ambivalent
submissiveness and adolescent self-punishment and spite in
Friedrich's decision—whether it was made in response to his
father's command or was his own voluntary choice. For the irony
turned out to be that there was nothing temporary about it at all;
with minor but significant modifications, a permanent pattern of
his life was becoming clear. Finally, he found additional support
and encouragement when he learned that the popular poet
Ferdinand Freiligrath was at the moment employed as a clerk in a
Barmen business establishment. Engels' youthful poetry immediately turned into imitations of Freiligrath.

It may be useful at this point to introduce some further material
in support of the assertions I have made about the indistinct
distribution of roles between Engels senior and junior, particularly in certain moments of decision. The first source of such
material is one of the younger Engels' surviving pieces of
"creative" effort. It dates from the same year I have been
discussing, 1837, and is a fragment of a romance in prose, "*Eine
Seeräubergeschichte* [A Pirate Story]." For the most part it is a
Byronic imitation, with glancing references to Homer. As far as

its literary interest goes, it's not quite up to the level of *A Bishop among the Bantus*.[9] It opens in a harbor on Salamis in the year 1820—the year of Engels' birth. Two sailors are discussing a young man who is standing off to one side. One sailor describes him to the other as "the new passenger who was taken on [*engagiert*]" by the captain the evening before. The captain, he goes on, wants to make him a member of the ship's crew or company; and indeed has disclosed his intention of drowning the young man in the sea if he refuses to join them and persists in his plan to go traveling to Istanbul instead. It does not require very much literary acuity to penetrate into the "allegorical" intention of such statements; the correspondences are transparently one to one, with almost no complicating displacements. And so it continues; the ship pulls out of the harbor, and the captain invites the young man below where he offers him wine and a deal.

"Now, listen, I would like to make you a proposal. But what's your name? And where are you from?"

"I am called Leon Papon, and I am from Athens. And you?"

"Captain Leonidas Spezziotis (from Spezzia) [sic]. But listen, you probably take us to be honest merchants? Well, we are not. Take a look at our cannons, open and concealed, our ammunition, our arms-room, and you will easily realize that we follow our shop-keeping activity only as a pretext. And you shall see that we are different and better people, namely genuine Hellenes, people who still know how to treasure freedom—in short, corsairs. . . ."

The captain then proceeds to say that he likes young Leon and that "you remind me very much of a dear son who was shot before my eyes by the infidels last year." Therefore, he proposes to the youth "that you become one of us and fight with us together for the freedom of the Hellenes." To which the latter replies: "What are you saying? Corsairs? I become one of you? On the spot! I shall be able to revenge myself on the murderers of my father!"

[9] See Graham Greene, *The Heart of the Matter* (London, 1948), Bk. II, pt. 1, ch. 1.

One resists the impulse to discuss analytically this degree of innocence. Engels not only identifies the two characters through their names, but throughout the balance of the story confuses them consistently through pronominal references, and on several occasions identifies one with the name of the other. (That they are not in the story "really" father and son, but that one resembles the dead son and the other has a dead father who has also to be revenged, merely serves to indicate what the reality really is.) Moreover, they are only ostensibly merchants; in actuality they are Hellenes, heroic fighters for freedom. This latter is a nicer stroke, for what young Engels is, unconsciously I believe, trying to do is to assimilate the life and work of commerce to the earlier heroic phase of the bourgeois revolution. Still the doubleness noted earlier is very much in evidence. Leonidas then shows Leon around the ship; and Engels' description of the provisions, supplies, clothes and arms alternates between Homeric catalog and a merchant's periodical inventory, inclining more toward the latter; a tendency that is confirmed when they capture a Turkish ship that is loaded with cotton, and sell it to an English businessman! The story becomes increasingly bloody and increasingly incoherent, and finally breaks off without being able to develop any further than what has been suggested. Apart from the fusions, identifications and wish-fulfillments, the chief impulse of the story seems clearly to be a desire for reconciliation with his father.[10]

For the next year Engels remained in Barmen, working apparently at his apprenticeship in his father's firm. In August 1838 he was sent to Bremen, again on his father's initiative, in order to further his business training. The next bit of evidence is to be found in the first surviving letter that Engels wrote from there; it is dated on the 28th and 29th of the month and is addressed to his favorite sister, Marie. He tells her that on the

[10] *Werke*, Ergänzungsband, Pt. 2, pp. 510–521.

latter morning a barber had come to the house of the Orthodox
pastor with whom Engels was living; the pastor had suggested
that Friedrich allow himself to be shaved, since his appearance
was "utterly frightful." Friedrich had turned the suggestion down
for the following reason. His father had told him, he writes, that
"I should allow my razor to remain sealed until I need it." Engels
senior had left Bremen two weeks before this, and during that
interval, the son continues, his beard cannot have grown to such
an extent. Indeed, he affirms, he will not shave himself before he
has grown a raven-black mustache. He then reminds his sister of
the story of the razors. Their mother had said that "Father should
give me a set of razors." Father had answered "that would really
be to tempt or seduce [*verführen*] me, and had bought me them
himself in Manchester." However, the son concludes, "I will not
use them, out of principle." [11] One now understands rather better
why the corsair captain was called Leonidas; and as for the rest,
the ambivalences and ambiguities are distributed with bewildering even-handedness. Leon and Leonidas are at this moment
being represented as Alphonse and Gaston. The father anxiously
and reluctantly confers manhood upon his son, who accepts it
gratefully only in order to hand it back into his senior's
safekeeping. This amusing little incident has a positive sign next
to it. It will be represented again and again, in a series of negative
analogues, throughout the life of Engels senior and even after he
is dead.[12] The dynamics, however, remain the same.

In Bremen, Friedrich Engels worked in the office of Consul
Heinrich Leupold, a business-friend of his father and the head of a
textile-exporting firm. He remained there until Easter 1841. The
years in Bremen were also to serve as useful preparation for the
experience of Manchester, which was, as A. J. P. Taylor has

[11] *Werke*, Ergänzungsband, Pt. 2, pp. 326f.

[12] There are striking similarities in the way both Friedrich Engelses behaved toward
their respective sets of brothers when it came to matters of inheritance and the family
business.

aptly observed, "the last and greatest of the Hanseatic towns." [13] Of closer pertinence is the rapid intellectual development that Engels now began to undergo. He soon came under the influence of Karl Gutzkow, writer and editor, and one of the central figures in the literary-democratic movement that called itself Young Germany. Through Gutzkow, Engels became further acquainted with the writings of Ludwig Börne, a more overtly political and radical literary critic and journalist; Börne had belonged to an earlier generation (he died in 1837), but his essays had influenced the opinions of the first Young Germans. Gutzkow was at this time living in Hamburg and editing from there the *Telegraph für Deutschland*; it was in the pages of this newspaper that Engels' earliest essays appeared, first anonymously, later pseudonymously. At the same time Engels was going through the final phases of a rapid and thorough deconversion from the religion of his family; this development was furthered and assimilated into additional intellectual significance by his reading in the spring of 1839 of David Friedrich Strauss's *Life of Jesus*.[14] A few months later he found himself involved in the overwhelming experience

---

[13] A. J. P. Taylor, "Manchester," *Encounter*, VIII, 3 (March 1957), 3.

During the latter part of the eighteenth century Manchester's export trade with the Continent had expanded rapidly. The best European markets for British textile goods were in Germany and Italy. Hamburg and Bremen were the chief northern ports through which these goods passed, being transshipped from there either as consignments to certain mercantile houses throughout northern and central Europe, or distributed in a variety of ways to be sold at the great seasonal fairs that were held in many of the larger towns. See A. P. Wadsworth and J. deL. Mann, *The Cotton Trade and Industrial Lancashire, 1600–1780* (Manchester, 1931), pp. 164ff.; A. Redford, *Manchester Merchants and Foreign Trade, 1794–1858* (Manchester, 1934), pp. 25–31, 94ff.

[14] "For Germany . . . the criticism of religion is the premise or presupposition [*Voraussetzung*] of all criticism." K. Marx, "Zur Kritik der Hegelschen Rechtsphilosophie: Einleitung," *Werke*, I, 378; also in *Marx and Engels on Religion* (Moscow, 1957), p. 41.

Strauss's *Life of Jesus* (1835–1836) furthered such criticism through its application of myth theory to the Gospels; it denied historical reality to the supernatural parts of the account, and interpreted the development of early Christianity in generally Hegelian terms. The work produced a great sensation at the time. It was published in English in 1846; the anonymous translator was Mary Anne Evans, who was soon to become George Eliot.

of Hegel, going through that reconversion to new ideas, beliefs and ideologies through which successive generations of young persons discover their historical tasks and possibilities. It was without question the most important intellectual experience of his life, as it was for others both before and after him.[15]

Engels was now nineteen years old. His first published essays, the "Letters from the Wuppertal," appeared anonymously in the *Telegraph für Deutschland* in March and April, 1839—in a few months he would begin to use the pseudonym Friedrich Oswald. They are of passing interest here both because they are his earliest published efforts and because they anticipate *The Condition of the Working Class in England*. The first of these reports begins with a description of the valley itself, with the narrow Wupper flowing between smoking factories and yarn-covered bleaching-grounds. The waters of the river are purplish and dark red, not from bloody battle or from shame over the goings-on of men in the region, although there are plentiful grounds for such blushes; the river is simply discolored by the many dye-works that line its banks. He then goes on to describe the buildings, houses and churches in the valley, and concludes with the remark that in general the external appearance of the valley makes a very friendly impression. As on first sight so do the journeymen who can be seen of an evening marching in the streets singing their songs. On closer inspection, however, the observer will perceive that they are drunk, that the public houses are full to overflowing, that numbers of the workers who are turned out when the drinking places close at eleven sleep it off in the gutters, that some of them, particularly the carriers, have no permanent jobs or lodgings and spend the night anywhere, even sleeping on

---

[15] For an account of the various intellectual influences which played upon Engels during these years, see Mayer, I, 18–118; also Franz Mehring, *Karl Marx* (Ann Arbor, 1962), pp. 9–108, *passim;* David McLellan, *Marx Before Marxism* (New York, 1970), *passim;* a fundamentally unsympathetic account is also to be found in Peter Demetz, *Marx, Engels, and the Poets* (Chicago and London, 1967), pp. 9–33.

dunghills. Even the songs they sing are of a low and obscene character and are not the folk songs known through Germany and "of which we can be proud." The proximate cause of this demoralization, Engels was to write years later, was the sudden flooding of the lower Rhineland at about this time with cheap spirits from Prussia.[16]

One of the fundamental causes for this general state of affairs, he continues, is factory work, and he goes on to describe concisely the bad conditions under which the workers, especially the domestic hand-loom weavers, are compelled to live. He describes their generally deteriorated health—tuberculosis and venereal disease were widespread—and speaks of the large number of children of school age who are deprived of instruction and are forced to grow up in the factories, an injustice which he attributes wholly to the manufacturers' greed: one cannot overlook an unconscious reference to his own circumstances. Indeed, he goes on, "the rich factory owners have highly elastic consciences, and no Pietist will go to Hell for ruining one child more or less—especially if he goes to church twice every Sunday." Still worse, he asserts, is the fact that the Pietists themselves are the harshest factory owners and use their religious convictions to grind down the workers even further. As for the workers, they are hopelessly trapped: "those who do not fall into the hands of the Pietists, fall under the influence of alcohol." He then proceeds to delineate the Pietist world of Barmen-Elberfeld, summarizing its religious doctrines, composing character sketches of the leading clergymen, analyzing at length their influence upon the various orders and levels of schools in the district, and describing the kind of education that the children of the middle classes have been exposed to.

Its after-effects can be traced in the older generation of Barmen businessmen. As for education in its widest sense [*Bildung*]—not an

[16] Mayer, I, 12–13.

idea. In Barmen and Elberfeld an educated man is understood to be someone who can play whist and billiards, knows how to chat about politics, and is able to turn a pretty compliment. These people lead a terrible life, and yet they are at the same time so pleased with it all: daylong they sink themselves in the figures of their account-books, and they do so with a frenzy and an interest that is scarcely believable; in the evenings they gather together at stipulated hours to play cards, gossip about politics, and smoke, only in order to return home at the stroke of nine. So it goes every day, without variation. . . . The young people have been fairly taken in hand by their fathers and show every promise of becoming just like them. Their subjects of conversation are rather uniform; the young Barmers tend to speak more frequently about horses, those from Elberfeld about dogs; at the very most some of the local female beauties are passed in review, or they prattle about business matters—and that is all. Once every half-century, they speak about literature. . . .

And he concludes by reviewing further the cultural desert that is his native heath.[17]

It is perfectly clear that the young man who wrote this is getting back at his parents and their world; but it is also clear that he is not yet prepared to do so in his own name, which is also

[17] *Werke*, I, 413–432. There was, however, an oasis in the waste. Years later, Engels recalled that "for us narrow-minded, philistine Wuppertalers, Düsseldorf was always a little Paris, where the pious gentlemen of Barmen and Elberfeld kept their mistresses, went to the theatre and lived it up royally. But the sky is always leaden where one's own reactionary family lives. Moreover, the advancement of industrial development, which has spread to Düsseldorf as well, is extremely oppressive and deadly boring throughout all of Germany, so that I can well imagine that the Wuppertal's dreariness and wretchedness have now conquered Düsseldorf as well." *Werke*, XXXIII, 485.

In this connection it is pertinent to recall that "at the beginning of modern times it was by no means the capitalistic entrepreneurs of the commercial aristocracy, who were either the sole or the predominant bearers of the attitude we have here called the spirit of capitalism. It was much more the rising strata of the lower industrial middle classes. Even in the nineteenth century its classical representatives were not the elegant gentlemen of Liverpool and Hamburg, with their commercial fortunes handed down for generations, but the self-made parvenus of Manchester and Westphalia, who often rose from very modest circumstances." Max Weber, *The Protestant Ethic and the Spirit of Capitalism*, trans. T. Parsons (New York, 1930), p. 65.

theirs. He is not prepared to accept or assert the identity that he has inherited from his father even as he rebels against it and begins to transform it in the direction of new responsibilities. Moreover, as I have already suggested, the structure of the "Letters from the Wuppertal" is a nuclear prevision of the later work. Here he begins by describing the physical circumstances of the valley and the towns, goes on to the condition of the working people, and then describes the life and culture of the Wuppertal middle classes. *The Condition of the Working Class in England* will follow exactly the same structure of progression with this difference—the proportions will be reversed. In the "Letters from the Wuppertal" by far the largest part of the essay is devoted to the sardonic representation of the middle class; in *The Condition of the Working Class in England*, the middle class will be there again at the end, but this time reduced to the confines of a single chapter. This shift in proportions signifies something more than an increment in knowledge on the part of Engels; it suggests as well a shifting in identifications and a new and altered balance of psychic forces. And by that time he had gotten used to writing under his own name.

Engels left Bremen in the spring of 1841 and returned to his parents' home in Barmen. His father apparently wanted to send him next to Milan, where he would continue his business training, but this scheme came to nothing. After several months characterized by desultory traveling and regular squabbling with his father, he arrived at the temporary solution of volunteering for his year of military service, although he could have evaded it without trouble. It was, to be sure, another way of putting off a final decision; at the same time it was also an expedient way to get to Berlin, to the university there, and to the yeasty intellectual life of the Young Hegelians, into whose cause of religious and cultural radicalism he at once precipitated himself. It was, in addition, one step closer to the life of political activity. To the poet and literary critic concealed within the broadcloth of the young businessman, there succeeded the young philosophical radical inside the uniform of a guardsman in the regiment of Household Artillery; years later in Manchester the revolutionary socialist leader inside the pink coat of a fox-hunting man would also make his due appearance. In the meantime, however, Engels hastened to attend the Berlin event of the year. To put down the obstreperous Young (or Left) Hegelians, the Prussian government had brought over from Munich the aged Schelling, long-time opponent of Hegel and all his works, and had installed him to lecture in philosophy. The particular contents of Schelling's lectures are of little importance now. But seated in the audience that heard them were a number of young men; in addition to Engels, there were Kierkegaard, Burckhardt and Bakunin. None of them was known to any of the others, and yet one feels that one would have to seek carefully indeed to find another such occasion on which as much of Europe's intellectual future was gathered casually together under one roof. What had symbolically brought them there was what in fact their radically divergent futures would reveal—the final decomposition of the Hegelian synthesis, which may with extreme simplicity be described as itself the culminating systematic effort to bring the classical German enlightenment to a transcendent conclusion, while subsuming within itself the explosive and subversive new powers of the romantic upheaval. It was a moment of historical poignancy; a great cultural divide had been permanently crossed.[18]

Nevertheless, Engels did not spend his time repining over this cultural loss. During his year in Berlin, he audited other lectures at the university, consorted with *Die Freien*—the Freemen— among whom Left Hegelianism and bohemian buffoonery were becoming indistinguishable, passed temporarily beneath the influence of such luminaries as the Bauers and Max Stirner,

[18] Walter Lowrie, *Kierkegaard* (1938), pp. 233–235; Werner Kaegi, *Jacob Burckhardt: Eine Biographie* (Basel, 1950), II, 191–192; E. H. Carr, *Bakunin* [1937] (New York, 1961), pp. 99, 105; Karl Löwith, *From Hegel to Nietzsche: The Revolution in Nineteenth Century Thought* [1941] (New York, 1964), pp. 115–121.

attacked Schelling in several pamphlets, and managed easily to keep up with his military duties along with numerous other extracurricular commitments. He read Ludwig Feuerbach's recently published *Essence of Christianity*—as Marx was doing at about the same time—and responded to its importance. He also read Moses Hess' *The European Triarchy*, of which more in a moment. Yet beneath all this encouraging activity of development, matters were not so unruffled as they appeared from the surface. We can observe something of this in a letter Engels wrote to Arnold Ruge[19] on June 15, 1842, covering a review-essay that he was sending to the editor of the *Deutsche Jahrbücher*. There had been some previous correspondence in which Ruge had obviously addressed his correspondent as *Geehrter Herr Doktor*. Toward the end of his letter of reply, Engels pauses for a moment and then drops in the following sentence: "Incidentally I am not a doctor and can never become one; I am only a businessman and a royal Prussian Artillerist; therefore kindly spare me that title." The sense of fatedness contained in this statement, along with its mixture of sadness and irony, its self-effacing modesty and directness, is both touching and characteristic of one side of this young man. Having made such a statement, however, Engels was unable to let the matter rest there, and a month later, on July 26, he returns to worry it further. He writes to Ruge in explanation of why he has not sent in anything to be published.

I have taken the decision to renounce all literary activity for some time and instead to study all the more. The reasons for this are obvious. I am young and autodidact in philosophy. I have learned enough to form a point of view for myself and to stand up for it if necessary—but not

[19] Ruge (1802–1880), a Left Hegelian of an older generation, was the editor of various periodicals dealing with contemporary issues. In Paris for some months during 1843 and 1844, he worked together with Marx as co-editor of the *Deutsch-Französische Jahrbücher*. Marx's rapidly developing socialist views were not, however, to Ruge's liking, and the two soon parted ways.

enough to act in its behalf with success and adequacy. Indeed more demands are going to be made upon me just because I am a philosophical commercial-traveller [*philosophischer Musterreiter*] and have not bought the right to philosophise through a doctoral diploma. I think that if I were once again to write something, and then under my own name, that I should be able to satisfy these demands. And besides I mustn't now fragment my time too much, since it will probably be shortly taken up again by business work.

It is not hard to discern the ambivalence crowded into these sentences. Engels is clearly looking forward with melancholy apprehension to the date just a little more than two months in the future when his military service will end and he will return to Barmen. The suspension of literary activity has in part to do with that, in part to do with preparing himself unconsciously for a change in both the direction and subject matter of his writing. And in any event, the suspension was to last for all of four months. In addition, he picks up again the rankling truth of his being an autodidact, but along with the continuing self-deprecation there is an intensified irony. He may only be a businessman [*Kaufmann*] and philosophical commercial traveler, but then he realizes that a doctor's diploma and right, in Germany, to philosophize are largely a matter of buying [*erkauft*] as well. He has after all spent close to a year more or less within the precincts of a German university and has been able to observe at first hand what doctors of philosophy both young and old can be like. Yet this final renunciation of the wish to be a doctor of philosophy (which may be, I suggest, the real renunciation both mentioned and screened in the first sentence of the letter) is immediately followed by the resolution that if and when he writes again it will be under his own name—that is to say, within a firmer and more distinct self, although it will not be a self without strain and conflict.[20]

[20] Engels did not in fact publish anything under his own name until 1844. In addition, had he known that Ruge on one occasion had called himself "a wholesale merchant of

In a sense not yet perceived by Engels, there was more to being a philosophical commercial traveler than his use of the phrase portended. Charles Fourier, whom Engels would in the future regard with special warmth as one of his and Marx's forerunners, had been a traveling salesman when he was inspired by the law of passionate attraction that was destined to bring about an era of universal happiness.[21] Even more, only a few years before Engels embarked upon his career, Balzac had discerned in the traveling salesman an apotheosis of the new social organization.

The commercial traveller, a personage unknown to antiquity, is he not one of the most curious figures created by the manners and customs of the present epoch? is he not destined, in some order of things, to mark the great transition which, in the eyes of critical observers, welds the period of material development and improvement to that of intellectual development and improvement. . . . Is not the commercial traveller to ideas just what our stage-coaches are to packages and men?

This is from the opening of "The Illustrious Gaudissart" (1833), a brilliantly funny story, in which Balzac goes on to say, anticipating certain famous passages in Marx:

Since 1830 more especially, ideas have become property; and, as a writer clever enough not to publish anything has said, there are stolen today more ideas than handkerchiefs. Perhaps, some day, we shall see a Bourse for ideas; but already, good or bad, ideas are quoted, are gathered in, are of consequence, are carried and sold, are realized and bring in profit. . . . In becoming a matter of commerce, intelligence and its products naturally obey the laws of other manufacturing interests. Thus it happens that ideas conceived in their cups in the brains of some of

intellectual wares," the irony would not have been lost on him. See Franz Mehring, *Karl Marx*, p. 17.

[21] Frank E. Manuel, *The Prophets of Paris* (New York, 1965), pp. 197–248; *Anti-Dühring*, Pt. III, ch. 1.

these Parisians . . . were delivered, the day after their cerebral birth, to certain travelling salesmen charged with presenting skilfully, *urbi et orbi,* in Paris and the provinces . . . announcements and prospectuses. . . .

The Gaudissart of the title was at first a champion salesman of hats. In the story he moves into a higher line of work and is employed by the directors of *Le Globe,* the organ of the Saint-Simonian doctrine, to sell subscriptions in the provinces— whence flows the fun.

Further yet, while Engels was living in Manchester, the most popular novelist then alive was publishing *Martin Chuzzlewit.* Had Engels read it, he would have been interested to come across M. Todgers' "Commercial Boarding-House." The commercial gentlemen who lodge there are of varying "turns," some theatrical, some debating, some literary, some philosophical. And indeed "one gentleman, who travelled in the perfumery line, exhibited an interesting nick-nack, in the way of a remarkable cake of shaving soap which he had lately met with in Germany." (ch. 9) No doubt the identical cake of soap used by Engels to shave with the razors presented to him by his father. The irony that continually plays about the figure of the traveling salesman is not to be segregated from his central place in the imagination or actuality of the new society. The irony is connected as well with a permanent uncertainty or difficulty of judgment. A passage written by Engels many years later may be usefully referred to. In the introduction to *Dialectics of Nature,* he refers briefly to the Renaissance, the heroic inception of the bourgeois era.

The men who founded the modern rule of the bourgeoisie had anything but bourgeois limitations. On the contrary, the adventurous character of the time inspired them to a greater or less degree. There was hardly any man of importance then living who had not travelled extensively, who did not command four or five languages, who did not shine in a number of fields.

He then mentions Leonardo, Dürer, Machiavelli and Luther to support this contention, and continues:

The heroes of that time had not yet come under the servitude of the division of labour, the restricting effects of which, with its production of onesidedness, we so often notice in their successors. But what is especially characteristic of them is that they almost all pursue their lives and activities in the midst of the contemporary movements, in the practical struggle; they take sides and join in the fight, one by speaking and writing, another with the sword, some with both. Hence the fullness and force of character that makes them complete men. Men of the study are the exception—either persons of second or third rank or cautious philistines who do not want to burn their fingers.

It is impossible to determine to what degree, if at all, this is a passage of self-description and self-reference. The traits singled out tally with those that may fairly be ascribed to Engels himself; and yet there is nothing in the tone of the writing that suggests such an intention. And where, in this context, does a "philosophical commercial traveller" belong? In the 1870's Engels had at last left Manchester and was out of the business for good. In 1842, however, the larger ironies of the term, those that are directed away from the self, are still to be worked out.

The catalytic role played by Moses Hess (1812–1875) in the lives of both Engels and Marx was at this period of considerable importance. The more radical of the Young Hegelians had at this moment adopted the humanism of Feuerbach as their working point of view.[22] It was Moses Hess who proposed to them that the

[22] This humanism—sometimes referred to rather redundantly as anthropological humanism—had as its point of departure a critical view of religion in general and Christianity in particular, whose supersensible Deity it regarded as an alienated projection of man. It went on to criticize certain rationalistic elements in Hegel's philosophy in similar terms, observing that even in Hegel's system man is characteristically expropriated. In place of this alienated, expropriated and isolated creature, Feuerbach wanted to substitute man as a "sensible being," man as representative of a natural species in whom thought is secondary to concrete sensuous existence, at the center of the universe.

fulfillment of this humanism was to be found first in its fusion with French social theory and socialism, most notably embodied in Saint-Simon. German theory and French practice, the revolution in philosophy and the revolution in politics, were to be brought together and then carried forward to their next stage of development in the third member of the European Triarchy. In 1841, Hess affirmed that the advent of the social revolution which would begin and have its center in England was at hand. Engels read *The European Triarchy* and was converted, as in his own way was Marx. In view of the critical events that continued cumulatively to unfold in England throughout 1842, it was by no means a witless conviction.[23] Engels left Berlin at the beginning of October, having finished his year's military service—he received an excellent report from his company commander—and on the way to Barmen, he stopped off in Cologne to visit the editorial offices of the *Rheinische Zeitung*. There for the first time he met Hess, who reported on this meeting shortly afterward: "We talked of questions of the day. And Engels, who had been a revolutionary from the year one, departed from me a passionate communist"—which, translated from the jargon then current to the jargon now in use, means that according to Hess, Engels, who had until then been a revolutionary libertarian in the tradition of 1789, departed from their conversation a radical egalitarian or socialist. Thus, in the words of George Lichtheim, the modern historian of the origins of socialism, "it is not too much to say that

[23] "In 1842, probably the most distressed year of the whole nineteenth century, it was estimated that in Leeds at least twenty thousand people were living on incomes averaging only 11¼ d. per week. Conditions were as bad in Manchester and in Sheffield. 'The picture which the manufacturing districts now present,' wrote the *Manchester Times*, 'is absolutely frightful. Hungry and half-clothed men and women are stalking through the streets begging for bread.' " Donald Read, *Press and People, 1790–1850* (London, 1961), p. 20; quoting *Manchester Times* for July 9, 1842. See also G. Kitson Clark, "Hunger and Politics in 1842," *Journal of Modern History*, XXV (December 1953), 355–374; George Rudé, *The Crowd in History, 1730–1848* (New York, 1964), pp. 179–191; R. C. O. Matthews, *A Study in Trade-Cycle History: Economic Fluctuations in Great Britain, 1833–1842* (London, 1954), pp. 137ff.

in 1842 Hess literally converted Engels to communism—two years before Engels and Marx had entered upon their lifelong partnership." [24]

He was on his way back to Barmen only to prepare for his journey to Manchester. Once again there are two accounts of how this next step was taken. On the one hand, we are told, Engels was convinced by Hess' prophecies along with the continuing disturbances throughout England in general and Lancashire in particular that the revolution was just around the corner; and seizing upon his father's interest in the Manchester firm founded by Peter Ermen—Engels senior had bought in as a partner in about 1837—took the occasion as a pretext for visiting in person the scene of the imminent apocalypse. On the other hand, Mayer states that according to a police report of the 1850's, Engels senior wanted to remove his son from the enlightened and rationalistic atmosphere that he had been moving headily about in, and that the father had threatened to deny his son all further support if he did not cross over to England. The stories do not actually contradict each other, but as before it is difficult to separate out the two agents or to gauge the realities of their relative powers. What is certain is that Engels left Barmen for England and Manchester in the latter part of November. His father thought, or hoped, that his son would complete his commercial training in that world center. The son looked forward to being at the center of the working-class movement, which was in its turn, as he then was coming to conceive it, the focus of the world history of his time; there he would be able to take active part in the approaching great events. Both father and

---

[24] G. Lichtheim, *The Origins of Socialism*, pp. 277–279, 171–184. This work is to be highly recommended, though it is difficult and extremely compressed. In spite of the fact that the learned author has in the past referred to himself, like Hazlitt before him, as having once "declined into a journalist," and in spite of the fact that he buries about half of what he has to say in footnotes of unendurable length, his work is condemned to distinction.

See also Mayer, I, 100–118; Edmund Silberner, *Moses Hess: Geschichte Seines Lebens* (Leiden, 1966). Hess, like Engels, was both the son of a manufacturer and an autodidact, although the form of pietism from which as a youth he had to free himself was Judaic.

son were right and wrong, and faintly comical; it is almost as if they were, together, resolutely marching backward into the future. Engels would complete his training as a businessman, but not in a manner that his father could ever be satisfied with. There was to be no revolution in England, but Manchester was certainly the right place to be—imagine what world history might look like if Engels senior's plan to send young Friedrich to Milan had not fallen through. On one matter father and son were in agreement: Manchester was the place.[25]

On his way to England Engels stopped off once again in Cologne to revisit the offices of the *Rheinische Zeitung*. The historic first meeting between him and its young editor, Marx (who at twenty-four was two years older than Engels), took place, with appropriate coolness, since Marx was just then in the midst of breaking altogether with the philosophical gang of post-Hegelians in Berlin, whence Engels had just come. Nevertheless, it is apparent that Engels arranged to send some articles from England, and no sooner was he off the boat than he began firing back rockets—his first two pieces for the *Rheinische Zeitung* were dated November 29th and 30th and were written in London. They make amusing reading today, since Engels could have written them without ever having left Barmen. English freedom? Simple despotism. English modernity? In no

---

[25] In some senses Engels never gave up his conviction that the revolution would take place next Thursday. In 1892, George Julian Harney, with whom he had been friends for almost forty years, wrote to him: "You are the Prince of Optimists. You always see the Universal Revolution just coming round the corner. My sight is not so good, nor my hope so sanguine." Peter Cadogan, "Harney and Engels," *International Review of Social History*, X (1965), 97. What this kind of fixed belief has to do with the processes of projection and wish-fulfillment, and how both are related in the mind of a revolutionary thinker to the higher ego functions of reality-testing and locomotor activity, are relevant questions that I am technically incompetent to discuss.

Engels was intermittently aware of this fixed tendency in himself. In an article on the Blanquist refugees from the Paris Commune of 1871, he sets down a number of observations on Blanquis as a "man of action" and optimist about the revolution that is always about to happen, which suggest a genuine self-consciousness on his part. *Werke*, XVIII, 529ff.

country in the world does feudalism continue to exist with such uninterrupted power. Chartism? "A contradiction in itself," since it is trying to attain "a revolution by legal means." He didn't bother to unpack his bags or his perceptual faculties until he got to Manchester shortly thereafter.[26] But as one reads the dispatches, reports and articles that over the next twenty months he wrote for the *Rheinische Zeitung*, the *Schweizerischer Republikaner*, the *Deutsch-Französische Jahrbücher*, and *Vorwärts!* one can make out distinctly the continuing rapid development of a young man who has now found his métier and himself, who can use his eyes as well as his abstract rationality, and who is capable of thinking for himself. Although he was never to be anything but a radical critic of English society, he was by the end of his nearly two-year stay able to write a passage such as this:

England is unquestionably the freest—that is, the least unfree—country in the world, North America not excepted. As a result, an educated Englishman has a degree of independence about him that no Frenchman, let alone a German, can boast of. England's political activity, its free press, its naval supremacy, and its gigantic industry have worked toward developing in each individual the inherent energy of the national character; in this character the most determined energy exists side by side with the calmest deliberateness, so that in this respect as well the continental peoples lag infinitely far behind. English military and naval history is a series of splendid victories. . . . In literature only the classical Greek and German literatures are comparable. In philosophy at least two immeasurably great names—Bacon and Locke—show forth in the empirical sciences. And if the question arises as to what people has *done* the most, then it cannot be denied that the English are that people.[27]

[26] During the summer of 1842, a few months earlier, another young German had passed through Manchester on his English travels. Otto von Bismarck's report on his experiences therein has a good deal more to say about the size, care and fodder of English cavalry horses than it does about Manchester—although one has to recall that he was writing to his father, an old officer of horse himself. See Johannes Penzler, *Jugendgeschichte des Fürsten Bismarck* (Berlin, 1907), pp. 121–123.

[27] "Die Lage Englands, II," *Vorwärts!* Sept. 18, 1844; *Werke*, I, 569–570.

He was still an autodidact in philosophy, although it is evident that he has been doing his homework in other subjects.

Engels' experiences in Manchester may be divided into two conventional kinds: those that were expressed in physical activity and direct observation; and those that have primarily to do with reading and writing. The distinction is altogether arbitrary, for the years 1842 through 1845 constitute in Engels' life a period of intense activity and rapid psychic and intellectual integration. That period culminates and concludes in two truly creative episodes—his writing of *The Condition of the Working Class in England*, and the establishment of his lifelong association with Marx.

The economic distress that had prevailed throughout most of Britain since 1837 had reached its worst point in the summer of 1842; the Plug Plot strikes had been a spontaneous outbreak on the part of the textile workers—a fact thoroughly understood at the time by Carlyle, but that Engels, regarding England from Berlin through the rose-tinted binoculars of Moses Hess, had taken as the opening scene of the great rebellion.[28] What still remained—and it was plenty—of that depression in trade seems to have been the first observation that stuck in Engels' mind on his arrival. "When I arrived in Manchester at the end of November, 1842," he writes, "there were everywhere crowds of unemployed still standing at street corners, and many factories were still standing idle. Between then and the middle of 1843 those who had been lounging at street corners through no fault of their own gradually disappeared, as the factories came once again into activity." (102)[29] The Ermen and Engels mills were then

[28] In fairness to both men, it should be added that Carlyle went on to say that if something weren't done in short order to improve the condition of the working class it would indeed be the prelude to a revolution. See also Donald Read, "Chartism in Manchester," in Asa Briggs, ed., *Chartist Studies* (London, 1959), pp. 29–64.

[29] Engels may have slightly misdated the day of his arrival, since his second report to the *Rheinische Zeitung* carries the dateline "London, den 30 November."

located near the outlying district of Pendleton, their Manchester offices in Newmarket Buildings, Market Street.[30] We know that Engels spent part of the time during his stay working at the mills (185), and it is more than likely that his training also included work in the city offices and visits to the nearby Exchange. We do not know exactly where Engels lived, but there is one sentence that is of some help in this connection. In his discussion of child labor in calico printing, he states that "in the neighborhood of my lodgings near Manchester there was a calico printworks that was often still lit up late at night when I returned home," and he goes on to describe what has been reported to him of the effects on the children who were employed there of these long hours of labor. (220) From this kind of information—along with more presently to come—one gets a sense of regular and prolonged walking, of a young man getting to know the city from the ground—and from below the ground—up.

Engels was quite explicit about this. In his dedication to "the Working Classes of Great-Britain," which he wrote in English on the day he completed the manuscript, and prefixed to the original German edition of 1845, he stated that during his stay in England he purposefully "forsook the company and the dinner-parties, the port-wine and champagne of the middle-classes, and devoted my leisure hours almost exclusively to the intercourse with plain Working Men; I am both glad and proud of having done so." The deliberateness of this intention arose from his judgment that although he might read all the documents that were to be had, this was not enough. He wanted, he says, "to see you in your own homes, to observe you in your every-day life, to chat with you on your condition and grievances, to witness your struggles against the social and political power of your oppressors." He wanted, in other words, "more than a mere *abstract* knowledge of my subject." And because he had acted consciously

---

[30] W. O. Henderson and W. H. Chaloner, "Friedrich Engels in Manchester," *Mem. and Proc. Manchester Literary and Philosophical Society*, XCVIII (1956–1957), p. 14.

upon this want, he "was induced to spend many a happy hour in obtaining a knowledge of the realities of life." (7) The realities of life in this context are set over against not only the "fashionable talk" and unrealities of middle-class existence; they are opposed as well, indeed primarily, to "mere *abstract* knowledge."

It may be suggested that in a passage such as this we are witness to the beginning of a break in and simultaneous transformation of the German cultural tradition of philosophical-critical-social theorizing. How historic an occurrence this was, becomes more distinct if we recall that Marx was at the same period going through a very similar experience. It detracts nothing from Engels' merit to say that the transformation attained its fullest articulation in the subsequent writings of Marx. Moreover, it stands to Marx's credit that he instantly recognized the truth of what Engels in his experience had realized before him—that it was only through an intimate acquaintance with the concrete realities of English social and economic existence and with the body of writings that had sprung up as the theory of that existence that such a transformation could be finally achieved. Engels himself remained persistently aware of this circumstance. In his preface to the first German edition he wrote that England was the only place in which such a project could be undertaken. This was so because of the advanced character of its industrial and social development and because of the unique richness of documents and official reports and inquiries. But the converse also applied: all the well-meaning efforts of the German middle class to deal with social questions by founding societies "to improve the conditions of the workers" come to nothing because they "proceed continually from preconceptions about the proletariat that are as ludicrous as they are absurd." And they do so because "so little is known of the way in which the proletariat really lives in Germany today." (3–4) It was not the burghers alone, however, who blundered about in darkness. On March 17, 1845, two days after he had sent the completed manuscript off to the publishers, Engels in Barmen wrote Marx in Brussels a long letter whose last paragraph begins: "Otherwise there's nothing new here. The bourgeoisie talks politics and goes to church; the proletariat does—we know not what, and hardly can know it. [*das Proletariat tut, wir wissen nicht was, und können's kaum wissen.*]"

In Manchester, Engels went into action along several fronts. He made himself known to the Chartists there, attended their meetings, read their literature, and became friendly with one of the leading members of the Manchester branch of the association, James Leach. (151f.)[31] In his dual capacity of "philosophical commercial-traveller," he became acquainted with Lancashire and more remote districts. On one of these more wide-ranging journeys, which took place in the autumn of 1843, he traveled from Bradford to Leeds. He may have done so at Leach's suggestion, for one of Engels' purposes on this trip was to introduce himself to George Julian Harney, sub-editor of the *Northern Star* (who was actually performing all the duties of editor) and a friend of Leach's. Years later, Harney remembered the Engels of this first visit as "a tall, handsome young man, with a countenance of almost boyish youthfulness, whose English, in spite of his German birth and education, was even then remarkable for its accuracy." [32] The two seemed to have hit it off

---

[31] In later years, Engels' excellent memory occasionally played him tricks. In May 1872 Engels spoke on the Irish question before the General Council of the International Workingmen's Association. In the course of this speech, he said that "he recollected the time when he saw Feargus O'Connor and the English Chartists turned out of the Hall of Science in Manchester by the Irish." The event referred to occurred in March 1842, months before Engels arrived in England. The Irish in question who did the turning out were members of Daniel O'Connell's Irish National Repeal Association, a moderate working-class organization deeply hostile to Chartism.

Engels' notes for this speech are reprinted in Karl Marx and Frederick Engels, *Ireland and the Irish Question: a Collection of Writings* (New York, 1972), pp. 302ff. See also Donald Read, "Chartism in Manchester," *Chartist Studies*, ed. Asa Briggs, pp. 50–52; N. McCord, *The Anti-Corn Law League* (London, 1958), pp. 102f.; Donald Read and Eric Glasgow, *Feargus O'Connor: Irishman and Chartist* (London, 1961), pp. 93f.

[32] George Julian Harney, "On Engels," in *Reminiscences of Marx and Engels* (Moscow,

well at once—their friendship was to continue, with interruptions caused by political differences, until Engels' death in 1895—and soon Engels was contributing pieces to the *Star* on German affairs as "Our Own Correspondent." [33] The first two of these were slightly cut versions of articles that had already appeared in Robert Owen's *New Moral World* in November 1843. Before that, however, Engels had reported in the June 9 *Schweizerischer Republikaner* on the Sunday meetings of the socialists in the Manchester Hall of Science; he was much impressed by the large numbers of people that congregated there and by the Owenite speakers, particularly James Watts. His dispatch is none the less uncertain and slightly confused. And no wonder. He could hardly have been expected to know at once that the Owenites were then in the last phase of a transition that changed a socialist organization into a secular church—hence the extraordinary amount of time at these meetings given to polemics against organized religion.[34]

These polemics were regarded with alarm in certain religious quarters, and among the means enlisted to oppose such militant anti-clericalism on the part of the manufacturing population were magnetico-phrenological demonstrations which proved the existence of God and the error of Owenite materialism. In the winter of 1843–1844 Engels witnessed such a demonstration, enacted by the mesmerist Spencer Hall and a young girl with whom he traveled.

---

n.d.), pp. 192f. The interesting question of Engels' relation to English and to languages in general cannot be discussed here.

[33] A. R. Schoyen, *The Chartist Challenge: a Portrait of George Julian Harney* (1958), pp. 129–131, and *passim;* also Peter Cadogan, "Harney and Engels," *International Review of Social History,* X (1965), pp. 66–104.

[34] *Werke,* I, 473–477; also G. D. H. Cole, *The Life of Robert Owen* (London, 1930), pp. 293ff.; M. Beer, *A History of British Socialism* (London, 1953), I, 160ff.; J. F. C. Harrison, *Robert Owen and the Owenites* (London, 1969), *passim;* Sidney Pollard and John Salt, eds., *Robert Owen: Prophet of the Poor* (London, 1971), *passim;* R. Laurence Moore, *European Socialists and the American Promised Land* (New York, 1970), pp. 3–24.

The lady was sent into a magnetico-sleep and then as soon as the operator touched any part of the skull corresponding to one of Gall's organs, she gave a bountiful display of theatrical, demonstrative gestures and poses representing the activity of the organ concerned; for instance, for the organ of philoprogenitiveness she fondled and kissed an imaginary baby, etc. . . . right at the top of the skull he [Hall] had discovered an organ of veneration, on touching which his hypnotic miss sank on to knees, folded her hands in prayer, and depicted to the astonished, philistine audience an angel wrapt in veneration. That was the climax and conclusion of the exhibition. The existence of God had been proved.

Engels reports that he and an acquaintance then set out to see if they could reproduce these phenomena.

A wideawake young boy of 12 years old offered himself as subject. Gently gazing into his eyes, or stroking, sent him without difficulty into the hypnotic condition. . . . To set Gall's cranial organs into action was the least that we achieved; we went much further, we could not only exchange them for one another, but we also fabricated any amount of other organs, organs of singing, whistling, piping, dancing, boxing, sewing, cobbling, tobacco-smoking, etc., and we could make their seat wherever we wanted . . . we discovered in the great toe an organ of drunkenness which only had to be touched in order to cause the finest drunken comedy to be enacted.

What Engels describes as the "frivolous skepticism" of his behavior in this episode serves in fact as a reminder to the reader that he had been associated not long before with the anarchic antics of the *Freien,* and that although he was a serious he was not a solemn young (or old) man.[35]

---

[35] *Dialectics of Nature* (New York, 1963), pp. 298ff. Mesmerism and magnetism were originally used in quite the opposite cause. See Robert Darnton, *Mesmerism and the End of the Enlightenment in France* (Cambridge, Mass., 1968). Engels' account is rather too simple in its polarities. He neglects to mention that Saint-Simonians and Fourierists alike

Other evidence makes it apparent that, in addition to his activities among the Chartists and the Owenites, Engels was getting acquainted with the agitations against the New Poor Law, the factory reform movement, the Anti-Corn Law League, the Trades Union question, and the issues involved in sanitary reform—that is to say, he immersed himself in the turbulent political life of the period and traced in his own daily experience its conflicts and vicissitudes.

The Condition of the Working Class contains the full results of this experience. In May 1843, for example, the men at a local brick-works went out on strike. The dispute escalated into armed and bloody violence, and on the night when the climactic riot and shoot-out occurred, Engels seems to have been there. His account of the actions and movements of the rioters, at both the scene of the shooting in Manchester and along their line of retreat to Eccles, three miles away, is so close and circumstantial as to suggest either that he was actually there or that he had spoken at length to someone who had been. (256f.)[36] Most of all, however, he undertook to investigate Manchester on his own—on his own time and in his own way. He was himself aware of the intensity

waded hip-deep in mesmeric fluid, and that although many Owenites may have been opposed to spiritualism and phrenology, Robert Owen became a convert after 1853 and held conversations with Thomas Jefferson, Benjamin Franklin and the Duke of Wellington.

Marx offers this suggestive comment on the early Utopian socialist sects and their relation to science and pseudo-science: "The first phase in the struggle of the proletariat against the bourgeoisie is marked by the sectarian movement. This is justifiable at a time when the proletariat is not yet sufficiently developed to act as a class. Isolated thinkers subject the social antagonisms to criticism and at the same time give a fantastic solution of them which the mass of the workers have only to accept as complete, to propagate and to put into practical operation. . . . In short, they represented the infancy of the proletarian movement just as astrology and alchemy represented the infancy of science." "Die angeblichen Spaltungen in der Internationale" [1872], *Werke*, XVIII, 32–34. See also a handsome paragraph in Marx's first draft of *The Civil War in France*, in Karl Marx and Friedrich Engels, *Writings on the Paris Commune*, ed. Hal Draper (New York, 1971), p. 163.

[36] The account of the incident given in the *Northern Star* is not as detailed as the one provided by Engels.

and systematic rigor with which he pursued this project. He wrote that he knew Manchester "as intimately as I know my own native town—more intimately than most of its inhabitants." (51)[37] He gained this intimacy by taking to the streets, at all hours of the day and night, on weekends and holidays.[38] He took to that network or web of pathways along which a city moves and that constitutes the principal means for observing and understanding it. Or ought to. For one of the chief components of the distress commonly felt by many people in modern cities is their sense that the city is unintelligible and illegible. The city is experienced as estrangement because it is not perceived as a coherent system of signs, as a surrounding communicating to us in a language that we know. After London, Manchester was the central site of that experience in Great Britain. The discontinuities and obscurities, the apparent absence of large, visibly related structures, the disorganizations and disarticulations seem to compose the structure of a chaos, a landscape whose human, social and natural parts may be related simply by accidents, a random agglomeration of mere appearances. It was into this prototypical anxiety-creating modern scene that Engels thrust himself.[39]

But he did not take this plunge alone. He was accompanied on his expeditions into the inner recesses of the city by Mary Burns, and it was she who inducted him into certain working-class

[37] In this connection, Engels uses the word *"Vaterstadt,"* a common enough term, but bound in this particular context to attract and accumulate other meanings.

[38] For example, on Whitsunday, 1844, Georg Weerth, a young German workingman and aspiring poet, who was employed in Bradford and whom Engels had befriended (among other things, he supplied Weerth with books), came over to Manchester and spent a day in the company of his compatriot, whom he described as "a German philosopher who has buried himself in that dark city." The daylight hours were consumed by their wandering all about the city, which Weerth describes as far-flung, extensive, straggling. Georg Weerth, *Sämtliche Werke* (Berlin, 1957), V, 125, 128.

[39] See Eliel Saarinen, *The City: its Growth, its Decay, its Future* [1943] (Cambridge, Mass., 1965), pp. 345f.; also Kevin Lynch, "The City as Environment," *Cities*, ed. D. Flanagan, et al. (New York, 1965), pp. 192–201.

circles and into the domestic lives of the Manchester proletariat.[40] Thus Engels learned how to read a city in the company—or through the mediation—of an illiterate Irish factory girl. He learned to read it with his eyes, ears, nose and feet. He learned to read it with his senses, the chief inlets, as Blake almost said, of mind in the present age. There should be nothing very disquieting about this coming together of young Engels' passage into the hidden regions and meanings of Manchester and the developing course of his first extended sexual relation.[41] The erotic, the social, and the intellectual passions regularly reinforce one another, or mingle in common interanimation; or, put in another way, the social and intellectual passions can acquire additional forces, derived and displaced from their original erotic matrix. There is much more than can possibly be gone into here; the complexity of the material is equaled only by how little of it there is to go on. Two things, however, may be observed. Engels' relation with Mary Burns, which was to last all her life, represents a further shifting and consolidation in conscious and unconscious identifications. As a boy, he had often given his little savings to "the poor." As a young man, he has now decided in more ways than one actively to throw his lot in with labor, with the working class or proletariat. The difference between an identification with "the poor" and an identification with the "working class" represents, among many other things, the measure in which an idealistic and rebellious young man could appropriate for himself a traditional historical masculine identity and maintain that identity even in the role of insurrection against the world in which it was grounded.[42] At the same time, that

[40] Mayer, I, 128, 136, 381. Very little about Mary Burns has come to light. Mayer's sources of information were oral communications from Eduard Bernstein and Karl Kautsky.

[41] This is not a discovery to be credited to Freud. "As she went along the crowded narrow streets, she felt how much of interest they had gained by the simple fact of her having learnt to care for a dweller in them." North and South, ch. 13.

[42] Erik H. Erikson, Gandhi's Truth (New York, 1969), pp. 90, 194 and passim, throws out some interesting hints in this regard.

identification was not of such a kind that it moved Engels to adopt the style of life of the proletariat, or to do the next most convenient thing, choose that style of life most frequently resorted to by young middle-class men of his time and culture who had come to similar decisions about the direction of their lives, namely, the style of Bohemianism. Instead he chose to live with Mary without marrying her (and without wholly living with her either), and to be a respectable revolutionary and respectable Manchester businessman all at the same time.[43]

The distinction in identifications can be generally rephrased in another way. Identification on the one side with that part of society conceived of as "the poor" and expressed by means of sympathy, charity, benevolence and philanthropy is opposed on the other by an identification with that part of society conceived of as "the proletariat" and expressed in such activity as embodies the "revolutionary daring . . . [of] the defiant phrase: *I am nothing and I should be everything.*" K. Marx, "Contribution to the Critique of Hegel's Philosophy of Right," in *Early Writings*, ed. T. B. Bottomore (London, 1963), p. 56. These two conceptions are polar and purified extremes joined by a continuum of mixed attitudes; the differing unconscious derivations of both, however, ought to be kept in mind in considerations of reforming and revolutionary characters, at least those of middle-class origins.

[43] Whatever one wants to conclude about the character of Engels' relation with Mary Burns, and with her sister Lizzie, who kept house for the two of them while Mary was alive and took Mary's place after her death in 1863, it is safe to say that nothing about it was simple. One need only recall that Engels' favorite sister was named Marie and that his mother was named Elizabeth (and referred to as Elise) to refresh one's sense of the depths of meaning that are determined in such matters.

On the other side, this complexity is nowhere more clearly revealed than in the one incident whose historical notoriety has to do with the fact that it is the sole occasion that has survived in which Engels recorded himself as hurt and slighted by Marx and over which the two had a momentary falling out. On January 7, 1863, Engels in Manchester wrote to Marx in London that Mary Burns had suddenly and unexpectedly died, of either a heart attack or a stroke. "I cannot tell you how I feel," he wrote; "The poor girl loved me with her whole heart." Marx, who was at that moment in the throes of one of his domestic economic crises, responded to Engels' announcement in the most cursory way, and then went on to expand at length about his own miseries with butchers, bakers, the rent, etc., concluding, characteristically, that "work *under such circumstances* is clearly impossible." Engels was naturally wounded by such a response and in his reply to Marx—which he delayed for almost a week—took care to remark that even his "philistine acquaintances" in Manchester had shown on this occasion "more sympathy and friendship than I could expect." Marx allowed ten more days for cooling off before he answered, apologetically, awkwardly, but with an effort of forthrightness. Engels then wrote back in answer to this effort at peacemaking:

Engels' reading during this period was not only accessory to these experiences but constitutive of them as well. The text of *The Condition of the Working Class* demonstrates that he had done considerable homework in parliamentary papers, in books and pamphlets prepared by private and individual investigators, and in current newspapers and periodicals. The articles that he wrote for the *New Moral World* indicate that he was keeping vigorously abreast of theoretical developments on the Continent.[44] His early interest in literature seems to have been sustained, at least in the social novels and novelists. Soon after he arrived in England, he was struck by the perception that there was one department of knowledge of which he and his fellow Germans were woefully, if understandably, innocent; this was political economy, a pursuit in which the British were at that time the world's leading theoreticians and practitioners. He set about to make good on these arrears; the first result of his efforts, an essay entitled "Outlines of a Critique of Political Economy," was written toward the end of 1843 and was printed in 1844 by Marx and Ruge in the single issue of the *Deutsch-Französische Jahrbücher* that ever managed to get off the press.[45] In this original essay, however, one can already

---

I thank you for your candor. You understand yourself what sort of impression your earlier letter made on me. No one can live so long with a woman without being terribly moved by. her death. I feel that with her I buried the last of my youth. (*Werke*, XXX, 309–318)

Making every allowance one can for the genuineness of Engels' grief, the likelihood that other utterances about Mary have not survived, and further accidents, these are still astonishing remarks. One can expect and put up with a certain amount of self-reference on such occasions. But Engels' remarks on the death of Mary are nothing but self-references—including what ought to be recorded as some kind of classic in the socialist tradition of the relations of the sexes—"The poor girl loved me with her whole heart." Marx's response is in a league by itself, but I find it difficult to conclude that this entire episode is not suffused with class feelings and discriminations (in all directions, including both Marx and his wife) and that Engels' response on the death of Mary Burns was not differentially at least a class response, and a common, coarse and typical one at that.

[44] *MEGA*, I/2, 435–455.

[45] *Werke*, I, 499–534; a translation is to be found in Karl Marx, *Economic and Philosophical Manuscripts of 1844*, ed. Dirk J. Struik (New York, 1964), pp. 197–226. The degree to which Engels' essay anticipated and influenced Marx is undecided and has provided matter for some scholarly dispute. What seems to be beyond debate is that both young men were independently developing along similar tracks and toward similar

hear the voice and discern the vision of that writer who at this moment was exercising a decisive influence on Engels and to whose work Engels was to devote his next essay. I mean of course Carlyle.

Past and Present was published at the beginning of April 1843. Engels must have read it soon afterward, since he mentions Carlyle's name and quotes one of his phrases in a "London Letter," published on May 16, 1843, in the *Schweizerischer Republikaner*.[46] He read *Chartism* as well, and before the year was out was at work on a review essay of *Past and Present* which also first appeared in the *Deutsch-Französische Jahrbücher*. This much is known and generally agreed upon, as in a general way is there agreement that Engels read Carlyle to some effect. Yet the character of that effect has not, to my knowledge, been examined adequately.[47]

Engels was in the first place favorably predisposed toward Carlyle because of the latter's earlier exertions on behalf of German literature. Between 1824 and 1831, as translator, essayist and general advocate, Carlyle had served as the "Voice of Germany" in England.[48] Carlyle's familiarity with modern German thinking and writing and his appropriation of them in his own writing, made him a natural and logical choice as a model

---

young men were independently developing along similar tracks and toward similar conclusions. Engels' reading in the political economists appears to have been slightly in advance of Marx's, as was his ability to put down the results of his reading more promptly in clearer—as well as simpler—formulations.

[46] J. A. Froude, *Thomas Carlyle: A History of His Life in London 1834–1881* (New York, 1898), I, 244; *Werke*, I, 468.

[47] One extended effort to discuss this subject occurs in Peter Demetz, *Marx, Engels and the Poets*, pp. 34–40, and is a howling instance of how not to do it. Unfortunately this is not the place to catalog the errors and inaccuracies in Demetz's account. One example will have to do. Toward the end of his discussion Demetz calls Engels out for his ignorance; in recommending Carlyle "to his liberal friends," Engels did not realize that he was holding up "an arch-Tory as an exemplary political figure." It is difficult to decide which characterization is further from the mark: the misunderstanding of the Carlyle of 1843, or the misunderstanding of what the term Tory—let alone arch-Tory—meant at that time.

[48] See C. F. Harrold, *Carlyle and German Thought* (New Haven, 1934); René Wellek, "Carlyle and German Romanticism," *Confrontations* (Princeton, 1965), pp. 34–81; G. B. Tennyson, *Sartor Called Resartus* (Princeton, 1965), pp. 66–125.

and figure of transition for a young man who was himself in transit between one culture and another. Even more, Engels perceived, or constructed, a distinct analogy between the course of Carlyle's life and his own. Like Engels, Carlyle had dedicated the first part of his career to German literature. "For the past several years," however, Engels continues, Carlyle "has chiefly occupied himself with the social condition of England—he, the only educated man of his country to do that!—and as early as 1838 wrote a smaller work: *Chartism*." [49] In that parenthetical clause Engels projects himself into his conception of Carlyle. At a cooler moment, Engels might have known better. Surrounded as he was by stacks of Blue Books and reports, he still did not pause to take thought. Who did he think the Commissioners and Assistant Commissioners were?—artisans? journalists? philosophical commercial travelers? And in fact, the truth of that clause is to be read in the statement that at the end of 1843 Friedrich Engels was the only educated man (known to himself) of his country who was chiefly occupied with such matters. Moreover, the analogy/identity has another side to it, which comes into view when we note that Carlyle was exactly the same age as Friedrich Engels, Sr. The identity reveals in turn an identification, part of which may be summarized as follows: Thomas Carlyle spent the first years of his career in bringing to England what Germany has done; Friedrich Engels, Jr., will spend his first mature years in bringing to Germany what has been done in England. Yet what has been done in England, in contrast, is by no means a wholly positive addition to the world's substance; it is a positive addition which is at the same time filled with horrors; it is, in some measure, and in reality, the work of his own father, a work to which the son perforce continues to contribute his less than willing daily share of hours. Hence—and it is a big hence, flowing from all this and from all that has gone before it—the need for a figure like Carlyle and the complex services to which Engels put him.

[49] *Werke*, I, 528.

This crossed, counterpointed and ambivalent series of reciprocations was expressed once more in what I take to be its final and clarified form. Toward the end of *The Condition of the Working Class*, Engels pauses and drops a long footnote of explanation and amendment. He has pilloried the English bourgeoisie for several hundred pages, but he wants it understood that although he has used specific examples of how certain individual manufacturers have mistreated their working-people, he has throughout had the intention of speaking of them only as a class, and the examples are only "intended to illustrate how this *class* thinks and how it behaves." His animus, in other words, is not directed toward persons. By the same token, he has been unable to mention those members of the middle classes who are "honourable exceptions" to the general rule of their order. He now mentions some of them, including certain radical Lancashire manufacturers and members of Parliament, and on the other side the "humane Tories," Disraeli and his "Young England" associates, and Lord Ashley. He ends with a salute and valedictory to Carlyle. It is a handsome peroration, which begins by stating that Carlyle stands "wholly isolated" [*ganz einsam*], even among the critics of English society. (If we keep in mind Engels' circumstances at the moment he was writing this, it is difficult once again not to sense the same projection.) And he goes on amid the praise to characterize Carlyle as a "Germano-Englishman" [*Deutsch-Engländer*]. (351)[50] Shortly after Engels returned to Barmen in the autumn of 1844, he began to contribute pieces on the progress of socialism and communism on the Continent to the *New Moral World*. The first of these was printed on October 5th, and Engels signed it "Anglo-German."[51]

All this demonstrates something of the nature of Engels' positive predisposition toward Carlyle and something of its psychic workings-out. It tells us nothing about the substance upon which that predisposition rested. For that we have to turn to

---

[50] Engels apparently did not know that Carlyle was Scottish.
[51] *MEGA*, I/4, 338.

Past and Present itself and to Engels' review-essay, which begins at full tilt.

Among all the thick books and thin pamphlets that have been published in England during the last year for the amusement or edification of the "educated world," . . . [*Past and Present*] is the only one worth reading. All the multi-volumed novels, with their sad and amusing complications, all the edifying and contemplative, the learned and unlearned commentaries on the Bible—and novels and edifying books are the two staple commodities of English literature—all these you can leave quietly unread. Perhaps you will find a few geological or economic, historical or mathematical books which contain a grain of something new—yet these are things that are studied, but not *read;* these are dry, specialized science . . . plants whose roots have long since been torn from the common human ground from which they drew their nourishment. You may seek as you will, Carlyle's book is the only one which touches upon human strings, which expounds upon human circumstances, which develops a sign of a human point of view.[52]

These are high marks indeed; even for a reviewer of twenty-three, they still seem excessive.[53] And Engels does not modify these hyperbolics until he has finished his account, which consists chiefly of quotations, of Carlyle's work—at which point he is two thirds of the way through a long essay. What is there, then, that is moving Engels so strongly? In the first place, there is no work of the period which communicates a sense of the crisis more acutely than *Past and Present*; furthermore, Carlyle does not regard the crisis exclusively or even primarily as economic or material, in either its origins or its nature, although he does not for a moment overlook the importance of these categories. He represents it as general and social, inclusive on the one side of the

[52] *Werke*, I, 525.

[53] As I mentioned earlier, *Martin Chuzzlewit* was being published during 1843; volume one of Ruskin's *Modern Painters* appeared as well.

material and economic, and on the other of the spiritual and moral. As we sometimes say today, he understands it as *systemic*. Carlyle responded to the long drawn-out agonies of the thirties and forties by describing it as the life-and-death struggle of a whole system of existence; although he did not use the term, he represented the reality unmistakably as the first great historical convulsion of modern industrial capitalism.[54]

Engels was not, however, impressed only by the high degree of generality of Carlyle's insights. He was equally taken by Carlyle's extraordinary ability to discover the precise concrete equivalents for such conceptions, resonant and symbolic instances that made these abstractions into something more than diagnostic or analytical formulations. *Past and Present* is full of such images, most of them drawn, it might be added, from the life of urban distress. There are the mother and father at Stockport Assizes, "arraigned and found guilty of poisoning three of their children, to defraud a 'burial-society' of some £3 8s. due on the death of each child." Such events, remarks Carlyle, "are like the highest mountain apex emerged into view; under which lies a whole mountain region and land, not yet emerged." There are the Lancashire cotton workers: "a million of hungry operative men . . . rose all up, came all out into the streets, and—stood there. What other could they do? Their wrongs and griefs were bitter, insupportable, their rage against the same was just: but who are they that cause these wrongs, who that will honestly make effort to redress them? Our enemies are we know not who or what; our friends are we know not where! How shall we attack any one, shoot or be shot by any one?" Yet the huge inarticulate question

---

[54] The orthodox tradition has in general paid very little attention to Carlyle, apart from repeating the ritualized ideological clichés about his later politics. Exception is to be made for Georg Lukács, who in a Preface written in 1962 for a new printing of *The Theory of the Novel* [1920] (Cambridge, Mass., 1971) offered these appropriate comments on "romantic anti-capitalism. Originally, say in the young Carlyle or in Cobbett, this was a genuine critique of the horrors and barbarities of early capitalism—sometimes even, as in Carlyle's *Past and Present*, a preliminary form of a socialist critique." P. 19.

that they put, "What do you mean to do with us?" remains unanswered. There is the unforgettable "great Hat seven-feet high, which now perambulates London Streets," the topmost point to which English puffery has been observed to reach. "The Hatter in the Strand of London, instead of making better felt-hats than another," mounts this huge contrivance "upon wheels; sends a man to drive it through the streets; hoping to be saved *thereby*. He has not attempted to *make* better hats, as he was appointed by the Universe to do, and as with this ingenuity of his he could very probably have done; but his whole industry is turned to *persuade* us that he has made such!" But there is something still worse than the falsehood and effrontery of such puffing: "that we natives note him little, that we view him as a thing of course, is the very burden of the mystery." Or there is Dr. Alison's poor Irish widow in Edinburgh, petitioning the Charitable Establishments for help, being refused everywhere, finally sinking down and dying from typhus, and infecting "her Lane with fever, so that 'seventeen other persons' died of fever there." It is all very curious, Carlyle remarks.

The forlorn Irish Widow applies to her fellow-creatures, as if saying, "Behold I am sinking, bare of help: ye must help me! I am your sister, bone of your bone; one God made us: ye must help me!" They answer, "No; impossible; thou art no sister of ours." But she proves her sisterhood; her typhus fever kills *them:* they actually were her brothers, though denying it! Had human creature ever to go lower for a proof? [55]

---

[55] *Past and Present*, Bk. I, chs. 1, 3; Bk. III, chs. 1, 2. In his essay, Engels quotes three out of these four passages.

The hat business (which has already made one appearance in "The Illustrious Gaudissart") was to turn up again in a related context. David Ricardo once drew an analogy between diminishing the cost of production of hats and diminishing the cost of subsistence of men. Marx quotes the passage and then comments: "Doubtless, Ricardo's language is as cynical as can be. To put the cost of manufacture of hats and the cost of maintenance of men on the same plane is to turn men into hats. But do not make an outcry at the cynicism of it. The cynicism is in the facts and not in the words." *The Poverty of Philosophy* (New York, 1963) pp. 50f.

The principle animating such moments is one that is central to almost all the great Victorian critics. It consists for the most part in rescuing and restoring a phrase, incident or image from what would otherwise be ephemeral and dead. The sources from which such material was regularly annexed were newspapers, Blue Books, or documents of a similar nature—the very idea of the ephemeral on the one hand, and on the other an early form of evidence or information logically assembled, codified and prepared for storage, that is to say, for historical disappearance or death. Part of the genius of the great Victorian critics as a "school" or group—including the novelists preeminently among them—has to do with their ability to scan such material with an eye to picking out of it bits and moments of a special kind. Either because of their own inherent linguistic structure or because of what the Victorian critics *as writers* could do with them, these bits and moments were then inserted at critical junctures in the arguments, polemics and exhortations that they were conducting. As writers they were performing one of their quintessential functions: they were taking dead writing and transforming it back into living writing. Or we can say that they were transforming information into a present history whose structure they were simultaneously inventing. The imaginary line that runs from Dr. Alison's Irish widow in Edinburgh to Matthew Arnold's "Wragg is in custody" may be considered as axial in the intellectual consciousness of the period. It is as close as nineteenth-century English critical prose comes to writing or language as praxis—however dismaying that conclusion might have been to Arnold himself.[56] Engels learned much in this regard, as

[56] It is also the antithesis of the Flaubertian ideal ambition for writing. Such a conclusion might also help in part to explain why it was common in the later nineteenth and early twentieth centuries for educated people to state in print that Dickens, Carlyle and others had been directly responsible for social reforms. One had to unlearn the misapprehensions contained in the conceptual form of such statements before one could appreciate the truth of perception that they also carried. What such statements unknowingly testified to was the character of the relation of writing to praxis which a number of the chief Victorian

both his essay on Carlyle and *The Condition of the Working Class* demonstrate. And so did Marx, as volume one of *Capital* abundantly suggests.

But this is not all that Engels learned. He found in Carlyle insights of a kind, formulated with a force, passion, and penetration that were not, in my opinion, to be found anywhere else at that moment. And Marx himself was then in the midst of learning how to write in this manner. Perhaps the most convenient way of demonstrating this contention is simply to set down a few passages from *Past and Present*, and when it is applicable, juxtapose to them passages from the writing of the young Marx and Engels. We may as well start with something so transparent that no juxtaposing is necessary:

Supply-and-demand is not the one Law of Nature;
Cash-payment is not the sole nexus of man with man. . . . (III, 9)

Or there is this:

To whom, then is this wealth of England wealth? Who is it that it blesses; makes happier, wiser, beautifuler, in any way better? . . . As yet no one. We have more riches than any Nation ever had before. Our successful industry is hitherto unsuccessful; a strange success if we stop here! In the midst of plethoric plenty, the people perish; with gold walls, and full barns, no man feels himself safe or satisfied. (I, 1)

Which may be juxtaposed to this:

. . . if all the members of the modern bourgeoisie have the same interests inasmuch as they form a class as against another class, they have

---

writers had attained. G. M. Young seemed to be hinting at something like this when he suggested, in a discussion of actual reform: "Directly, Carlyle contributed little; but the atmospheric effect of his insistence on personality, immaterial values, and leadership was immense." *Portrait of an Age* (London, 1953), p. 55n.

opposite, antagonistic interests inasmuch as they stand face to face with one another. . . . From day to day it thus becomes clearer that the productive relations in which the bourgeoisie moves have not a simple, uniform character, but a dual character; that in the selfsame relations in which wealth is produced, poverty is produced also . . . that these relations produce . . . the wealth of the bourgeois class, only by continually annihilating the wealth of the individual members of this class and by producing an ever-growing proletariat. (*The Poverty of Philosophy* [1847], p. 123)

Or to this:

When the fluctuation of competition is small, when demand and supply, consumption and production, are almost equal, a stage must be reached . . . where there is so much superfluous productive power that the great mass of the nation has nothing to live on, that the people starve from sheer abundance. For some considerable time England has found herself in this crazy position, in this living absurdity. ("Outlines of a Critique of Political Economy" [1844], pp. 216–217)

Here are two other passages from *Past and Present*, both of which Engels translated.

We call it a Society; and go about professing openly the totallest separation, isolation. Our life is not a mutual helpfulness; but rather, cloaked under due laws-of-war, named "fair competition" and so forth, it is a mutual hostility. We have profoundly forgotten everywhere that *Cash-payment* is not the sole relation of human beings; we think, nothing doubting, that *it* absolves and liquidates all engagements of man.(III, 2)

And yet I will venture to believe that in no time, since the beginnings of Society, was the lot of those same dumb millions of toilers so entirely unbearable as it is even in the days now passing over us. It is not to die, or even to die of hunger, that makes a man wretched; many men have died; all men must die—the last exit of us all is in a Fire-Chariot of Pain. But it is to live miserable we know not why; to work sore and yet gain nothing; to be heart-worn, weary, yet isolated, unrelated, girt in with a cold universal Laissez-faire: it is to die slowly all our life long, imprisoned in a deaf, dead, Infinite Injustice, as in the accursed iron belly of a Phalaris' Bull! This is and remains forever intolerable to all men whom God has made. Do we wonder at French Revolutions, Chartisms, Revolts of Three Days? The times, if we will consider them, are really unexampled. (III, 13)

Over against these, we can set this:

But the *community* from which the worker is *isolated* is a community of a very different order and extent than the *political* community. This community, from which *his own labor* separates him, is *life* itself, physical and spiritual life, human morality, human activity, human enjoyment, *human* existence. *Human existence* is the real community of man. As the disastrous isolation from this existence is more final, intolerable, terrible, and contradictory than isolation from the political community, so is the ending of this isolation. And even a partial reaction, a *revolt* against it, means all the more, as *man* is more than *citizen* and *human life* more than *political life*. Hence, however *partial* the *industrial* revolt may be, it conceals within itself a *universal* soul: no matter how universal a *political* revolt may be, it conceals a *narrow-minded* spirit under the *most colossal* form. ("Critical Notes on 'The King of Prussia and Social Reform'" [1844])[57]

Or this:

private property isolates everyone in his own crude solitariness . . . because . . . everyone has the same interest as his neighbor. . . . In this discord of identical interests—which is precisely a result of such identity—is consummated the immorality of mankind's condition until now; and this consummation of competition. ("Outlines of a Critique of Political Economy," p. 213)

Carlyle's attacks on political economy and the condition of

---

[57] *Writings of the Young Marx on Philosophy and Society*, ed. Lloyd D. Easton and Kurt H. Guddat (New York, 1967), p. 356; *Werke*, I, 408. In this passage one can also make out the persistence in the Marx of 1844 of Feuerbach.

England provided Engels with a number of powerful insights. Among the most important of them was a conception that Carlyle had hit upon brilliantly and developed unsystematically and that Marx was subsequently to work out with extraordinary severity. This was the conception of reification—*Verdinglichung* is Marx's term—that process in modern industrial society in which personal relations between men take on the de-authenticated form of objective relations between things, in which men come to be primarily related to one another by means of and in the commodities they exchange.[58] In a broader sense Carlyle's writing had a releasing or triggering effect on Engels. Intellectually isolated in England, his association with Marx still hidden in the unknown future, he responded to the example of Carlyle as did other young men of his time; he was stimulated into further thought and legitimated in his bolder speculations. All the same, the influence was not a dependency, and Engels made it explicitly clear that he was not prepared to follow Carlyle beyond a certain critical point. He stopped short at the religiosity, questioned the Gospel of Work as by-passing certain qualitative distinctions, and demurred at the more excessive passages of medievalism.[59] He was a young man on his own and his own man. If Carlyle at first served him as a figure of transition between one culture and another, then he served him as well in the next great transition that Engels was to experience, the beginning of his relationship with Marx.[60]

[58] See among many others Georg Lukács, *History and Class Consciousness* [1923] (London, 1971), pp. 83–222; H. Marcuse, *Reason and Revolution* (New York, 1941), pp. 279ff.

[59] *Werke*, I, 539ff. It should be noted that Engels does not repudiate all Carlyle's medieval references, comparisons and contrasts, but only those that seem to him uncritically one-sided.

[60] Numerous other lines of connection can be drawn between Marx and Engels and Carlyle, of which I choose only one. When it came to questions of organization and authority, and particularly when it came to questions of authority raised by Bakunin and

Engels left Manchester at the end of August 1844 and traveled home to Barmen by way of Paris, where he stopped for a visit of about ten days. It was during this time that he and Marx established their friendship—they were now twenty-four and twenty-six years old respectively—a compact that they sealed by drafting some passages of what was to be their first joint work, *The Holy Family*—although the title they had given it was *A Critique of Critical Criticism.*[61] Profoundly moved and energized by this experience, Engels returned to his family's home with the resolve of pulling up stakes almost at once and making his way back to Paris and Marx. Once he was there, however, it was immediately evident that he could not do so without causing such commotion and distress in his family that it would probably have caused a break between them and him, a course that he was

---

his followers, they could speak and write in phrases and tones that may seem shockingly familiar. Engels writes *re* the Bakuninists: "How these people propose to operate a factory, run a railroad, or steer a ship without one will that decides in the last resort, without unified direction, they do not of course tell us." Or again: "All socialists are of the opinion that the political state and with it political authority will disappear as the result of the coming social revolution; and this means that public functions will lose their political character and be transformed into the simple administrative functions of watching over the true interests of society. But the anti-authoritarians demand that the authoritarian political state be abolished at one stroke, even before the social conditions which give rise to it have been destroyed. They demand that the first act of the social revolution be the abolition of authority. Have these gentlemen never seen a revolution? A revolution is certainly the most authoritarian thing there is; it is the act through which one part of the population imposes its will on the other part by means of rifles, bayonets and cannon—authoritarian means if such there be at all; and if the victorious party does not wish to have fought in vain, it must maintain this domination by means of the terror which its arms inspire in the reactionaries." *Werke,* XXXIII, 389: XVIII, 308 ("Von der Autorität").

Marx's and Engels' negative comments on Carlyle are well known. They refer for the most part to the Carlyle who has gone sour, are appropriately curdled themselves, and are in my judgment generally correct.

For example, in a review of Carlyle's generally regrettable *Latter-Day Pamphlets* (1850), Marx wrote with what for him was a kind of wry sadness: "The genius has gone to the devil; only the cult remains." *Werke,* VII, 255–265.

[61] The other title was substituted by their publisher, although Marx had used the expression among his intimates.

unwilling to take. He broke silence after three weeks, and in his first letter to Marx reports that he has been sitting about amusing himself with friends and family. This amusement seems to have been divided into two parts. Engels found himself surrounded with a number of amicable young ladies, and appears to have soon become embroiled with one of them with the prospect of marriage in view. At the same time, his favorite sister, Marie, had become engaged to Emil Blank—a young communist living in London—and the Engelses' house was all bustle and noise. In these circumstances, he remarks, work is out of the question, as is the possibility of his speedy return to Paris. It is more likely that he will have to occupy himself by knocking about in Germany for six months or a year before he can find a way of extricating himself from the general small-mindedness and superstitious apprehensions of the world by which he is surrounded. It was, we should also recall, his first extended stay with his family since 1838.[62]

He soon turned to purposeful activity. He resumed his connection with Hess, then in Cologne, and along with him and other radically minded members of the local middle classes, engaged in organizing meetings, giving speeches and writing propaganda for the approaching revolution. When he reported in *The New Moral World* on the "Rapid Progress of Communism in Germany," he was forced to concede that this progress had been strictly confined to recruits from the middle class, a fact, he went on to explain, "which will perhaps astonish the English reader, if he do not know that this class in Germany is far more disinterested, impartial, and intelligent, than in England, and for the very simple reason, because it is poorer." [63] We will not pause

[62] *Werke*, XXVII, 5.

[63] *MEGA*, I/4, 340. A year earlier, Engels—like Marx—had still been convinced that communism could come to Germany by force of thought, reason and truthfulness alone, and in one of the most poignant passages in the early literature of socialism, declared his faith in this eventuality.

to examine the logic of *that* one. Nevertheless, he continues, it is only a matter of moments before the working classes come in too. Wherever he has traveled in the Rhineland, "there was not a single place where I did not find at least half-a-dozen or a dozen of out-and-out Socialists." In order to secure this kind of evidence, however, there was no need to travel at all: "Among my own family—and it is a very pious and loyal one—I count six or more, each of which has been converted without being influenced by the remainder." [64] Or more! He is counting by threes if not by sixes. One would be inclined to deplore Engels' incessant whistling in the dark, this incurable habit of substituting wish-fulfillments for judgments, were it not so patently insepara-ble from the resiliency, the good humor, and the continual availability of executive energies, all of which made possible a lifetime devoted to an extrapersonal cause.

By the middle of November, Engels was able to report to Marx that progress was being made on several fronts. He had convinced himself that revolutionary agitation on a considerable scale was now in train. At the same time he was still unable to leave

---

Thus, philosophical Communism may be considered for ever established in Germany. . . . All persecution and prohibitions have proved ineffectual, and will ever do so; the Germans are a philosophical nation, and will not, cannot abandon Communism, as soon as it is founded upon sound philosophical principles: chiefly if it is derived as an unavoidable conclusion from their *own* philosophy. And this is the part we have to perform now. Our party has to prove that either all the philosophical efforts of the German nation, from Kant to Hegel, have been useless—worse than useless; or, that they must end in Communism; that the Germans must either reject their great philosophers, whose names they hold up as the glory of their nation, or that they must adopt Communism. And this *will* be proved; this dilemma the Germans *will* be forced into, and there can scarcely be any doubt as to which side of the question the people will adopt. . . . The Germans are a very disinterested nation; if in Germany principle comes into collision with interest, principle will almost always silence the claims of interest. The same love of abstract principle, the same disregard of reality and self-interest, which have brought the Germans to a state of political nonentity, these very same qualities guarantee the success of philosophical Communism in that country. (*MEGA*, I/2, 448f.)

[64] *MEGA*, I/4, 340–341.

Barmen for Paris, since that would entail a rupture with "my entire family." (Including the six?) The contradictions between these two assertions are mollified in some measure when Engels adds—ambiguously enough to be sure—in his next sentence that besides there is this love affair about which he first has to do something conclusive.[65] But more important, he had gotten down to his book:

I am buried over my ears in English newspapers and books from which I am putting together my book on the condition of the English proletarians. I think it will be ready by the middle or end of January, since I got through the most difficult work, the ordering of the material, about 8–14 days ago. I shall compile for the English a fine bill of indictment [Sündenregister: lit., list of sins]; I shall accuse the English bourgeoisie before the entire world of murder, robbery, and all sorts of other crimes on a mass scale, and I will write a preface for it in English as well. . . . By the way, it is of course understood that when I beat the bag I mean to hit the donkey, namely, the German bourgeoisie, to whom I say clearly enough that they are just as bad as the English, only not as courageous, as consequent, and as accomplished in methods of sweating.[66]

By the time the third week in January came, Engels had fallen slightly behind the Stakhanovite schedule that he had set for himself. His love affair had come to an unpleasant end, but he begs Marx to spare him the trials of explanation, since he has already suffered enough. "I am glad that at least I can work again, and if I were to recount the whole mess for you, I'd be wrecked for the evening." All the same, now that he is back on the tracks, he expects to be finished within no more than two or three weeks. Indeed he counsels Marx, whose work was advancing at what for him was a painfully slow rate, to follow the example that he, Engels, was setting: "Therefore get going . . . do it as I do; set

[65] The ambiguous sentence reads: *"Zudem hab' ich eine Liebesgeschichte, die ich auch erst ins reine bringen muss."*

[66] *Werke*, XXVII, 9, 10.

yourself a time by which you positively *intend to be finished,* and make arrangements for early publication." [67]

Heartening enough, no doubt, but in the course of this letter Engels comes back again to his situation in Barmen and provides an account of a different nature. The passage is lengthy, but it tells us much about what was happening.

. . . there are no opportunities at all here to give even occasional vent to one's high spirits, and I am leading such a life as the most splendid Philistine could only wish for—a quiet, tranquil life, full of godly bliss and respectability. I sit in my room and work, hardly go out at all, and am as substantial as any German. If this keeps up I am afraid that God will overlook my writings and let me into heaven. I can assure you that here in Barmen I am about to acquire a good reputation. But I am sick of it as well. I want to get away from here by Easter, and will probably go to Bonn. I allowed myself to be persuaded by the advice of my brother-in-law and the doleful faces of both my parents to have another go at the business [*Schacher*] [68]; and for the last few weeks have put in some time working at the office. Prospects connected with the love affair prompted me to it as well. But I was sick of it before I ever started working. The *Schacher* is too horrible, Barmen is too horrible, the waste of time is too horrible. Above all it is too horrible to remain not only a bourgeois, but a manufacturer to boot, a bourgeois actively engaged in

[67] Engels continued in the future to cheerfully chide Marx over his dilatory scholarly progress. In 1851, for example, he closed one such extended letter of advice with the plea, "Show yourself to be a little bit of a businessman this time." *Werke,* XXVII, 375.

[68] There is no precise equivalent for the word *Schacher* in English. Some of its meanings are caught in such approximations as huckstering, haggling, chaffering, petty trade, low business—but not its particular tonality of contemptibleness. It is a word whose ultimate origin was Hebrew, and it was taken over into German from the Yiddish. Marx and Engels use it regularly and unsparingly, as in the following: *"Welches ist der weltliche Kultus des Juden? Der* Schacher. *Welches ist sein weltlicher Gott? Das* Geld." "Zur Judenfrage," *Werke,* I, 372. In what follows I shall for the sake of precision and expressive force retain the untranslated word in place.

As for Yiddish itself, Engels expressed what was almost certainly their commonly held prejudice when he described it as a "horribly corrupted German." "Poles, Tschechs and Germans," *New York Tribune,* March 5, 1852, reprinted in *Germany: Revolution and Counter-Revolution* (New York, 1969), p. 55.

opposing the working classes. A few days in my old man's factory were enough to bring before my eyes such horrors as I have tended to let grow dim in my mind. I had of course reckoned on remaining in the *Schacher* only as long as it suited me, and then writing something prohibited by the police in order to nip across the border in passable style. But I can't even stand it till then. If I did not have to record each day in my book the most horrible stories about English society, I believe that I would have already gone sour; but this at least has kept my fury boiling. Perhaps it is conceivable for a communist to remain in his external condition a bourgeois and *Schacher*-beast, as long as one *does not write;* but to carry on communist propaganda on a wide scale and to engage simultaneously in *Schacher* and industry simply will not work. Enough. I'll leave here at Easter. And on top of all this add the enervating existence in a thoroughly radical-christian-prussian family— it isn't possible any longer. In the end I might become a German philistine and introduce philistinism into communism.[69]

The youthful perplexities and confusions combined with sudden penetrations of self-awareness are both familiar and refreshing. As, even amid his hyperbolic utterances of conflict, anguish, and aggression is Engels' unflagging good nature. The representation is one of flux and multiply directed ambivalence, beneath which there emerges once again a fixed purpose and sense of self. But the purpose and identity themselves contain built-in conflict. On the one hand he is leading the life of a bourgeois mouse, although he is all the while writing a bomb of a book. On the other he is determined to decamp in a hurry, although complicated feelings for his family—including the abortive marriage—have helped him to persuade himself to return to the business, in a part-time capacity at least; apparently he is still at it and hating it. The connection between these last two opposing tendencies begins to be revealed if we first reverse their order. Engels had made one last half-hearted effort to please or appease his father—and to a lesser extent, one surmises, his

[69] *Werke,* XXVII, 17f.

mother. Like many other efforts of this kind and in such a context, however, it seems equally to have been unconsciously designed to convince everyone in sight of its hopeless impossibility. Engels senior seems to have been convinced, and Mayer tells us that he put aside his deeply cherished and long-held ambition of seeing his eldest son a member of the business, and offered him instead and at long last the opportunity to pursue scholarly studies, along with appropriate support. Which accounts for the reference to Bonn.[70]

Although Engels still seems to be flirting with the idea, it was all too late, about five years too late to be exact. But in his present mood so was virtually everything else. He admits to having partially repressed or blotted out his sense of the terrible realities of factory conditions—even as he is transcribing daily those horrors from his English experiences. He planned to stop in the business only so long as it suited him, but he was sick of it before he ever began again. Most of all, however, was the unsupportability he now ascribed to his general circumstances; it was unsupportable to exist in divided and contradictory social roles, in a divided selfhood and identity. It was bad enough to be a permanent lifetime member of the bourgeoisie, but it was unbearable to be a manufacturer as well in active, objective opposition to the working classes on whose side one's feelings and convictions were enlisted. Worse yet, and more impossible, was being all this and writing revolutionary propaganda for the working classes to boot. Yet not only is Engels describing here precisely the existence he has pursued since at least 1842; he is anticipating with equal precision the circumstances he was to live in from 1850 to 1870. He is in essence describing his style of life in two of the most important periods of his career. The fact that he now declares this identity to be unbearable seems less

[70] Mayer, I, 218f. The offer of support excluded funding of communist or revolutionary activities. Latter-day parents may be relieved to learn that the small-time blackmail concealed within the offered educational option is by no means original with them.

important than the clarity of insight that characterizes the
declaration, a clarity of definition that, it may be suggested,
helped him to go on bearing the unbearability.

There is a further irony. In speaking about the discrepancy
between his external condition [*äusseren Lage*] and his authentic
beliefs and activities, Engels is casting back to the decision he had
made at the time of his leaving school in 1837. Then he had been
content to assert that his external role as a man of business was
compatible with a projected internal alternative existence as poet,
writer and man of letters. He had persisted in this style for some
eight years by now, and we may doubt whether the change from
the writer of literary-social criticism to the writer of political and
revolutionary tracts and essays can be solely accountable for the
intensified sense of strain and discontent. It is more likely to have
been brought about by his having to live in such intimate
proximity to his parents, and for the first time in years; that, and
of course the new, related and rapidly developing friendship with
Marx. As for Engels' humorous closing reflection about philistinism, he was perhaps saying more than he knew. One might
add that among Marx's and Engels' many contributions to
communism was exactly their infusion into it of a powerful dose
of philistinism. They brought to it philistine seriousness, philistine
moral conviction, philistine rationality and methodical application. Which is only another way of saying that Marxism is the
grandest of bourgeois social philosophies. Matthew Arnold would
have disapproved, but he might have understood.

Engels' next letter to Marx dates from a month later, February
22, 1845. He has in the interval learned of the orders of expulsion
issued in Paris against Marx and others connected with the
Vorwärts!, and of Marx's removal to Brussels, and writes to say
that as soon as the news reached him he opened up a subscription
"to divide communistically among us all the extra expenses which
you have been caused." Should this amount prove insufficient to
set Marx up in Brussels, he goes on to add, "I should like to point
out that as a matter of course the honorarium which I hope to

receive soon, at least in part, for my first English thing [that is, for *The Condition of the Working Class in England*] is at your disposal with the greatest pleasure. In any case I don't need it myself for the moment, since the old boy is obliged to lend me some. The *canaille* shall at least not have the pleasure of causing you pecuniary embarrassment as a result of their infamy." Engels had not yet sent the manuscript off, nor would he do so for another three weeks, at which date he rephrased his offer, promising Marx that as soon as he received the 100 Talers that the publisher had promised him on receipt of the manuscript, he would forward the sum to Marx.[71] Apart from what has become for us the retrospective predictability of Engels' openness and generosity, there are other matters touched on in these statements that require noting. They have to do with the pathos, the comedy, the extravagance that were to persist in informing relations between the two Friedrich Engelses. From the very outset, Engels senior was willy-nilly implicated in the detestable activities of his son and his son's great associate; he was implicated in his person and his money and was to remain so until his death and after. His son's selfless openhandedness toward Marx is an ironic reflex of the pathos of the prosperous father's predicament with respect to his son.

The large and well-known historical ironies of the future have already been prepared. Marx was to do the research and much of the writing of *Das Kapital* in the British Museum; and he was in considerable measure to be supported during these years by money earned by Engels junior in the Manchester factories of Ermen and Engels. Friedrich Engels senior had subsidized the writing of *The Condition of the Working Class in England*; moreover, the entire work had been written in his own house, under his own roof. Nothing could have been more appropriate.

In the meantime, with the manuscript in its final stages, the younger Engels turned to more active forms of political behavior.

[71] *Werke*, XXVII, 19, 24.

He writes Marx a glowing account of how revolutionary agitation is going swimmingly in Elberfeld. Meetings are held, and everyone attends them, except, of course, for the proletariat. Hess lectures, readings from Shelley are given, Engels reads one of his own political essays. New supporters are being won every day. That these are all the worst kinds of philistines, who normally are interested in nothing outside of themselves, that not a single one of them is a workingman, are matters too trivial to be discussed. In any event, he is only going to stop for another four weeks in Barmen, and then at the beginning of April on to Bonn.[72] But there was to be no Bonn, and Engels' euphoric inconsequentiality barely serves to mask his deeper but unstated purpose—which is to join Marx in Brussels. To this end, he continued and intensified his overt agitational activities in Barmen-Elberfeld.

Engels has left us another account of these entertaining proceedings. It appeared as the last of the Letters on Continental Socialism that he sent to the *New Moral World*, and was printed in May 1845, after he had arrived in Brussels. "Having been unable, for a time, from certain causes, to write you on the state of affairs in Germany," is the winning way it opens. The Prussian government, he continues, has cracked down on the middle class reforming "Associations for the Benefit of the Working Classes," largely because most of them have become infested with communists, who have, from the inside, exposed the ignorance and absurdity of these would-be philanthropists. Engels then goes on to detail the events of February in Elberfeld, "the centre of the manufacturing district of Rhenan Prussia." Regular communist meetings having been held here, "the Communists of this town were invited by some of the most respectable citizens to discuss their principles with them." The first of these meetings took place in February and was, Engels remarks, "more of a private character."

[72] *Werke*, XXVII, 20, 22.

About forty or fifty individuals assisted, including the attorney-general of the district, and other members of the courts of law, as well as representatives of almost all the leading commercial and manufacturing firms.

The meeting began with the appointment of a chairman. Moses Hess

then read a lecture on the present state of society, and the necessity of abandoning the old system of competition, which he called a system of downright robbery. The lecture was received with much applause (the majority of the audience being Communists); after which Mr. Frederick Engels (who some time ago had some papers on Continental Socialism printed in your columns) spoke at some length on the practicability and the advantage of the Community system. He also gave some particulars of the American colonies and your own establishment at Harmony in proofs of his assertions.

There followed an animated discussion which lasted until one in the morning. The second such meeting took place a week later,

in the large room of the first hotel in the town. The room was filled with the "respectables" of the place. Mr. Koettgen, chairman of the former meeting, read some remarks on the future state and prospects of society, as imagined by the Communists, after which Mr. Engels delivered a speech in which he proved (as may be concluded from the fact, that not a word was offered in reply), that the present state of Germany was such as could not but produce in a very short time a social revolution; that this imminent revolution was not to be averted by any possible measures for promoting commerce and manufacturing industry; and that the only means to prevent such a revolution—a revolution more terrible than any of the mere subversions of past history—was the introduction of, and the preparation for, the Community system.

Following this heady stuff there was further animated discussion along with some "Communist poems, by Dr. Müller of Düsseldorf." A third meeting was held a week after this, at which "Dr.

Hess again lectured, and besides, some particulars about the American communities were read [probably by Engels] from a printed paper." A fourth meeting was scheduled for the next week, but a few days after the third meeting

a rumour was spread through the town that the next meeting was to be dispersed by the police, and the speakers to be arrested. The mayor of Elberfeld, indeed, went to the hotel-keeper, and threatened to withdraw the license, if any such meetings in future should be allowed to take place in his house. The Communists instantly communicated with the mayor about the matter, and received, the day before the next meeting, a circular directed to Messrs. Hess, Engels and Koettgen, by which the provincial Government, with a tremendous amount of quotations from ancient and written laws, declared such meetings to be illegal, and threatened to put a stop to them by force, if they should not be abandoned. The meeting took place next Saturday, the mayor and the attorney-general (who after the first meeting had absented himself) were present, supported by a troop of armed police, who had been sent by railroad from Düsseldorf. Of course, under such circumstances, no public addresses were delivered: the meeting occupied themselves with beef-steaks and wine, and gave the police no handle for interference.

But such measures only rebounded to serve the communist cause. The government's ascription of such importance to the communists magnified that importance, brought them publicity, numerous requests for information, "and a great many of those who had come to the discussion ignorant or scoffing at our proposals, went home with a greater respect for Communism. This respect was also partially produced by the respectable manner in which our party was represented; nearly every patrician and moneyed family of the town had one of its members or relatives present at the large table occupied by the Communists. In short," he concludes, "the effect produced by these meetings upon the public mind of the whole manufacturing district was truly wonderful." [73] The only thing more wonderful than that effect,

[73] *MEGA* I/4, 344ff.

one is prompted to remark, is the temperament that could compose such a report, out of such material, with such pronounced pleasure in its own exertions.

By the middle of March, then, developments had come to this: first, Engels had gotten his manuscript safely out of the house; and second, things had been brought to such a pass in the Engels household that something had to give. It did—with the timely intervention of the local police—but before Engels finally felt forced to take off for the Belgian border, he paused and composed for Marx a last representation of what his life at home had become. In its vigor, directness and complex tonality it represents the young Engels at his best.

I am indeed living a genuine dog's life here. All the religious fanaticism of my old man has been rearoused by the Communist meetings and by the "dissolute character" of several of our local Communists with whom, naturally, I associate. And his fanaticism has been increased by my declaration, definitively made, of giving up the *Schacher*. Moreover, my open appearance in public as a Communist has brought out in him a superb bourgeois fanaticism. You can imagine my position. Since I am leaving in a fortnight or so, I don't want to start up any row. I let everything pass over my head; they are not used to this, and so their fortitude increases. If a letter comes for me, it is sniffed at from all sides before I ever get it. Since they know that these are all Communist letters, there is on each occasion such a putting on of faces of pious misery that it is enough to drive one crazy. If I go out, the same faces. If I sit in my room and write—naturally, about Communism, they know that—more of the same. I cannot eat, drink, or sleep, I cannot let loose a fart, without the same accursed pious countenances standing there in front of my nose. Whether I go out or stay at home, keep silent or speak, read or write, laugh or not, it makes no difference. Whatever I do, my old man immediately puts on this infamous grimace. What is more, he is so dense that he lumps Communism and Liberalism together as "revolutionary" movements—and—despite all that I say in reply to him—regularly holds me responsible for all the infamies perpetrated by the English middle classes in Parliament.

To top it all off, it is now the pious season at home. A week ago today a brother and a sister of mine were confirmed; today the entire kindred have traipsed out for Holy Communion. The Lord's body has done its work, and this morning's doleful faces surpassed everything. To complete my run of bad luck, I spent last night with Hess in Elberfeld, where we went on about Communism until two in the morning. Naturally today long faces about my staying out so late, and intimations that I was probably in the pokey. At last someone summons up the courage to ask where I had been.—With Hess.—"With Hess! Good God!" Pause. Rising Christian despair in every face. "What company you choose to keep!" Sighings and so forth. It is enough to drive one mad. You cannot imagine the malice that is in this wild Christian hunt after my soul. All my old man needs to do now is to discover the existence of the "Critical Critique"; he is quite capable of showing me the door. At the same time there is this perpetual anger in myself in seeing that nothing will help with these people; that they absolutely *want* to worry and torture themselves with their fantasies about hell; that one cannot bring them to consider the most pedestrian principles of justice. My mother is at bottom a lovely human being; it is only in relation to my father that she has no independence. I really love her, and were it not for her it would not occur to me for a moment to make even the slightest concession to my fanatical and despotic old man. Even so my mother is continually worrying herself sick; in particular, every time she gets upset over me she immediately comes down with a headache that lasts for a week. It is to be tolerated no longer, I have to get away and hardly know how I can bear the next few weeks of my being here. Yet somehow I'll be able to manage.[74]

In this passage the writer of *The Condition of the Working Class* is distinctly present. Overt commitment and personal engagement are inseparably combined with analytical self-consciousness; they are indeed what make it possible for Engels to attain the distance from himself, the perspective, required for this dramatic representation. The fullness of his presence in this scene implies the ripeness with which his retraction from it impends. His

[74] *Werke*, XXVII, 26f.

dramatization of it in words prepares for and foreshadows his future absence from it in reality, just as in the future his and Marx's political writings will be dramatic gestures that anticipate and prepare for the disappearance of bourgeois society. Yet the drama represented herein is not an undifferentiated form but a specific instance of a historical sub-genre: the Engels household in Barmen is the theater of middle-class domestic-cultural comedy.[75] Comedy but not farce. For it is striking how *real* these people remain to Engels. The father cannot understand the first thing about his son's activities, except that they are scandalous and wrong; but the son's anger is not deflected into parody, farce or mockery. Instead he keeps on being angry, he keeps on arguing and communicating, he keeps on caring—for them as well as himself. And the comedy consists in part in his exasperated awareness of this, in his putting up with it, in his complicity in it. It would never occur to him to make the slightest concession to his father, but then there is his mother, whom he loves, sick headaches and all. He is about to break with them—finally and for good as he believes—but there is no hint that the rupture will entail cessation of communication, or of feelings.

As a corollary of all this, there is conveyed in this letter, as in others, what I can only call Engels' extraordinary sense of personal security. One is tempted to attach this virtue to the family life and culture that Engels is in the course of decisively repudiating, although there is not enough evidence to permit one to do so. This security is most manifest in the absence from Engels' writing of such expressions, locutions, tones and turns of voice that might suggest what in such situations we have learned to expect, some deep sense of anxiety. In particular he does not feel anxiety about his aggressive urges or theirs; he does not believe that his anger, intense and explicit as it is, will lead to murder or is the equivalent of it, nor does he believe anything of

[75] Just as for Marx, Cromwell rehearsed and revivified Old Testament epic, and the men of the first French Revolution were engaged in a modern version of Roman tragedy.

the kind about his father either. This discrimination of realities is grounded upon and compounded out of that same exceptional sense of security and trust which was now beginning to inform what was to be his almost forty-year relation with Marx, a relation unprecedented in its kind (so far as I am aware) and for which I can find no name. It is a relation of friendship and collaboration; of fraternal and filial loyalties; of servitude within equality and equality within servitude; of common actions undertaken to a common end; of unswerving attachment to an impersonal ideal which was yet embodied in the person of a single man. It was all these and none, for it was something more as well, for which, as I say, I can find no single term or name.[76] But it is difficult to conceive of how Engels could have made this exceptionally profound and enduring investment of himself had there not been much in the past on which he could continue to rely. On the one hand, he was a young man intent upon burning his bridges behind him. On the other, he knew in some part of himself that those bridges were built of fireproof material. We can put it another way. It does not detract too much from the existential reality of his decision to say that he was jumping into the abyss with a parachute. Or perhaps it does; perhaps that is one of the ways of distinguishing between the qualities of existential and historical choices in their classical modes, between the post-Hegelian Kierkegaard and the post-Hegelian Marx and Engels.

For once again the break did not occur in such a way as to conform to the usual expectations of how these generational dramas ought to take their course, and in the decision-making that

[76] Perhaps the most "creative" as well as the most puzzling circumstance about that relation (especially on Engels' part) is the almost complete absence from it—or from all the records of it that remain—of ambivalence. And since ambivalence is by practical definition a constituent of virtually every kind of human relation—and particularly such relations as friendship, partnership and collaboration—there is on the face of it something exceptional and mysterious in both a cultural and personal sense in a relation in which the ambivalence is not merely minimal, muted or nonoperational, but seems as good as nonexistent.

went on, both Engelses—surely unconsciously—saw to it once
more that the long-enduring symbiotic connection of father and
son should throughout it all be preserved. As things grew daily
more tense between them, the local police continued to show a
conspicious interest in the activist son. The imminent scandal of
an arrest in the family home provided exactly the kind of external
intervention that allowed both to get off the hook, allowed a break
without a breaking. For Engels senior it got his troublesome son
out of the house, out of the region, and out of the clutches of
Hess—who was at least an evil of known quantity. For the son, it
got him across the border to Brussels and to Marx, with whom he
had wanted all along to be. The decision was again a "joint" one
in all the extensions of that ambiguous term: both had made
concessions without conceding anything. As a final touch, or
more of the same, Engels senior eventually agreed to provide his
son with a regular allowance, an offer which the son gladly
accepted.[77] So Friedrich Engels junior went off to Brussels, where
he prospered simultaneously as revolutionary and remittance
man. And Friedrich Engels senior continued to subsidize the
revolution, the next fine fruit of which would be the joint
production known to us as *The German Ideology*.[78]

Engels thus rounds off the first major phase of his career. In this
account of its coda I have deliberately stressed the ironies and
continuities that are appropriate to anything so complex as a life
of this kind, and that prevent us from falling into the error of

[77] "He had proposed to continue a reduced allowance to young Jolyon, but this had
been refused, and perhaps that refusal had hurt him more than anything, for with it had
gone the last outlet of his penned-in affection; and there had come such tangible and solid
proof of rupture as only a transaction in property, a bestowal or refusal of such, could
supply." John Galsworthy, *The Man of Property* (London, 1906), ch. 2.

[78] The allowance was to be remitted quarterly; additional sums for special expenses such
as traveling were petitioned for separately. Enough money was procured during the next
years for Engels to take Marx to England during the summer of 1845, to bring back Mary
Burns to live with him in Brussels, to support them together, and to pay for trips to Paris.
This rough accounting does not include whatever might have been spared for Marx and
family.

regarding continuous phases of a process as segmental units. But the real rounding-off had been achieved internally, and its principal effort was the writing of *The Condition of the Working Class in England*, as the finished book was its principal result. It is to this achievement that we now must turn.

The Condition of the
Working Class (I)

Of the strange and to a certain extent unnatural conditions
of life, not paralleled in any former state of history, which
have thus arisen, there is no account of the purely historical
kind, bearing the stamp of genius, which can be cited to the
reader. The historian of genius who shall deal with the
nineteenth century is probably not yet born—has certainly
not yet written.[1]

Engels' account of Manchester is a central part of the
intellectual and imaginative vision that is *The Condition of the
Working Class in England*. And that account must be understood
within the context of the work as a whole. In his Preface to the
first German edition, Engels puts forward a number of claims,
two of which are at this juncture pertinent. First, he asserts, this
work could only have been written about England. It is only in
England that working-class conditions may be found to exist in
their "classical form" in their fullest realization. Moreover, it is
only in England that adequate material has been collected for any
kind of exhaustive representation of these conditions, as it is only

---

[1] George Saintsbury, *Manchester* (London, 1887), p. 101. These remarks appeared in
the same year in which Engels' work was first published in English.

in England that this material has been set on record and so to speak "confirmed" in large numbers of official inquiries and reports. (3)[2] Second, this work is the first in or out of England that attempts within the compass of a single volume to deal with all the various types of workingmen. (4) If we leave aside the crowing which is an indispensable function of such prefatory assertions, part of the significance and connectedness of these statements begins to emerge when we consult Engels' dedication "To the Working Classes of Great Britain," written in English on the same day as the German Preface.[3] Toward the end of this short personal testament, Engels rises to salute these subjects of his study, and his friends. "I found you to be more than mere *Englishmen*, members of a single, isolated nation, I found you to be MEN, members of the great and universal family of Mankind, who know their interest and that of all the human race to be the same. And as such, as members of this Family of 'One and Indivisible' Mankind, as Human Beings in the most emphatical meaning of the word. . . ." (8) After all these centuries of soul-destroying political claptrap, it is difficult to read these phrases with the attention they merit. Nevertheless, they do suggest Engels' larger position at this moment in his development. They make it clear that he is simultaneously looking back to 1789

[2] More than twenty years later Marx was to repeat this assertion in the Preface to the first German edition of *Capital*. Well known as these sentences are, they bear rereading.

The social statistics of Germany and the rest of Continental Western Europe are, in comparison with those of England, wretchedly compiled. But they raise the veil just enough to let us catch a glimpse of the Medusa head behind it. We should be appalled at the state of things at home, if, as in England, our governments and parliaments appointed periodically commissions of inquiry into economic conditions; if these commissions were armed with the same plenary powers to get at the truth; if it was possible to find for this purpose men as competent, as free from partisanship and respect of persons as are the English factory-inspectors, her medical reporters on public health, her commissioners of inquiry into the exploitation of women and children, into housing and food.

[3] Or at least identically dated March 15, 1845. In the original edition the dedication was printed before the Preface.

and forward to an 1848 that has not yet occurred and about which, therefore, very little can specifically be said. Nevertheless, the universal invoked and asserted is precisely what his work as a whole has to demonstrate—it is a virtual hypothesis to be tested out in historical experience. The descriptive or characterizing term used with the greatest frequency throughout *The Condition of the Working Class* consists of variations of the word "demoral-ize"—demoralized, demoralizing, demoralization and so on. What Engels is requiring of himself is the demonstration that this demoralized state is in accord with those grand universal affirmations. And more than in accord. That state must compose the indispensable precondition of those affirmations and provide the actual conditions as well as the means of their realization. It is a very large order.

Engels turns to his task in a historical Introduction. Starting out with the technological innovations of the middle of the eighteenth century, there came into being an "industrial Revolution." [4] The consequences of this development were of an unprecedented magnitude, for it was a revolution that "transformed the entire structure of civil society. The world-historical meaning of this transformation is only now beginning to be understood." [5] Since

---

[4] In adopting, along with others, the model of the French Revolution, Engels was following the lead of the French theorists of the late 1820s.

[5] "Civil society" reads in German *"bürgerliche Gesellschaft."* This much-vexed term has been also translated, naturally, as "bourgeois society," and carries its troubled history irreparably with it. It was taken into German in the eighteenth century from the "civil society" of English political economists, and it is in German that its ambiguity is most richly exploited, most notably in Hegel. See *Hegel's Philosophy of Right*, trans. T. M. Knox (Oxford, 1942), pp. x, 122ff. Marx and Engels struggled manfully to clarify the term, as in the following:

Civil society embraces the whole material intercourse of individuals within a definite stage of the development of productive forces. It embraces the whole commercial and industrial life of a given stage, and, insofar, transcends the State and the nation, though, on the other hand again, it must assert itself in its foreign relations as nationality, and inwardly must organize itself as State. The term "civil society" emerged in the eighteenth century, when property relations had already extricated themselves from the ancient and medieval communal society. Civil society as such

England is the classical ground of this momentous upheaval, it is also the place in which one can study in all its fullness "the development of its principal result, the proletariat." (9)[6] It is this emergence, this production, this creation of a new human being and of a new class of social beings that is the explicit object of the present work.

Although it is not to his purpose to write a history of the Industrial Revolution, Engels believes it necessary to establish some conception of the prehistoric state of the English workers, of their general condition before the great transformation. To this end, Engels turned to the work of Peter Gaskell, *The Manufacturing Population of England* . . . (1833) and got a representation of English preindustrial rural society. It is in fact and of course a construction, a myth, and Engels has been duly and abundantly twitted for his innocence on this score.[7] The life he

---

only develops with the bourgeoisie; the social organization evolving directly out of production and commerce, which in all ages forms the basis of the State and of the rest of the idealistic superstructure, has, however, always been designated by the same name. (*The German Ideology* [Moscow, 1964], pp. 48f.)

As a result, *"bürgerliche Gesellschaft"* in Marx and/or Engels can still mean either civil society or bourgeois society, and the meaning intended is regularly governed by the context in which the usage occurs.

That such meanings were by no means unknown to English writers may be suggested by the following from Hazlitt: "The *Times* is not a *classical* paper. It is a commercial paper, a paper of business, and it is conducted on principles of trade and business. . . . It is not ministerial; it is not patriotic; but it is *civic*. It is the lungs of the British metropolis; the mouthpiece, oracle, and echo of the Stock Exchange; the representative of the mercantile interest." "The Periodical Press" (1823), in *Selected Writings*, ed. R. Blythe (Penguin, 1970), pp. 259f.

[6] "The modern working class is the product of the machine. . . . It is the result of the development of productive energy. It is the creation of the machines. No machines would mean no working class." J. Kuczynski, *The Rise of the Working Class* (New York, 1967), p. 51.

And to extend the metaphor, not the proletariat alone. A great granddaughter of Robert "Parsley" Peel, the manufacturer-founder of that family's fortunes, once remarked that "the only ancestry we care about is the shuttle." Norman Gash, *Mr. Secretary Peel*, p. 24.

[7] One is, however, entitled to ask where in 1845 Engels might have conveniently found a reliable description of English social structure and history in the eighteenth century. In

describes is the familiar one of small-scale farming and domestic industry. The basic form of property was still land, and competition of the lower orders among themselves did not exist because of the rural dispersion of their homes and the economy that supported them. Their lives were comfortable, peaceful and uneventful; they were pious and honest men; and their material condition was better by far than that of their successors.[8] Their hours of work were not excessive; they had time for traditional recreations; and their health and that of their children were good. Socially their world was laid out for them: it was prescriptive and patriarchal. "They regarded the squire—the most important landlord in the district—as their natural superior. They sought him out for advice and counsel. They laid their little disputes before him, and treated him with all the deference that such a patriarchal relation entails." These circumstances were to be found in their homes and cottages as well; family life was traditional, orderly and religous; "children grew up in idyllic simplicity and in happy intimacy with their playmates." In this communal "seclusion and retirement," they were undisturbed by

---

addition, members of the twitting party occasionally forget themselves so far as to be able to write: "It is true, again, that most workers were free in some measure to determine their hours of work and play . . . holidays were numerous and well observed. Many domestic workers were accustomed to give Sunday, Monday, and sometimes Tuesday, to idleness and sport." T. S. Ashton, *The Industrial Revolution* (London, 1948), p. 51. For further material, discussion and controversy, see P. Mantoux, *The Industrial Revolution in the Eighteenth Century* (London, 1928; rev. ed., 1961); J. L. and B. Hammond, *The Village Labourer* (London, 1911); K. Polanyi, *The Great Transformation* (New York, 1944); F. A. Hayek, ed., *Capitalism and the Historians* (London, 1954); N. J. Smelser, *Social Change in the Industrial Revolution* (London, 1959); E. J. Hobsbawm, "The British Standard of Living, 1790–1850," *Econ. Hist. Review*, 2nd Series X (1957); R. M. Hartwell, "The Rising Standard of Living in England, 1800–1850, *Econ. Hist. Review*, 2nd Series XIII (1961); E. J. Hobsbawm and R. M. Hartwell, "The Standard of Living during the Industrial Revolution: A Discussion," *Econ. Hist. Review*, 2nd Series XVI (1963); E. P. Thompson, *The Making of the English Working Class* (1963) surveys the general scene.

[8] It is not clear here whether Engels means as their "successors" [*Nachfolger*] the industrial proletariat or the agricultural laborers of the mid-nineteenth century. He probably means both.

the excitements of "spiritual and intellectual activity," nor were the larger conditions of their life broken in upon by "violent perturbations." They walked in the path of the Lord, and their "unassuming modesty and humbleness" made them favorably disposed toward their social betters.[9]

This is, to be sure, mythology—although if we were to produce a similar passage from the writings of Edmund Burke, ten thousand ideological swords would leap from their scabbards to defend it on theoretical if not empirical grounds. What happens next, however, is something else again. Engels proceeds to another construction, but it is a construction of an altogether different character and quality.

By the same token, however, they were also spiritually dead; they lived only for their petty private interests, their looms and little gardens, and knew nothing of the mighty events that moved through mankind in the world outside. They were contented with their quiet, plant-like existence, and but for the Industrial Revolution would never have emerged from this existence, which to be sure was snugly-romantic enough, but was none the less an existence unworthy of human beings. Indeed they were not human beings, but were merely laboring machines in the service of the small number of aristocrats who had until then directed the course of history. The Industrial Revolution has carried this development to its logical conclusion as well, made over the workers altogether into mere machines, and taken from them the last remnants of independent activity. Yet it was exactly by means of this development that the workers were driven to think and to demand for themselves a human station in life. (11f.)

It may not be excessive to suggest that in this passage, at this moment, a new mode of conceptual reflection and analysis has been turned upon English events and history. Before the great

[9] Interestingly enough, a number of radical plans for social reorganization in the first half of the nineteenth century projected a "new" society based upon small independent holdings of land, subsistence farming, and cooperative local organization of institutions. Feargus O'Connor's Chartist Land Plan was such a scheme.

change the English rural population lived in a settled and customary order which rewarded them in the foregoing ways. The indisputable actuality of these rewards was at the same time not to be separated from the fact that they were part of a semblance; the appearance of their humanity was at once real and less than real—it was, in other words, an appearance in the formal sense of the term. The great change annihilated that appearance and the real satisfactions that went along with it; in so doing it carried the contradictory reality concealed within that appearance to its next phase of development, a phase which is both the logical extension of what preceded it as well as its nullification. Deprived of that semblance which yet sustained them, separated from what they felt to be a unity of existence in which they, like natural beings, had sunk their roots, the workers are compelled to confront their dispossession. Regarding what they have lost, what is now absent to them, they begin as well to see what was absent from their previous state, although they did not then know it. Reflection begins in loss and disappearance, and from this there follows their demand, made now for the first time, for an *authentic* human existence. Their loss of the semblance of humanity has led them to recognize at last its substance, and to actively desire it.

If this sounds like literary criticism and strikes the reader as being incompatible with modern historical analysis, then, one is prompted to remark, so much the worse for both disciplines. As well as for a third, which in the language of literary criticism I have been attempting to paraphrase and adapt. For what Engels has done here, in the opening pages of the work, is to bring the Hegelian method of thinking to bear upon this momentous development in English history. And, good pupil of a great master, he has done so by introducing straight off the principal and most potent Hegelian category and instrument of analysis— the negative. Negativity and the forms of negation are the protean powers in Hegel's system. Whether we find them in the logical and ontological categories of "otherness," or in the story of the fall of man being read as the fall into consciousness, or of the history of human thought being conceived as a serial drama of separations, losses and estrangements, these notions remain the central, dissolving and self-dissolving focus of the entire system, the unsteady axis about which it perpetually rotates. Engels is making a direct application of this category to the English industrial workers, to their condition as he has seen it and to their history as he has imagined it. What he has seen in them is deprivation, suffering, anguish, negation in all its most palpable forms and on a gigantic scale. What he is asserting is that their achievement of final and full humanity can only proceed through such terrible historical intensities. And now we are in a position to understand slightly better his reasons for saluting the English industrial workers in his dedication as the embodiment of the universal; they are for him, as they were becoming for Marx, the universally negated. As a class of men they had been deprived of everything except their humanity, and even that existed for them in an estranged and unachieved form. Universally negated, they represented in turn the power of universal negation, and out of this immense and dreadful convulsion there would emerge a final, positive . . . what? As in Christianity, and other systems of historical vision, it is difficult to reconcile man's historic suffering with the promise of a better future, to hold in balance the actualities of humanity's historical experience of oppression against that positive imagination held out in reciprocation.

Without Contraries is no progression. That is all very well for a visionary poet—one hears the rising objection—but Engels is working the other side of the intellectual street. Both parts of this argument are inadequate and incorrect. On the one hand there is the strong current tendency in various branches of academic literary criticism to deny to literature any essential cognitive value; this tendency I take to be both intellectually recessive and theoretically insupportable. Its insupportability comes into view as soon as one admits that literature is, among many other things, a historical phenomenon and that therefore it plays a part—and a most important part—in the historical development of conscious-

ness. On the other there is the tendency, still strong in certain
quarters, but weakened in others, to judge such a work as Engels'
either on strictly empirical grounds—did he get every datum,
every statistic, every detail right—or on the grounds that the
predictions of future developments made by him in the course of
the work were falsified by what actually happened. These
objections seem to me to fall beneath the level of theoretical
consideration.[10] Engels was in a general way applying and
adapting the systematic, coherent, consequent Hegelian style of
analysis to a complex, apparently unsystematic and possibly
incoherent massive aggregate of experiences and materials of
disparate orders; to an English social reality notorious for its
capacity to withstand theoretical incursions. The return on such
an undertaking is to be found in new or augmented *meaning,*
insights organized, connected and developed. Meaning does not
imply internal consistency or coherence alone; it does imply a
coherent regard which can be assessed by various empirical and
critical—though not scientific—means. In short it remains within
the field of our common, complex discourse, a field which
includes literature, history, most of philosophy, and most of the
social and behavioral sciences; happily for some of us, less so for
those who have been trying for so long now to make their escape
into science.

Having made this first large theoretical assertion, Engels then
goes on rapidly to summarize the early history of the Industrial
Revolution. No one thing that he adduces is particularly new, but
I have not seen an account from the time that is as succinct, as

[10] "Only 'prophetic' vision, or subsequent study of a completed period, can grasp the
unity underlying sharp contradictions. One would be misunderstanding the role of
perspective in literature, though, if one were to identify 'prophetic' understanding with
correct political foresight. If such foresight were the criterion, there would have been no
successful typology in nineteenth century literature. For it was precisely the greatest
writers of that age—Balzac and Stendhal, Dickens and Tolstoy—who erred most in their
view of what the future would be like." Georg Lukács, *Realism in Our Time* (New York,
1964), p. 56.

wide-ranging, and as coherently conceived. His underlying
theme is, expectably, the idea of change. The first group of
technological innovations set in train a series of elaborate
differentiations; these changes are themselves and in turn connected. Thus, for example, the first improvements in spinning not
only altered the relations between weaving and spinning, and
weavers and spinners; it affected the division of labor in the
family as well, and therefore had consequences in the structure of
the household, and its internal balance of forces. (12f.) And
analogous developments followed the assembly of large numbers
of power-driven machines in factories. Such changes were
accompanied by demographic shifts, population increases, alterations in the conditions of employment, in the nature of wealth,
and so forth. Although Engels begins with and concentrates upon
the cotton industry—both the place of "take-off" and the branch
of industrial activity with which he was most intimately familiar
—he does not neglect parallel developments in other branches of
textile manufacture, in metalwork, minerals, and mining, in
agriculture, and in transport: roads, canals, and railways. Nor
does he fail to mention developments in commerce and the
expansion of overseas and colonial markets. All these are
connected in the sense that they act and react upon one another
and in the sense that they form parts of a large, exceptionally
complex and continually changing coherent whole. They are *not*
connected in the sense that a single cause is isolated to which all
subsequent changes can be dependently ascribed; and they are
not connected in the sense that they are all subsumed within a
single explanatory system, as, say, in Comte and Spencer.
Multiple determinations are accompanied by independent variables.[11]

[11] For recent workings-out of this inexhaustibly complex development, see Phyllis
Deane, *The First Industrial Revolution* (Cambridge, 1965); E. J. Hobsbawm, *Industry and
Empire* (New York, 1968), pp. 1–88; David S. Landes, *The Unbound Prometheus*
(Cambridge, 1969), pp. 1–123; Peter Mathias, *The First Industrial Nation* (New York,
1969); John W. Osborne, *The Silent Revolution* (New York, 1970).

Nevertheless, nothing in English life has been left unaffected. "Everything," writes Engels, "was drawn into this universal whirlpool (or vortex) of motion." (21) [*In diesen allgemeinen Strudel der Bewegung wurde alles hineingerissen.*] It is a characteristic figure (Is Engels recalling his native Wupper?) and combines lateral with circular motion, movement that is forward and outward with movement that is centripetal and downward, as it combines something from the observable world of nature with something from Newtonian physics. Yet it is not a figure that can do adequate service for long, and toward the end of the Introduction, as he begins to summarize, Engels tries once more in an expanded passage to discover the language and so invent the conclusion (they are two phases of a single process) that he is seeking.

Such in brief is the history of English Industry over the last sixty years, a history that has no counterpart in the annals of mankind. Sixty or eighty years ago, England was no different from any other country, with its little towns, a few simple industries, and a thinly distributed but proportionately large agricultural population. Today England is a unique country, with a capital city of 2-½ million inhabitants, with colossal factory towns; with industries that supply the entire world, making almost everything by means of the most complex machines. It has an industrious, intelligent and dense population, two-thirds of whom are engaged in industry. These consist of quite different classes than existed in the past, and indeed make up a quite different nation, with other customs and other needs. The Industrial Revolution has the same importance for England as the political revolution for France and the philosophical revolution for Germany. . . . The most momentous result of this Industrial Revolution is the English proletariat. (23f.)

[*Die wichtigste Frucht aber dieser industriellen Umwälzung ist das englische Proletariat.*]

Nothing like it has ever happened before; the character of the transformation has been radical, extensive and thoroughgoing. Its significance is to be appraised in world-historical terms. The language Engels finds is until the very end notably unfigurative—the unprecedented magnitude of the event is its own intensifier.[12] Yet among the qualitative changes has been the creation of a new nation, with new classes; and these new classes are made up of new men. It is at this point that Engels introduces a metaphor. These men as a group represent an organic result [*Frucht*] of a nonorganic if not inorganic process. The metaphor, as it so often does, suggests the presence of a theoretical crux.

But Engels carries it one step further. It was "through the introduction of machinery," he writes, that the proletariat "was called into existence." (24) [*das Proletariat durch die Einführung der Maschinen ins Leben gerufen wurde.*] [13] Even more, "the first proletarians belonged to manufacture and were begotten directly through it." (27) [*Die ersten Proletarier gehörten der Industrie an und wurden direkt durch sie erzeugt.*] Here is the new human family, its new genealogy, its new myth of creation, and its new family romance—and all the old ambiguities. For they were not begotten, created, caused, produced or generated *by* industry, but *through* it; they belonged to it, and yet they were its foster children and inmates, its natural and unnatural offspring.[14] Engels' emphasis falls again on the unprecedented eruption and interruption of human affairs that has occurred. It is an upheaval

---

[12] Dickens found an intensifier. In *The Old Curiosity Shop*, ch. 43, when Nell and her grandfather are brought by barge to the great industrial town, they "passed through a dirty lane into a crowded street, and stood, amid its din and tumult, and in the pouring rain, as strange, bewildered, and confused, as if they had lived a thousand years before, and were raised from the dead and placed there by a miracle." It is as if the pre-industrial world were antediluvian, or as if the Industrial Revolution were itself the Flood rather than the new world constructed after the subsidence of the waters.

[13] He is here casting back to the first sentence of the Introduction, where he wrote that "The history of the English working classes begins in the second half of the eighteenth century with the invention of the steam engine and of machines for manufacturing cotton." (9)

[14] See the fire-watcher's narrative in *The Old Curiosity Shop*, ch. 44, for a similar contemporary representation.

that has not yet reached its climax, that is, even as he is writing, reaching its newest critical point of intensity. And he closes this Introduction by referring again to the deepening suffering of the working class, to the increasing distance between and polarization of the working and middle classes, to the deplorable ignorance of the middle classes about the misery of their laboring countrymen. Hence, he writes, the "smiling indifference" of the middle classes, even though "the ground beneath their feet is undermined and may give way at any minute." Indeed, "the imminence of this collapse is as certain as the laws of mathematics or mechanics." (26) Is this only wishful thinking on the part of the young insurrectionary, or is it already a foretaste of the much older Engels who will write with lamentably vain certitude about "dialectics of nature" and "scientific socialism"? The outcome may permit us to make a closer determination.[15]

Chapter II of *The Condition of the Working Class* has as its title "The Industrial Proletariat" and is precisely three pages long. Since no other chapter in the book bears this title, we are justified in inquiring into what appears to be an oddness or anomaly of construction. Engels begins by stating that although the working class may be divided into groupings—depending upon their time of historical emergence and the kind of work in which they are engaged—it is of some advantage to examine its condition as a whole before proceeding to a detailed examination of the special characteristics of each branch of industry. He then steps back and isolates what he evidently considers to be the four main variables that went into the making of the working classes. Three of these are technological: the intensification of the division of labor, the use of water power and steam power, and the introduction of modern machinery. They are, he writes, "the three great levers"

---

[15] See G. Lichtheim, *Marxism, An Historical and Critical Study* (London, 1961), pp. 234–243; Z. A. Jordan, *The Evolution of Dialectical Materialism* (London, 1967), *passim;* in fairness it should be noted that there are those, such as L. Althusser, *For Marx* (New York, 1970), who continue to prefer the later Engels.

that, since the middle of the eighteenth century, industry has used to "heave the world out of joint." In turn they are associated with a fourth development, the tendency in modern society toward concentration and centralization. This tendency is to be detected in the factory system itself, which centralizes and concentrates the operations of production in the interests of efficiency and cheapness. It is equally there in the concentration of property and capital in the hands of a small number of great owners. And it is there in the accompanying centralization of the population, or human capital, in new settlements—"Hence the extraordinary rapid expansion of the great factory towns." (26ff.) Concentration and expansion are taking place concurrently; increasing density and increasing scale are concomitant functions.[16]

At this point Engels was faced with a choice of values or priorities. He could go on to describe the general conditions of labor in the mechanized factory system, along with their consequences in the lives of the operatives and tenders of the machines. Or he could choose instead to represent first the conditions of life within the new circumstances of density and concentration, the new mass experience of what has come to be called urbanization. It is a matter of some significance, I believe, that he picked the second course. He offers a number of reasons in justification of this decision. It is in the great towns, he states, that "industry and commerce attain their fullest development," that "the concentration of property has reached its highest point," and that the influence of these upon the working classes may be "most distinctly and openly" observed. Moreover, it is here that

---

[16] The populations of the towns were increased because of high rates of reproduction and internal migration. In 1851, for example, only 55 percent of the inhabitants of the largest towns in Britain had been born there, and of those inhabitants who were over twenty years of age, only 39 percent had been born in the towns in which they lived. In a classic study of labor migration, A. Redford demonstrated how most of the internal migration covered only a short distance, the majority of the migrants to a large town coming from the immediately surrounding counties. In the case of Lancashire, more than two thirds of the migrants over twenty years of age came from adjacent counties and from Ireland. *Labour Migration in England, 1800–1850* (London, 1926), pp. 158ff. and *passim.*

the traditional English way of life has been "most radically obliterated." [*hier sind die Sitten und Verhältnisse der guten alten Zeit am gründlichsten vernichtet*] The very name "Merry England" has no meaning and has disappeared from memory.[17] In these towns there are essentially only two classes, the rich and poor, for the lower middle-classes are rapidly disappearing. The vast majority of the inhabitants of these urban centers, therefore, are proletarians. These are cogent enough observations, but they do not sufficiently account for the impulses, both personal and theoretical, that moved Engels to the choice that determined the structure of the entire work.

Neither of these impulses is particularly obscure, and their workings may be clearly discerned in Chapter III. This chapter, "The Great Towns," is without doubt the best and the most important section of *The Condition of the Working Class*; in my judgment it is the best single thing Engels ever wrote.[18] The success or failure of the whole conception of the work depends on it, and on how we judge it, and any critical, analytic discussion of the book must concentrate its demonstrations upon the material it brings forward. And we can propose forthwith what Engels' personal motives were in choosing to write about the great towns first. He was choosing to write about his own experience: to contend with it, to exploit it, to clarify it, and in some literal sense to create it and thereby himself. For in transforming his experiences into language he was at once both generating and discovering their structure.

[17] For further discussion see E. P. Thompson, *The Making of the English Working Class*, pp. 143, 229.

[18] I accede to Engels' judgment, in spite of considerable evidence to the contrary, that the Communist Manifesto was essentially the work of Marx. See, however, *The Birth of the Communist Manifesto*, ed. Dirk J. Struik (New York, 1971), which contains a good account of Engels' contribution along with translations of his preliminary sketches and drafts which formed part of the basis of the finished work. (One of these early drafts was only first discovered as late as 1968.) It may also be mentioned that the title *Communist Manifesto* is Engels' formulation. See *Werke*, XXVII, 107; Mayer, I, 259–290.

In one sense it is fortunate that Engels begins with London, for his representation of it supplies us with a standard of comparison for what he does subsequently. Recalling his first impressions from the autumn of 1842, Engels speaks of how imposing the metropolis appears as one sails up the Thames. The city itself is unique, for one can "roam for hours" without ever coming to "the beginning of the end, without meeting the slightest sign that might lead one to infer that there is open country nearby. This immense centralization, this agglomeration of two and a half million human beings on one spot has multiplied the power of this two and a half million a hundredfold; it has raised London up to the commercial capital of the world." [19] Yet this impression of overwhelming magnificence does not last; after a few days spent on the crowded streets of the city, after visiting some of its slums, the visitor begins to discover something of the sacrifices, of the human costs, that have bought these marvels of civilization.

the inhabitants of London have had to sacrifice the best part of their humanity . . . a hundred powers slumber dormantly in them, inactive and suppressed, in order that a handful of others might develop themselves more fully. . . . The very bustle and tumult of the streets has something repugnant in it, something that human nature feels outraged by. Hundreds of thousands of people from all classes and ranks of society crowd by each other. Are they not all human beings with the same qualities and faculties: Do they not all have the same interest in being happy? Must they not in the end seek their happiness through the same means and methods? Yet they rush past each other as if they had nothing in common, nothing to do with one another. They are in (tacit) agreement on one thing only—that everyone keep to the right of the pavement so as not to interfere with the crowds that stream in the opposite direction. Meanwhile it occurs to no one that others are worth even a glance. The brutal indifference, the unfeeling isolation of each

[19] For an excellent survey and account of the current state of research, see Francis Sheppard, *London 1808–1870: The Infernal Wen* (London, 1971); for a summary of the population of conurbations, see B. R. Mitchell and Phyllis Deane, *Abstract of British Historical Statistics* (Cambridge, 1962), p. 19.

individual person in his private interest becomes the more repulsive and offensive, the more these individuals are packed into a tiny space. We know well enough that this isolation of the individual—this narrow-minded self-seeking—is everywhere the fundamental principle of modern society. But nowhere is it so shamelessly unconcealed, so self-conscious as in the tumultuous concourse of the great city. The dissolution of mankind into monads, each of which has a separate purpose, is carried here to its furthest point. It is the world of atoms.

From this it follows that the social war—the war of all against all—has been openly declared. As in Stirner, men here regard each other only as useful objects. Each one exploits the other with the result that the stronger tramples the weaker underfoot, and that the few who are strong, the capitalists, seize everything for themselves, while for the many who are weak, the poor, there remains scarcely a bare existence. (30f.)

How are we to respond to such a vision? To begin with, we may remark that it is no disgrace on Engels' part to be overcome by London, to succumb to its immensity; his response, to be sure, is inadequate, but then so was almost everyone else's. Besides he could not have spent more than a few weeks there at the most, time enough to be thoroughly distressed by the unique city, but not enough to begin to take it in coherently. Observing the passage more closely, we may note that on one of its sides it isn't actually much of an advance on Wordsworth, the Wordsworth whose first residence in London occurred in 1790 and who recorded his impressions of that experience in Book VII of *The Prelude*.

> Above all, one thought
> Baffled my understanding: how men lived
> Even next-door neighbours, as we say, yet still
> Strangers, not knowing each the other's name.

> Rise up, thou monstrous ant-hill on the plain
> Of a too busy world! Before me flow,
> Thou endless stream of men and moving things!

Thy every-day appearance, as it strikes—
With wonder heightened, or sublimed by awe—
On strangers, of all ages; the quick dance
Of colours, lights, and forms; the deafening din;
The comers and the goers face to face,
Face after face. . . .

Oh, blank confusion! true epitome
Of what the mighty City is herself,
To thousands upon thousands of her sons,
Living amid the same perpetual whirl
Of trivial objects, melted and reduced
To one identity, by differences
That have no law, no meaning, and no end—
Oppression, under which even highest minds
Must labour, whence the strongest are not free.

(ll. 115–118, 149–157, 722–730)

The effect, despite all protestations, is not so much of confusion in the object as in the observing eye and mind. And the confusion is of not a simple disarray, as Wordsworth implies in his use of "blank"; it is rather an incapacity to differentiate, to discover articulated structures in—or impose them upon—the materials of experience, here half perceived but not half created.

The passage from Engels reveals similar if not identical tendencies. It begins without an organizing conception, and large parts of it consist of Engels' casting about for a notion that will intelligibly subordinate the material that keeps continually slipping away. And when toward the end he does hit upon such a notion—or structuring principle—the reader is inclined to think that this is the point at which he ought to have begun. The difficulty is in part that the experience, which for our purposes is the passage of writing, remains largely unmediated; it is not worked through and does not advance out of the logic of its immanent oppositions—which, as I have said, really come into view only toward the end. Still in the course of this uncertain movement Engels touches upon a number of matters which require comment. He begins by describing the deprived, uncomplete, unrealized humanity of the mass of London's inhabitants. It isn't that this assertion is untrue, but that half of it is missing. The integral positive moments of these negative judgments are at the moment inaccessible to him, and will not turn up until considerably later.[20] He next goes on to comment about the appearance and behavior of these moving city throngs. What Engels has to say reveals that he was at the same point of development that, in this same connection, Dickens had attained in *Nicholas Nickleby* (1838–1839). And it is by the roundabout way of some passages in that novel that I propose to develop further this explication of Engels.

When Nicholas and Smike escape from Dotheboys Hall and make their way to London, they take lodgings in the vicinity of Golden Square, in that densely subdivided house in which Newman Noggs and the Kenwigs family rent rooms as well. Out of pocket and confined in prospects, Nicholas decides upon a walk out of doors.

So, taking up his hat, and leaving poor Smike to arrange and rearrange the room . . . he betook himself to the streets, and mingled with the crowd which thronged them.

Although a man may lose a sense of his own importance when he is a mere unit among a busy throng, all utterly regardless of him, it by no

---

[20] They will not in fact turn up until he has completed his representation of Manchester, until, that is, he has produced the phenomenon in its fullness. In another place Engels addresses the matter with exemplary succinctness. Why is it, he asks, that in modern European national economies one does not look to the countryside for genuinely radical movements; "the agricultural population," he continues, "in consequence of its dispersion over a great space, and of the difficulty of bringing about an agreement among any considerable portion of it, never can attempt a successful independent movement; they require the initiatory impulse of the more concentrated, more enlightened, more easily moved people of the towns." *Germany: Revolution and Counter-Revolution* (New York, 1969), p. 16 [from an article that appeared in the *New York Tribune*, October 25, 1851]. These notions are today so familiar and venerable that it is difficult to recall that they were ever new.

means follows that he can dispossess himself, with equal facility, of a very strong sense of the importance and magnitude of his cares. The unhappy state of his own affairs was the one idea which occupied the brain of Nicholas . . . and when he tried to dislodge it by speculating on the situation and prospects of the people who surrounded him, he caught himself, in a few seconds, contrasting their condition with his own, and gliding almost imperceptibly back into his old train of thought again. (ch. 16)

What Dickens and Engels are both referring to is the uniform anonymity of the urban pedestrian mass, a condition which paradoxically rivets one's reflective attention upon that anonymous reduced phantom that is one's self. It is a condition that delivers us from one unreality to another: from the unreality of a nameless universal identity ("a mere unit") we pass directly over to the unreality of regarding our own apparition and its desires as all of reality and the only reality. As Dickens and Engels describe this condition, it appears both externally and internally as a contradiction, as a plenum that is yet empty.[21]

Further on, Dickens returns to this scene and undertakes to represent it on a larger scale and from an altered point of view. It is now London at night.

They rattled on through the noisy, bustling, crowded streets . . . now displaying long double rows of brightly-burning lamps, dotted here and there with the chemists' glaring lights, and illuminated besides with the brilliant flood that streamed from the windows of the shops . . . [containing objects of wealth and desire that] succeeded each other in rich and glittering profusion. Streams of people apparently without end poured on and on, jostling each other in the crowd and hurrying forward, scarcely seeming to notice the riches that surrounded them on every side; while vehicles of all shapes and makes, mingled up together in one moving mass like running water, lent their ceaseless roar to swell the noise and tumult.

---

[21] In Hegelian terms it would be a phenomenon making its appearance from the side of abstract, universal negativity.

As they dashed by the quickly-changing and ever-varying objects, it was curious to observe in what a strange procession they passed before the eye. . . . [objects of luxury and beauty as well as those that are associated with sickness, destruction and death]—all these jumbled each with the other and flocking side by side, seemed to flit by in motley dance like the fantastic groups of the old Dutch painter, and with the same stern moral for the unheeding restless crowd.

Nor were there wanting objects in the crowd itself to give new point and purpose to the shifting scene . . . pale and pinched-up faces hovered about the windows where was tempting food; hungry eyes wandered over the profusion guarded by one thin sheet of brittle glass—an iron wall to them. . . . Life and death went hand in hand; wealth and poverty stood side by side; repletion and starvation laid them down together. (ch. 32)

Although it is separated from the earlier passage by some two hundred pages, this extract none the less represents its logical development.[22] It renders explicit what was latent in the earlier descriptive scene—and, it might be added, what is latent in Engels' highly but unsatisfactorily compressed remarks as well. It begins, logically and actually, by substituting objects for people. The "double row" of street lamps is interspersed or "dotted" with other sources of light, and these in turn are assimilated to the "flood" of illumination that "stream[s]" from the shopwindows. As in the earlier passage, the discrete units are at the same time part of a moving, undifferentiated flood or stream. Yet the discrete units are related in still other ways; in the first place, they remain discrete units, for the nature of their relation to each other is precisely in being disjoined. They are rows, dots and patches of light that shine out separately from the dark disconnecting ground of night. Second, they are related by pure succession and contiguity, for the entire scene is in continuous motion. As this successive motion turns into a "flood that streamed,"[23] Dickens

22 See *Dickens: From Pickwick to Dombey* (New York, 1965), ch. 3, where I have tried to analyze Dickens' conception of society in *Nicholas Nickleby*.

23 As in so many of Dickens' better passages, the implicit conceptual sequences are

shifts focus from the lights as objects and sources of illumination to the objects they illuminate and that lie within them, the goods and products that rest invitingly in each separate shopwindow. Yet these enclosed and inapproachable entities become, as they are passed, parts of the stream and "succeeded each other in rich and glittering profusion." Having established this immediately relevant and intermediate term, Dickens then transforms the whole back into its human form. "Streams of people apparently without end poured on and on. . . ."

There is an ironic ambiguity here, though probably an unconscious one. The streams of people seem endless in numbers and flow from an apparently inexhaustible source. But they also, as in Wordsworth, seem to have no discernible end in view; they move in different directions but appear to exist without discernible purpose—they may in fact be directionless.[24] Moreover, they seem scarcely to notice the rich world of commodities that envelops them; that is to say, they seem not to notice the very objects of their desires and exertions. Although these objects are there lit up in the shopwindows, they and the people who jostle relentlessly past them appear for the moment to be windowless monads. Dickens then turns to consider the commodities themselves, which are organized by being "jumbled each with the

---

being partly enacted in the very movement of the syntax, which here embodies a series of trans-logically connected images. In other words, the syntax itself is operating in the way we ordinarily ascribe to the working of images.

[24] Dickens returned to this notion and brought it to a triumphant conclusion at the end of ch. 19 of *Bleak House*, one of his great set pieces called "Moving On."

Jo moves on, through the long vacation, down to Blackfriars Bridge, where he finds a baking stony corner, wherein to settle to his repast.

And there he sits, munching and gnawing, and looking up at the great Cross on the summit of St. Paul's Cathedral, glittering above a red and violet-tinted cloud of smoke. From the boy's face one might suppose that sacred emblem to be, in his eyes, the crowning confusion of the great, confused city; so golden, so high up, so far out of his reach. There he sits, the sun going down, the river running fast, the crowd flowing by him in two streams—everything moving on to some purpose and to one end—until he is stirred up, and told to "move on" too.

The passage, it should go without saying, merits the closest analysis.

other and flocking side by side"; they are a random assortment of contrasts connected by their spatial proximity, and Dickens associates them with the "fantastic groups" of the *Totentanz*, mistaking the nationality of Holbein the younger, but continuing to elaborate the notion of the transformation of objects, as the figure of Death in the woodcuts transforms the human figures he is juxtaposed to. Dickens is unwittingly playing with the theory of commodities.[25]

He then switches "objects" once more and finds them in the human part of the scene, "in the crowd itself." The monads let in windows, and hungry faces with their hungry eyes now regard those other objects that earlier in the passage were disregarded. But they regard them from the far side of their windows which, Dickens says, are the same as an iron wall. Thus these objects are once again contiguously related, but the contiguity is precisely the term of their disrelatedness as well. These circumstances correspond to the structure of urban society as Dickens has imaginatively represented it in *Nicholas Nickleby*—a series of private worlds which are never really connected. It is, we may recall, a very early moment in his development.[26]

[25] Dickens apparently had a lifelong special feeling for these pictures. One of the few surviving application-slips in his hand from the British Museum, dating from ca. 1832–1833, is for an engraving of them. See *The Letters of Charles Dickens*, ed. M. House and G. Storey, I, 9n. In "The Stroller's Tale," the first of the interpolated tales in *Pickwick Papers*, ch. 3, he refers to "The spectral figures in the Dance of Death, the most frightful shapes that the ablest painter ever portrayed on canvas. . . ." And in *Little Dorrit*, Bk. II, ch. 21, he has Miss Wade characterize Henry Gowan, the artist who cynically regards his talent and his art as mere commodities, as follows: "He was like the dressed-up Death in the Dutch series; whatever figure he took upon his arm, whether it was youth or age, beauty or ugliness, whether he danced with it, sang with it, played with it, or prayed with it, he made it ghastly." It recurs once more at the very end, in *The Mystery of Edwin Drood*, ch. 12.

[26] Nevertheless, compare: "The mutual and universal dependence of individuals who remain indifferent to one another constitutes the social network that binds them together. This social coherence is expressed in *exchange value*, in which alone each individual's activity or his product becomes an activity or a product for him." Karl Marx, *Grundrisse der Kritik der politischen Ökonomie* [1857–1858] (Berlin, 1953), p. 74; selections from this

Engels was, to be sure, incapable of this kind of local richness and depth of response: there is only one Dickens. But he was not merely conceptualizing abstractly either; and he and Dickens were both trying to shape their responses to these bewildering phenomena of urban behavior. In this connection, one of the things that both observed was developed to a possible conclusion by Georg Simmel. In his essay "The Metropolis and Mental Life," Simmel undertakes to analyze and explain the characteristic mental attitude of modern city dwellers toward one another. The term he uses to designate this attitude is "reserve": "If so many inner reactions were responses to the continuous external contacts with innumerable people as are those in the small town, where one knows almost everybody one meets and where one has a positive relation to almost everyone, one would be completely atomized internally and come to an unimaginable psychic state." The model in question has to do with frequency of stimuli. In the city, Simmel argues, they are of such an inordinate degree that one has to shut down or dampen responsive processes that in other situations presumably act without inhibition. (This latter inference is at least doubtful, as is the unqualified assertion about relations in small towns.) He is describing what is thought of today as a defensive adaptation; one behaves in an atomic way socially and externally in order to preserve one's internal wholeness and integrity. One thinks of Wemmick, the lawyer's clerk in *Great Expectations*, who every morning becomes less human and more mechanical in his appearance and behavior as he approaches his work in the central city, and every evening reverses the process as he approaches his home in an outlying suburb. At the same time, however, the "inner aspect" of that reserve is not a neutral indifference, but is rather composed of aversive impulses, feelings of "mutual strangeness and repulsion." Nevertheless, Simmel concludes, "what appears in the metropoli-

---

work have been translated by David McLellan under the misleading title *The Grundrisse* (New York, 1972); the foregoing sentences appear on p. 66.

tan style of life directly as dissociation is in reality only one of its elemental forms of socialization." [27] One feels that this last clause, true enough as far as it goes, ought to have about three further dialectical turns appended to it.

But Engels is not satisfied with delineating this mode of psychic distance, and he goes on to observe that the more closely packed together city dwellers are, the more pronounced become their indifference to and isolation from one another. The behavior he is referring to was in the nineteenth century classified under the head of "congregation," their term for what is nowadays described as density and its effects. And what Engels is in effect saying is that London is what has been recently called a "behavioral sink." [28] Indeed, Engels' method so far in trying to explain the experience of London has been to throw in everything he can think of, including the kitchen sink; and had he known of the behavioral sink he would have flung that in after it. Yet it is precisely at this point that he has also hit upon the organizing conception that he has a trifle hectically been seeking. After this the writing abruptly straightens itself out and moves directly to its argued conclusions.

The conception was itself something of a contradiction and was articulated in its original form by the great English and German Romantic writers. What they had as a group experienced was that an augmented sense of one's personal individual reality, of selfhood, might reciprocally entail an increased awareness of isolation and personal estrangement. The classical directive "Know thyself" might not lead to rationality and community but to their opposites. An access of radical subjectivity might end in the desolation of permanent incommunicability —of madness, muteness, drug-sustained reverie, or suicide— rather than in powers of communicativeness enriched by the

[27] *The Sociology of Georg Simmel*, ed. Kurt H. Wolff (Glencoe, Ill., 1950), pp. 415f.
[28] For a useful summary of research on the experiences of space and crowding from the points of view of social psychology, cultural anthropology and ethology, see Edward T. Hall, *The Hidden Dimension* (New York, 1966).

experience of that universal and aboriginal mental life that exists beyond the borders of everyday consciousness. Self-realization, in other words, might involve the loss of a socially active and vivid existence, and thus be a project of self-nullification as well. In general, the great romantics tended to emphasize the reciprocating and combinative influence of these different possibilities. They generally withheld from ascribing causal priority to one or the other, but tended to represent them in complex incremental interplay. We know now that what, among other things, they were experiencing with such preternatural acuteness—and representing in their first responses as personal singularity and idiosyncrasy—was the general form that society in their time was rapidly taking on. As happened so often in the nineteenth century, the immediate successors of the great romantics, the writers of the fourth, fifth and sixth decades, transposed these experiences directly into social terms. They did so in part because they had the experience of the romantics behind them—to assimilate and build upon—in part because society had by then become with unmistakable overtness what the romantics by and large figuratively anticipated.

Self-realization, then, had taken on the normative shape of the pursuit of self-interest. And the universal human search for the self—literally self-seeking—stood revealed in its current historical embodiment as a competitive activity in which one's personal quest was achieved by means of the defeat, sometimes relative, sometimes absolute, of the same quest in others. Moreover, this activity was restored to the status of classical rationality. Since society is nothing more than an aggregate collection of individuals, as McCulloch typically maintained, "it is plain that each in steadily pursuing his own aggrandizement is following that precise line of conduct which is most for the public advantage." [29] The subjectivity and irrationality of the romantics were at least

---

[29] J. R. M. McCulloch, *Principles of Political Economy* (London, 1825), p. 129, quoted in Elie Halévy, *The Growth of Philosophic Radicalism* (London, 1952 ed.), pp. 500f.

on one of their sides the negative, critical complement to such statements, statements which purported themselves to be the rational theory of this new rational world. The irrationality was also a response to the unreason that lay as yet concealed within the new social rationality and the behavior out of which it arose. The spontaneous composition of universal egoisms was to take place by means of unarmed combat, in that open space called the marketplace, wherein the circle had at last been squared; it was magic, it was "nature"; it was reason, it was madness; it was science and the rule of three, it was ideology and the rule of force. Or, as Marx was to remark later on, it all depended on how you read Ricardo; you could find in his works a profoundly reasoned theory of a society that functioned according to a self-acting principle, the identity of interests; or you could equally find there "an arsenal for anarchists, socialists, and all the enemies of bourgeois society." By the time Engels came to write, the cracks and fissures in the theory—not to speak of the social reality to which they referred—were gaping widely.[30]

As he finds the terms of these rich contradictions, Engels begins in the latter part of the passage to write with increased directness and force. This new clarity brings with it a sudden expansion of reference. Almost at once it becomes apparent that the enabling or springing allusion is in the first instance to Carlyle. The diction and tone are convincingly reminiscent; and the entire passage turns upon the alarming application of the idea of personal isolation within the context of socioeconomic activity, a recognizably Carlylean stragegy.[31] The allusions range backward and forward in time; backward to their historical inception in Hobbes and forward to their most recent and bizarrely mystified appearance in Max Stirner's *The Ego and His Own*, published while Engels was writing *The Condition of the Working*

[30] *Werke*, XXVIII, 504f.; translated in *Letters to Americans*, pp. 44f.

[31] I except Dickens, Balzac, Tocqueville and Marx, who had also by this time found other means of bringing these disparate orders of experience into conjunction.

Class.[32] Leibnitz is dragged in for metaphoric support, as are the classical atoms.[33] Nor is Hegel overlooked, the language and movement of the passage recalling such statements as the following, which Engels was certain to have read: "civil society is the battlefield where everyone's individual private interest meets everyone else's." [34] A few sentences further on, Engels tries in fact to compound Hobbes and Carlyle. On all sides, he writes, one can observe signs of "social warfare; the house of every individual person is in a state of siege," while at the same time "mutual plundering, under the protection of the law" is duly occurring on all sides. The theoretical state of nature at last reveals itself to be a refraction of the actual circumstances of society. This realization and its consequences, Engels confesses, are terrifying; the observer has nothing left to be surprised at, except for the fact that "the whole of these insane goings-on" manage somehow still to cohere. (31) [*dass das ganze tolle Treiben überhaupt noch zusammenhält.*]

The dominating conception, of course, is that of conflict and of war—and these in almost every imaginable manifestation. Yet it would be less than disinterested to reduce these conceptions at once to the status of metaphors or images. Matters of an extralinguistic meaning and importance are at stake, and realities which cannot be confined by language—though it is only through language that we can reflectively apprehend and express them— are involved. On the one hand, these conceptions are among the fundamental presuppositions of Engels'—and Marx's—style of

[32] Part III of *The German Ideology*, almost four hundred pages long, is devoted to a gleeful dismemberment of "Saint Max."

[33] The atoms continue to do yeoman service. Cf. *The Old Curiosity Shop*, ch. 44. Nell and her grandfather stand bewildered amid the noise and dirt of the industrial town. "They were but an atom, here, in a mountain-heap of misery, the very sight of which increased their hopelessness and suffering." Dickens' heart isn't in it, however, and his arithmetic is primitive. He can't even go so far with the theory as to think of them as *two* separate atoms; by making the two back into one, he defeats the purpose of the theory and reveals the other logic by which he really thinks.

[34] Hegel's *Philosophy of Right*, p. 189.

thinking, and constitute another considerable portion of their inheritance from Hegel. On the other, these conceptions refer cognitively to an immense body of social and historical experience and material; and an entire school of historical interpretation—not all of whose members can by any means be thought of as Marxists—has organized itself upon such categories. For example, the opening sentence of J. L. Hammond's and Barbara Hammond's *The Skilled Labourer, 1760–1832* (1919) reads, "The history of England at the time discussed in these pages reads like a history of civil war." In the third place, there is a considerable revisionist or "optimistic" school of historical interpretation which, grounding itself upon other theories—either explicit or tacit—of social-historical change, has challenged the first school and regarded the material in question with other meanings. There is no sense in pretending that this disagreement is going to be settled here or elsewhere. The evidence itself is no longer a matter of dispute; in a way it never really was. What is at issue is the existential character of various historians and social theorists, for these differing interpretations of the past are always a function of the present, refer to the present, and represent a present commitment. Perhaps the most useful thing one can do at such a juncture is to introduce a quotation or an authority that has not yet been considered in the context of this discussion. For instance, there is this from Max Weber:

In a market economy every form of rational calculation, especially of capital accounting, is oriented to expectations of prices and their changes as they are determined by the conflicts of interests in bargaining and competition and the resolution of these conflicts. In profitability-accounting this is made particularly clear in that system of bookkeeping which is (up to now) the most highly developed one from a technical point of view, in the so-called double-entry bookkeeping. Through a system of individual accounts the fiction is here created that different departments within an enterprise, or individual accounts, conduct exchange operations with each other, thus permitting a check in the technically most perfect manner on the profitability of each individual step or measure.

Capital accounting in its *formally* most rational shape thus presupposes the *battle of man with man.* And this in turn involves a further very specific precondition. No economic system can directly translate subjective "feelings of need" into effective demand, that is, into demand which needs to be taken into account and satisfied through the production of goods. . . . A need may fail to be satisfied not only when an individual's own demand for other goods takes precedence, but also when the greater purchasing power of others for *all* types of goods prevails. Thus the fact that the battle of man against man on the market is an essential condition for the existence of rational money-accounting further implies that the outcome of the economic process is decisively influenced by the ability of persons who are more plentifully supplied with money to outbid the others, and of those more favorably situated for production to underbid their rivals on the selling side.

It is thus clear that the formal rationality of money calculation is dependent on certain quite specific substantive conditions. Those which are of a particular sociological importance for present purposes are the following: (1) Market struggle of economic units which are at least relatively autonomous. Money prices are the product of conflicts of interest and of compromises; they thus result from power constellations. Money is not a mere "voucher for unspecified utilities," which could be altered at will without any fundamental effect on the character of the price system as a battle of man against man. "Money," is, rather, primarily a weapon in this battle, and prices are expressions of the battle; they are instruments of calculation only as estimated quantifications of relative chances in this battle of interests.

Jede *rationale Geldrechnung und insbesondere daher jede* Kapital-rechnung *ist bei* Markterwerb *orientiet an Preischancen, die sich durch Interessenkampf (Preis-und Konkurrenzkampf) und Interessenkompromiss auf dem Market bilden. Dies tritt in der Rentabilitätsrechnung besonders plastisch bei der technisch (bisher) höchst entwickelten Form der Buch-führung (der sog. "doppelten" Buchführung) darin hervor: dass durch ein Kontensystem die Fiktion von Tauschvorgängen zwischen den einzelnen*

Betriebsabteilungen oder gesonderten Rechnungsposten zugrunde gelegt wird, welches technisch am vollkommensten die Kontrolle der Rentabilität jeder einzelnen Massregel gestattet. Die Kapitalrechnung in ihrer formal rationalsten Gestalt setzt daher den Kampf des Menschen mit dem Menschen voraus. Und zwar unter einer weiteren sehr besondersartigen Vorbedingung. Für keine Wirtschaft kann subjektiv vorhandene "Bedarfs-empfindung" gleich effektivem, das heisst: für die Deckung durch Güterbeschaffung in Rechnung zu stellendem, Bedarf sein. . . . Die Voraussetzung des Kampfes des Menschen mit dem Menschen auf dem Markt als Bedingung der Existenz rationaler Geldrechnung setzt also weiter auch die entscheidende Beeinflussung des Resultates durch die Über-bietungsmöglichkeiten reichlicher mit Geldeinkommen versorgter Konsu-menten und die Unterbietungsmöglichkeit vorteilhafter für die Güter-beschaffung ausgestatteter—insbesondere: mit Verfügungsgewalt über bes-chaffungswichtige Güter oder Geld ausgestatteter—Produzenten absolut voraus.

Die formale "Rationalität" der Geldrechnung ist also an sehr spezifische materiale Bedingungen geknüpft, welche hier soziologisch interessieren, vor allem:

1. den Marktkampf (mindestens: relativ) autonomer Wirtschaften. Geldpreise sind Kampf- und Kompromissprodukte, also Erzeugnisse von Machtkonstellationen. "Geld" ist keine harmlose "Anweisung auf unbe-stimmte Nutzleistungen," welche man ohne grundsätzliche Ausschaltung des durch Kampf von Menschen mit Menschen geprägten Charakters der Preise beliebig umgestalten könnte, sondern primär: Kampfmittel und Kampf-preis, Rechnungsmittel aber nur in der Form des quantitaven Schätzungs-ausdrucks von Interessenkampfchancen.

One of the things that such a magisterial utterance—and it is a characteristic one—prompts one to observe is that commentators coming after Weber appear to have done their studious best to avoid having to deal with it.[35]

[35] *Wirtschaft und Gesellschaft*, ed. Johannes Winckelmann (Berlin, 1964), I, 65f., 77; *Economy and Society*, ed. Guenther Roth and Claus Wittich (New York, 1968), I, 92f., 107f. (slightly altered). Although this is the kind of passage that Weber's detractors from both the left and right manage almost uniformly not to refer to, one notable exception to

Nevertheless, for all the density and suggestiveness of Engels' passage about London, it is not an adequate representation—one has to supply too much to it, it does not unpack itself through its own inherent movement. Furthermore, it generalizes itself far too rapidly; London is left almost immediately behind and is forsaken instead for "society" itself. And it is not at all clear how one gets from the war of all against all to the concentration of all wealth in the hands of a few capitalists—or if clear, it isn't convincing. Engels seems to visualize some kind of aboriginal but unremittingly perpetuated free-for-all, in which a handful of ruffians have only now—why only now?—succeeded in grabbing everything for themselves. This is historically insufficient; and it harks back theoretically to the kind of argument sustained in Rousseau's *Second Discourse, On the Origin of Inequality*, which, brilliant and inflammatory though it is, exists in a world of altogether different historical and theoretical possibilities.[36] London, after all, is not the sort of place about which theories can be gotten up in a hurry; you cannot bring down a mammoth by shooting from the hip.

Engels then sets out to make a "more detailed examination of the conditions in which the social war has placed the propertyless class." Let us see, he continues, "what sort of reward society bestows in fact upon the working-man for his labour in the form of housing, clothing and food." Let us see in what sort of "an existence it maintains those who contribute the most to the existence of society." And he proposes to begin with housing.

---

this rule was Joseph A. Schumpeter, who wrote: "The whole of Max Weber's facts and arguments fits perfectly into Marx's system." *Capitalism, Socialism and Democracy* (London, 1947), p. 11. But then there appears to have been no stampede among social theorists to take up the challenge of this remark either.

[36] In that discourse, Rousseau imagined a purely hypothetical "state of nature." This concept enabled him to discuss what he intuitively perceived to be man's original and natural qualities as distinct from those characteristics that had been developed in him throughout the course of civilized history. The theoretical model implicit in this essay is an ahistorical one, although Rousseau tends to cast his radical reflections in historical form.

The reasons for his making this choice will presently appear.

He then discusses slums briefly and in a general way, describes from his own limited experience the rookery of St. Giles, mentions other kinds of London slums, such as those enclaves of the most bitter poverty that are to be found "nearby to the splendid mansions of the wealthy," and within the most respectable districts of town.[37] For example, an area hard by Portman Square was found to be such a "recess or lurking-place" of the utmost misery, packed with "a mass of Irish demoralized by dirt and poverty." (34) He then turns to his substantial collection of reports, documents and newspaper clippings, and begins to cite the usual hair-raising statistics about rents and densities. He delivers a long, telling quotation on Bethnal Green, summarizes and quotes from reports of coroners' inquests on persons who have died of starvation and in circumstances of utter destitution—all of these, he remarks, as typical as they are extreme. He moves on to the homeless. He evidently visited a number of the infamous cheap lodging houses, and writes a terrible paragraph about them; but they prove too much for his descriptive powers, and he breaks down in the midst of his exposition. Then there are the literally unhoused and unaccommodated, those who sleep in passages and arcades or who find shelter in parks or on the embankment. He has saved a long leader from the *Times* on this subject and quotes from it liberally. This rapid survey has filled only seven or eight pages; and the parade of horrors has just begun.

In the succeeding ten pages Engels follows the same procedure in even briefer compass for the other major cities of the United Kingdom. He begins with Dublin and then passes across to Edinburgh, for both of which he sets down relevant chilling extracts from Alison's *Observations on the Management of the Poor in Scotland* (1840),[38] Chadwick's *Sanitary Report* (1842), *The*

[37] For a thorough review, and bibliography, of this subject, see H. J. Dyos, "The Slums of Victorian London," *Victorian Studies*, XII, 1 (September, 1967), 5–40.

[38] Carlyle had used the same report to spectacular effect in *Past and Present*.

Artizan and *The Northern Star*.[39] He mentions Liverpool and
Bristol, and moves on to the industrial towns of Nottingham,
Leicester, Derby and Sheffield, and produces further extracts on
the courts and cellar-dwellings of Birmingham and the wynds of
Glasgow. As he turns to "the great industrial district of the center
of the British Isles, the densely-populated belt made up of the
West Riding of Yorkshire and South Lancashire," (47) the
writing once again returns to his personal experiences. With an
eye attentive to the lay of the land, the veteran young artillerist
sketches in brief the topographical situation of the region,
comments appreciatively on the valleys of the Aire in which
Leeds is situated, and on the houses of the industrial towns that lie
dotted about in these valleys and in those of the Calder—"the
houses built of rough grey stone seem so spruce and tidy in
comparison with the blackened brick buildings of Lancashire that
it is really a delight" to look upon them. This is the view from a
distance; a visit to these towns themselves, he sadly continues,
leaves one with "little enough cause of rejoicing." He then
introduces a long extract describing the sanitary conditions of
Leeds, the ghastly truth of which, he remarks, he confirmed by
his own personal observation. (47) Seven miles away is Bradford,
which Engels represents in much the same fashion, making clear
that he has spent some time—although not a great deal of
it—passing about the city and noting its particularities. And he
strongly implies as well that he has visited Huddersfield, Barnsley
and Halifax and made similar observations in these places.

One passes from the West Riding to South Lancashire by
crossing—over it on foot or through it by rail, and Engels
suggests that he has done both—Blackstone Edge, the highest
point of those hills and the watershed between the Irish and
North Seas. Engels has at last arrived in Manchester, and as he
does so his tone becomes for the moment appropriately elevated

[39] As well as numerous other sources which Engels' editors in German and English have
succeeded in identifying.

and ironic. We now, he says, "enter upon that classic ground on which English industry has wrought its masterpiece." (50) [*so kommen wir auf den klassischen Boden, auf dem die englische Industrie ihr Meisterwerk vollbracht hat*] A hundred years ago, this district was mostly marshland, thinly populated; today it is "sown over with towns and villages and is the most densely-populated region of England." Here and especially in Manchester, there is to be found what is at once both "the point of departure and the center" of British manufacture. Here "the modern art of manufacture has attained its consummation," its perfection or fullest realization. [*ihre Vollendung erreicht*] It was in the cotton industry that the revolutionary technological innovations were both first introduced and subsequently pressed to their most advanced limits. By the same inevitable token, the consequences of modern industry insofar as they affect the working classes "develop themselves here in the most integral and unalloyed ways, and the industrial proletariat appears in its most exemplary form." And it follows necessarily as well that two further concomitant developments have been carried here to their furthest point and to "the most distinct consciousness": "the degradation in which the worker, through the application of steam power, machinery, and the division of labour—has been sunk"—the application being almost literally made upon his being—and "the efforts of the proletariat to raise themselves up out of this degraded state." Engels then addresses his reader with a proposal. He is going to examine conditions in Manchester in greater detail, and for two reasons. First, it is "the classic type of modern industrial town." [40] And second, "I know it as intimately as I know my native town—and more intimately than most of its

---

[40] As late as 1927, this statement continued to be repeated and confirmed. "Among the towns mentioned on almost every page of this book, and to which the factory system owes as much as they owe to the factory system, the cotton towns show the earliest and the most remarkable development. And by far the most important and famous of them all, which remains today the classic type of an industrial town, is Manchester." P. Mantoux, *The Industrial Revolution in the Eighteenth Century*, p. 355.

inhabitants know it." The boldness of the claim is on a par with the quality of thought in the passage as a whole. With the exception of Tocqueville, there is to my knowledge nothing from the period that equals it in forcefulness, comprehensiveness and consequential power. Technological and social developments interlock and give rise to still further changes; and both are inevitably accompanied by collective transformations of consciousness which are themselves prerequisites of transformed behavior. And Engels has as yet hardly begun.

But he is still not ready to enter the city itself, or what most persons would regard as the city. Instead he steps back and regards Manchester as the center of a district of towns.[41] Such towns as Bolton, Preston, Wigan, Rochdale, Oldham, Ashton-under-Lyne, Stalybridge and Stockport surround Manchester and are connected with it in a complex variety of ways. As far as the working-class districts are concerned, these towns differ little from Manchester—

except that the workers possibly form an even larger proportion of the entire population. That is to say, these towns are wholly industrial, and all their commercial efforts are transacted in and through Manchester. They are dependent upon Manchester in every respect and are in

[41] At first, but only at first, this reminds one of Faucher. Seventy years later, when Patrick Geddes invented the term "conurbation," the district whose center was Manchester—he called it "Lancaston"—was one of his two primary examples of this development, Greater London being of course the other. *Cities in Evolution* (London, 1915), pp. 31ff.

One important reason for the concentrated distribution of the industry in this district had to do with the availability of power, first water and then steam. Lancashire is extremely well endowed with resources of water power; and the cotton district as it was finally settled in 1840 (and as it remains with only minor changes until today) was largely determined by the geographical shape of the Lancashire coal field. See H. B. Rodgers, "The Lancashire Cotton Industry in 1840," *Geographical Interpretations of Historical Sources*, ed. Alan R. H. Baker, et al. (London, 1970), pp. 337–355. For general considerations see Alfred Weber, *Theory of the Location of Industries* [1909], trans. Carl J. Friedrich (Chicago, 1929); A. Lösch, *The Economics of Location*, trans. W. H. Woglom and W. F. Stolper (New Haven, 1954); Walter Isard, *Location and Space-Economy* (New York, 1956).

consequence inhabited solely by workers, factory owners and small shopkeepers. Manchester, by contrast, possesses in addition to these a quite considerable commercial population, particularly in commission houses and high-class retail businesses. . . . Although nearly all these towns have between 30,000 and 90,000 inhabitants, they are virtually nothing but huge working-class quarters. These are interrupted only by [or interspersed only with] factories, a few main streets fronted with shops, and in addition a few gated and tree-lined lanes, along which, like villas, the gardens and houses of the factory owners are situated. The towns themselves are badly built, without regularity, rule, or order. They have filthy courts, lanes and back alleys. They are saturated with coal smoke and have a particularly dingy appearance, since the original bright red brick—the usual building material in these parts—has in the course of time turned black. Cellar dwellings are to be found everywhere. Wherever it is at all possible to do so, these subterranean holes are constructed, and a very considerable proportion of the population lives in them. (51)

Engels then goes on to devote some paragraphs to describing in brief Bolton, Stockport, Ashton-under-Lyne, and Stalybridge. Each of these has its own peculiarities—dependent in large measure upon geographical situation and the date at which the town either underwent rapid expansion or came into existence— but in general the condition of the workers' dwellings in these towns reproduces the conditions that apply in Manchester.

What Engels has described is a single huge complex, extending over a great space of earth and comprising upwards of a million persons. Manchester is surrounded by a series of sub-towns. They are related to it first by virtue of location and second by virtue of function. They are all like Manchester, only more so and less so. They are both more specialized and less differentiated than the central town. They are dependent on Manchester in the sense that their "higher" functions are located and directed from there, while they themselves are largely confined to performing the "lower" or fundamental functions—producing the wealth and reproducing the producers of that wealth—through which the whole is sustained. They embody a division of labor on an unprecedented mass social scale, and are immense industrial barracks or encampments. They are at this moment in their history almost purely functional or skeletal communities and have not yet provided themselves with such visible structures as make manifest those extra-economic institutions and activities through which communities of men are also ordinarily regarded as maintaining themselves, their ancestors and their children. They and their work represent a new, frightening and highly developed order of human existence. Yet what is most striking about this new complexity is its inexpungeable, contradictory uniformity— uniformity of life, of style, even of color. This uniformity is part of the experience of murderous, quasi-military discipline that generations of workingmen have had to undergo; but it is also what permits Manchester and its dependent communities to operate with such extraordinary, if lopsided, efficiency. In Engels' representation the complexity and uniformity are really held together.[42]

He is now prepared for Manchester itself. He begins by describing its geographical situation, Manchester proper lying on the left bank of the Irwell, between it and the two smaller streams, the Irk and the Medlock, that flow into it at this point, with Salford on the right bank of the Irwell bounded by a sharp bend of the river. On every side, however, the city extends itself, runs into, through and over what were formerly separate townships, such as Pendleton, the Broughtons, Hulme, Chorlton-on-Medlock and Ardwick. "The whole of this built-up complex," Engels writes, is what is "commonly called Manchester and contains about 400,000 people." Engels then proceeds to compose, in a single paragraph that runs to almost three pages in length, one of the most enduring and important statements ever written about the modern city.

---

[42] Manchester is "surrounded by a belt of growing towns all with the same functions and the same needs, and forming together as it were but one factory and one market." Mantoux, p. 50.

The town itself is peculiarly built, so that someone can live in it for years and travel into it and out of it daily without ever coming into contact with a working-class quarter or even with workers—so long, that is to say, as one confines himself to his business affairs or to strolling about for pleasure. This comes about mainly in the circumstances that through an unconscious, tacit agreement as much as through conscious, explicit intention the working class districts are most sharply separated from the parts of the city reserved for the middle class. Or, if this does not succeed, they are concealed with the cloak of charity. [*oder, wo dies nicht geht, mit dem Mantel der Liebe verhüllt werden*] [43]

If this is so, how does the city work? Engels turns at once to a description which is simultaneously an explanation and analysis.

In the center of Manchester there is a fairly extensive commercial district, which is about a half-mile long and a half-mile broad. This district consists almost entirely of offices and warehouses. Nearly the whole of this district is without permanent residents, and is forsaken and deserted at night, when only policemen on duty patrol its narrow, dark lanes with their bull's eye lanterns. This district is intersected by certain main thoroughfares in which an enormous volume of traffic is concentrated. The ground floors of the buildings along these streets are occupied by shops of dazzling splendor. Here and there the upper stories of such premises are occupied as residences, and these streets present a relatively lively appearance until late at night. With the exception of this commercial district, all Manchester proper, all Salford and Hulme, an important part of Pendleton and Chorlton, two-thirds of Ardwick, and certain stretches of Cheetham Hill and Broughton—all of these comprise a pure working-class district. This area [or district] extends around [or surrounds] the commercial quarter in a belt that is on the

---

[43] This last clause is given in Mrs. Wischnewetzky's rendering, which retains the obscure referential character of the German. Since Engels read through and made revisions in her translation, it is to be presumed that he let this sentence pass as perspicuous. It is indeed highly suggestive and one could associate out from it in all directions, but it remains not exactly perspicuous. Henderson and Chaloner invent a sentence in its place. "In those areas where the two social groups happened to come into contact with each other the middle classes sanctimoniously ignore the existence of their less fortunate neighbors." (54)

average one and a half miles in width. Outside, beyond this belt, live the upper and middle classes. The latter are to be found in regularly laid out streets near the working class quarter, in Chorlton and the lower-lying regions of Cheetham Hill. The upper middle class has situated itself in the remoter parts of Chorlton and Ardwick, or on the breezy heights of Cheetham Hill, Broughton and Pendleton, where its members live in villa-like houses surrounded by gardens. . . .

And so on. There is the organization. What remains is to set it in motion. This is done in the first instance by the system of transport, the omnibuses which run every fifteen or thirty minutes and connect these outlying areas with the center of Manchester. And the beauty of it all, Engels continues, is that the members of Manchester's monied aristocracy can now travel from their houses

to their places of business in the center of the town by the shortest routes, which run right through all the working class districts, without even noticing how close they are to the most squalid misery which lies immediately about them on both sides of the road. This is because the main streets which run from the Exchange in all directions out of the city are occupied almost uninterruptedly on both sides by shops, which are kept by members of the middle and lower-middle classes. In their own interests these shopkeepers should keep up their shops in an outward appearance of cleanliness and respectability; and in fact they do so. To be sure, these shops have none the less a concordant relation with those regions that lay stretched out behind them. Those shops which are situated in the commercial quarter or in the vicinity of the middle class residential districts are more elegant than those which serve to cover up the workers' grimy cottages. Nevertheless, even these latter adequately serve the purpose of hiding from the eyes of wealthy gentlemen and ladies with strong stomachs and weak nerves the misery and squalor that form the completing counterpart, the indivisible complement, of their riches and luxury.[44]

[44] "*das ergänzende Moment*" is what the old or former young Hegelian wrote. A beautiful illustration of Engels' thesis is to be found in the *English Note-Books* of

He then proceeds to a concrete demonstration, and conducts the reader along a number of the main streets and simply and irrefutably shows how the changes in character of the buildings that front the street indicate what is to be found behind them. He is in fact charting one series of connected and stratified variables within the social topography of the city.

By this means, Engels continues, "it is possible for someone who knows Manchester to *infer* the social character of a district from the appearance of the main street that it adjoins. At the same time, however, it is almost impossible to get from these main streets a view of the *real* working class districts themselves." He then moves toward his conclusion.

I know perfectly well that this deceitful manner of building is more or less common to all big cities. I know as well that shopkeepers must in the nature of their business take premises on the main throughfares. I know that in such streets there are more good houses than bad ones, and that the value of land is higher in their immediate vicinity than in neighborhoods that lie at a distance from them. But at the same time I have never come across so systematic a seclusion of the working-class from the main streets as in Manchester. I have never elsewhere seen a concealment of such fine sensibility of everything that might offend the eyes and nerves of the middle classes. And yet it is precisely Manchester that has been built less according to a plan and less within the limitations of official regulations—and indeed more through accident—than any other town. Still when I consider in this connection the eager assurances of the middle classes that things are going splendidly for the working classes, I cannot help feeling that the liberal industrialists, the Manchester "bigwigs," are not so altogether innocent of this bashful style of building. (56)[45]

Hawthorne, who came to Manchester in 1856 and then returned in 1857 for the Exhibition, rented a house first at Old Trafford and then on Chorlton Road, used the omnibuses exactly as Engels described, saw "many handsome shops," many fine paintings, and very little else—except for a sensational scene in Manchester cathedral. Nathaniel Hawthorne, *Works* (Boston, 1894), VIII, 285ff., 517–545; also *Our Old Home, Works*, VII, 169, 359ff.

[45] In the original German edition Engels wrote "big Whigs"; he later corrected this to read "big Wigs," a feeble enough pun in either form.

Unlike the earlier passage about London, this simply gives itself to the reader—such is its easy grasp of the material. In Manchester, as others had observed, the separation of classes had been driven to new extremes. What Engels added to this observation is that the separation had been built into the very structure of the city, and that this actual fabric both perpetuated such a condition and visibly expressed it. Even more, it had virtually effected the disappearance of one of the segregated classes; and the invisible poor of the mid-twentieth century was a reinvention of the invisible working classes of the mid-nineteenth. Yet how has this extraordinary phenomenon come about? In part, Engels says, it is through unconscious and unstated agreement, in part through deliberate intention—both of these, he intimates, applying to both groups, though not necessarily in equal proportions. The point to be taken is that this astonishing and outrageous arrangement cannot be fully understood as the result of a plot, or even a deliberate design, although those in whose interests it works also control it. It is indeed too huge and too complex a state of organized affairs ever to have been *thought up* in advance, to have preexisted as an idea.[46]

The city is a recognizably contemporary institution in other respects. It has already constructed for itself a central or inner core that is packed by day and deserted at night. This radical discrimination of function is equally borne out in the circumstance that those who during the day direct the city's workings

[46] "The first glance at history convinces us that the actions of men spring from their needs, their passions, their interests, their characters, and their talents. . . . Passions, private aims, and the satisfaction of selfish desires are . . . tremendous springs of action. Their power lies in the fact that they respect none of the limitations which law and morality would impose on them. . . . [At the same time] human actions in history produce additional results, beyond their immediate purpose and attainment, beyond their immediate knowledge and desire. They gratify their own interests; but something more is thereby accomplished, which is latent in the action though not present in their consciousness and not included in their design." G. W. F. Hegel, *Reason in History*, trans. Robert S. Hartman (Indianapolis, 1953), pp. 26, 35. (This is an augmented version of the Introduction to *The Philosophy of History*; an earlier translation of the whole work by J. Sibree remains widely available.)

from the center have moved away from there—where their homes originally were as well—and redistributed themselves as far from the center as the current means of transportation allow, on suburban heights. That is to say, as the city has rapidly and enormously expanded as an organization of production and a concentrated center of power and wealth, it has also deteriorated as a place in which to conduct other human and civilized activities. As the wealthier population have fled the center, they have leapfrogged over the vast working class and left them there massed, as it were, about that alternately dense and hollow core, in an immense unbroken belt in which they work and live. It is impossible at this point in history to disperse them, since they have to live within close walking distance of their places of work. Despite all these sudden shiftings and evolutions—the fearful concentration of the working class, the flight from the center to the periphery—things have worked themselves out in what is apparently tidy and orderly detail. Indeed the city reveals its social or class structure in each of its important spatial arrangements. These are most notable in those zones where the two extremes approach each other, or to put the same idea in another way, at their lines of division: which is where the middle middle and lower middle classes come in. Their houses lie outside the working-class belt, and between that belt and the more favorably situated suburban estates of the upper middle class. And their shops and small businesses are located along the main thoroughfares—acting so to speak as insulators for the city's system of communication. Their location in space, therefore, is at both critical junctures an intermediate one. And their intermediary position is not merely structural but functional as well. They are acting as buffers between the antagonistic extremes.[47]

[47] Compare, with appropriate allowances, this passage from George Orwell: "I was born into what you might describe as the lower-upper-middle-class. . . . a sort of mound of wreckage left behind when the tide of Victorian prosperity receded. . . . the layer of society lying between £2,000 and £300 a year: my own family was not far from the bottom. . . . In the kind of shabby-genteel family that I am talking about there is far more

These streets, then, are Manchester's Potemkin villages. Yet behind the façades there lies not the nothingness of trans-Uralic wastes, but a negative existence that is paradoxically a positive fullness, the indispensable creative source of all that positive wealth that lies beyond it. As Engels describes and analyzes them, those streets represent a collective effort of isolation, distancing and denial, and work socially to the same ends as the same unconscious defensive processes work toward in individual persons. All he has neglected to add is that when these symbolic aids were not available, it was possible to take to literal avoidance—the recourse adopted, for example, by the heroine of Mrs. Gaskell's *North and South*:

> The side of the town [i.e., Manchester] on which Crampton lay was especially a thoroughfare for the factory people. In the back streets around them there were many mills, out of which poured streams of men and women two or three times a day. Until Margaret had learnt the times of their ingress and egress, she was very unfortunate in constantly falling in with them. (ch. 8)

These ways of dealing with experience were not confined to Manchester or to the industrial towns or even to London. Some years earlier, in his essay "Civilization," John Stuart Mill had illuminated this subject from another point of view. "One of the effects of civilization (not to say one of the ingredients in it)," he

---

consciousness of poverty than in any working-class family above the level of the dole. . . . Practically the whole family income goes in keeping up appearances. . . . But the real importance of this class is that they are the shock-absorbers of the bourgeoisie. The real bourgeoisie, those in the £2,000 a year class and over, have their money as a thick layer of padding between themselves and the class they plunder; in so far as they are aware of the Lower Orders at all they are aware of them as employees, servants and tradesmen. But it is quite different for the poor devils lower down who are struggling to live genteel lives on what are virtually working-class incomes. These last are forced into close, and, in a sense, intimate contact with the working class, and I suspect it is from them that the traditional upper-class attitude toward 'common' people is derived." *The Road to Wigan Pier* (New York, 1958), pp. 153f., 156.

wrote, "is, that the spectacle, and even the very idea of pain, is kept more and more out of the sight of those classes who enjoy in their fullness the benefits of civilization." In the old cruel and heroic ages of Greece and Rome and of feudal Europe, this was not so. Today, however, all this has changed.

All those necessary portions of the business of society which oblige any person to be the immediate agent or ocular witness of the infliction of pain, are delegated by common consent to peculiar and narrow classes: to the judge, the soldier, the surgeon, the butcher, and the executioner. To most people in easy circumstances, any pain, except that inflicted upon the body by accident or disease, and the more delicate and refined griefs of the imagination and the affections, is rather a thing known of than actually experienced. This is much more emphatically true in the more refined classes, and as refinement advances: for it is in keeping as far as possible out of sight, not only actual pain, but all that can be offensive or disagreeable to the most sensitive person, that refinement exists. We may remark too, that this is possible only by a perfection of mechanical arrangements impracticable in any but a high state of civilization.[48]

It is a wonderfully intelligent passage and provides a useful context for Engels' remarks, as those remarks do in turn for

[48] *Essays on Politics and Culture*, ed. Gertrude Himmelfarb (New York, 1963), pp. 64f. The evolution in England of the method by which capital sentences were executed strikingly bears out Mill's contention. "In the eighteenth century offenders were usually driven in public procession to certain public places selected for the execution of all capital sentences. Sometimes they were put to death near the place of their crime. Later, public processions were abandoned in favour of executions—still carried out publicly—in front of prisons. Ultimately this system, too, was found unsatisfactory, and in the nineteenth century executions were withdrawn from the public view behind prison walls." This evolution "bears witness to a profound change in the attitude of public opinion towards crime and punishment." Leon Radzinowicz, *A History of the English Criminal Law and its Administration from 1750* (New York, 1948), I, 165. See also the study of the development of the mechanization of death in the slaughtering and meat-packing industries in Siegfried Giedion, *Mechanization Takes Command* (New York, 1948), pp. 209–245.

Mill's. Both are aware that they are discussing a special modern development; and both regard this development with an equally critical, not to say jaundiced, eye. What is striking about Mill's statement is that although it is written with the intention of the highest generality, the one thing that it fails to include is precisely the content of Engels' passage—the everyday world of labor and industry and the conditions of life in which it was sustained.[49] Furthermore, although Mill certainly sees the reciprocal and necessary connection between civilization or refinement and the concealment of pain, he does not press upon that connection with the same degree of force as Engels. For what Engels is saying is that the riches and luxury are not only connected with the hidden suffering and squalor. They are connected in such a way as to be integral components of a unified-diversified phenomenon, whose very separation is the clue to their unity, both of these manifestly made visible in the structure of Manchester's streets.[50]

Long before Ruskin declared that one has to read a building, Engels had demonstrated that one had to read a city—that a city could indeed be read. And yet, Engels says, doubling back upon himself, reading is *all* one can do from the main streets themselves. Those rows of shops, commercial buildings, pubs,

[49] I do not mean by this that the statements are opposed or contradictory of one another; they are not.

[50] As an illustration of what one type of modern sociological theorizing can do to the kind of insight that the passages from Mill and Engels represent, compare the following on the discrepancy between appearances and reality:

> We find that there are many performances which could not have been given had not tasks been done which were physically unclean, semi-illegal, cruel, and degrading in other ways; but these disturbing facts are seldom expressed during a performance. . . . we tend to conceal from our audience all evidence of "dirty work," whether we do this work in private or allocate it to a servant, to the impersonal market, to a legitimate specialist, or to an illegitimate one.

Erving Goffman, *The Presentation of Self in Everyday Life* (New York, 1959), p. 44. What in Engels and Mill is a rich blending of historically concrete instances that tend to reveal an emerging universal, has here been leached out into ahistorical generalities and empty inclusiveness. It is an instructive instance of what has been called the fallacy of misplaced abstractness.

warehouses and factories, different and discriminable as they are, are still ultimately coverings. They function, depending upon the context in which we regard them, as appearances, symbols or symptoms. They are the visible parts of a larger reality; they both reveal and conceal that reality; they are formations made up of displacements of and compromises between antagonistic forces and agencies. In order to get at the real things, one has to go behind such appearances—no nineteenth-century novelist could have put his theoretical case more distinctly.[51]

But before he does this, Engels doubles back upon himself once more. He is aware of the fact that this kind of thing can be found in other cities, and he is acquainted with such innocuous "explanations" of these arrangements as those that argue that the main streets are simply where shops and stores have to locate themselves, although there is some truth in these as well. Nevertheless, he has observed what he can only describe as the systematic exclusion of the working classes from the main streets of the city; at least what he is describing—the informal ghettoization of the working classes—seems to act with systematic thoroughness and consistency, although the ghetto is itself the largest part of the town. But he knows as well that Manchester has been built up without plan, without explicit designs, and largely even through accident. Indeed, as he remarks later on: "The big cities have sprung up spontaneously and people have moved into them wholly of their own free will." (135) It is at the same time impossible to observe how this entire set of arrangements works to the advantage of the controlling class of industrialists—and to hear them speak of how the lives of the

[51] And no twentieth-century one, for that matter. See *L'Emploi du Temps* (Paris, 1957), trans. *Passing Time* (1960) by Michel Butor. Butor systematically uses the city in ways that are strongly reminiscent of Engels. He even provides a map that in its details strikingly resembles the maps supplied by Engels; and he traverses his northern English industrial town with the intention of finding the center of its "complex network." The main difference between the two is that Engels believes that through systematic study one can get to know the essence of the city, or of its reality, while Butor, one hundred and twenty years later, does not.

working class are improving; lives which have been in effect excluded from their sight—without suspecting that these industrialists are not so entirely innocent of it all as they appear. Innocent in the sense of knowledge, in the sense of interest and implication, and in the sense of responsibility for behavior undertaken in the past, continued in the present and projected into the future.

It is an invincible conclusion. It dramatizes the triumph of the intellect and experience of a single young man; but it represents as well the coming to fruition in him of a sovereign mode of thought, in the secularized application of its method to a new field of experience. What Engels has perceived and created is a general structure; its form is that of a coherent totality, a concrete, complex and systematic whole, each one of whose parts has a meaning, and more than one meaning, in relation to all the others. These meanings begin to come into view when we realize that this total whole is, naturally, more than the sum of its parts, that it is made of its parts and their histories, and that the entire elaborated and coordinated structure is in motion. For Engels is describing a process whose properties are unique. As I have remarked before, this process is neither mechanical nor organic; it partakes of both and yet is neither and something other as well. The only names we can assign to it are the human or the social, or, what is the same thing, the human-social, since the two cannot in fact or theory be held apart. It was this singular process that Hegel's style of thinking explicitly and preeminently dramatized. And yet there is something oddly moving and appropriate in the fact that this, one of the early successful adaptations of the method of this most difficult and obscure of all philosophers, should fall to the lot of a young man who considered himself to be a virtual autodidact, who was the son of a factory owner, and that it should of all places have happened on the streets of Manchester.

Having thus constructively made out the macrostructure of the city, Engels prepares to go behind those main street frontages, to enter that dark, dense belt formed by Manchester's working class and their dwellings, and to examine it. In this examination he has two purposes in mind: to describe it literally as it is, and to determine whether he can discover in it some kind of corresponding microstructure. Before we follow him on this expedition, we may be prompted to ask ourselves a question. This question may appear superfluous in the asking, and it may still seem so after we have tried to answer it yet why should Engels have followed this procedure? Why should he have begun with the buildings along the main streets of Manchester and then gone on to discuss the buildings in which the working class lived? In short, are there some broader unstated, perhaps unconscious, theoretical bearings and meanings at work? It seems hardly necessary to say that I think there are.[52]

In the houses men build for themselves they are expressing a behavior which binds them in common with other living creatures and species. The nests and burrows of animals represent efforts at altering the environment; they introduce something utterly new to it, something that did not exist before but belongs to the creature who has made it. The purpose of this behavior is to create a surrounding suitable to the particular creature: shelter, protection, a stable microclimate, a site for breeding, etc. These structures tend to be specifically characteristic, and scientists can distinguish between closely related species, and even subspecies, of animals by examining these products of behavior that are in addition extensions of the creatures who made them. These structures are aboriginal embodiments of behavior, and represent in part how particular creatures relate themselves to the world about them. In other species this behavior is genetically controlled or "pre-programmed"; in man it is not. It still holds, however, that in this fundamental artifact of a house or dwelling place men

[52] It may be noted in anticipation that for Rousseau's natural man, the three necessities were "nourishment, a female, and repose," in *that* significant order. *The First and Second Discourses*, p. 116.

express a good deal of how they relate themselves—or of how they are related—to the world in which they live. And in the collective human artifact, the settlement, town or city, men as a group are expressing historically the character and quality of their existence, of the arrangements they have made, on the one hand, with the natural world, and on the other, with one another. Engels is thus on sound theoretical grounds when he remarks that the manner "in which the need for shelter is satisfied furnishes a measure for the manner in which all other necessities are supplied." (78)[53]

Engels—living in Barmen, and re-creating his experiences during the previous two years in order to transform them into writing and print—figuratively takes the plunge. But where in this essentially doughtnut-shaped belt is he to enter, and how is he to survey it with any coherence? His solution to this problem is as simple as it is sensible. At the northern limits of the commercial district—at about twelve on an imaginary clock—lying between that limit and the confluence of the rivers Irk and Irwell, and extending east along the banks of the Irk, is the Old Town, "a remnant of the old, pre-industrial Manchester. The original inhabitants and their children have moved to districts that are better built, and have left these houses, which were not good enough for them, to a tribe of workers containing a strong admixture of Irish." (57) Beginning with this section, which is conventionally, cartographically and historically an admirable place for starting out, Engels proceeds to box the compass, to

[53] In this paragraph I have summarized and drawn heavily on the writings of a number of behavioral scientists, such as N. Tinbergen, L. Calhoun, and J. R. Audy. I am in particular indebted to Audy's "The Environment in Human Ecology: Artifacts—the Significance of Modified Environment," *Environmental Determinants of Community Well-Being*, Pan American Health Organization Scientific Publications No. 123 (Washington, 1965), pp. 5–16.

The sense in which "artifact" in this context is used is very close to a reversal of the usage of eighteenth-century social and political theorists, who conceived of society as an artifact in the sense of a mechanical model. See J. H. Burrow, *Evolution and Society* (Cambridge, 1966), pp. 10f., 26, and *passim*.

traverse the belt of working-class districts in a clockwise direction, describing what he has seen as he goes along. What he has seen and what he describes varies from section to section, but these variations fall within a uniform context of mass immiseration, degradation, brutalization and inhumanization, the like of which had never before been seen upon the face of the earth.[54] We cannot follow him here in any detail but must select several of the more telling moments of his descriptive analysis.

As he stands in Long Millgate, one of the "better" streets of the Old Town, Engels sees himself surrounded by houses that are old, dirty and tumble-down; many are not even standing upright. Here, he says, one is "in an almost undisguised working-class quarter," since the keepers of the shops and pubs on such a street "make no effort to give their premises even a semblance of cleanliness." Yet these too are in a sense only façades, for they are as nothing compared to the alleys and courts that lie behind them, "to which access can only be gained by covered passages so narrow that two people cannot pass." (57)[55] It is almost as if one were actually penetrating into the heart of darkness. And once he is here, all Engels can do at first is to mutter, the horror, the horror. It is literally, he says, "impossible to imagine for oneself"—or to represent—the chaos, confusion, density, cramming and packing that exists in these spaces. Every available inch of ground has been built over; and the blame for this almost

---

[54] "Immiseration" is Joseph A. Schumpeter's apt translation of Marx's powerful coinage, "*Verelendung*." The historical derivation of this word connects it inwardly with Marx's earlier, explicit writings about alienation, or "*Entfremdung*," and demonstrates, in the fundamental terms of language, a deep continuity in his thinking.

[55] It should be noted that the use of façades as devices of concealment and estrangement was not limited to working-class districts alone. Some early nineteenth-century middle-class urban houses—one thinks of Nash and Wood—superimposed uniform street frontages masking separate houses whose interiors were freely designed by the individual purchasers of the subleases. And in Paris a number of Haussmann's great streets were designed in part with building speculators in mind. Behind the grand façades facing onto the broad avenues, space was used as sparingly as possible, with a minimum of distance between houses.

inconceivable overcrowding "is not only to be ascribed to the old buildings surviving from Manchester's earlier periods." It is in fact only quite recently, in modern times, that the practice has been followed of filling up every scrap of space that the old style of building had left. To prove his point, Engels then reproduces a "small section of a plan of Manchester"—it is the subdistrict he has just been writing about—and adds "it is by no means the worst spot and does not cover one-tenth of the Old Town." It is a pretty enough section, but at least to my unpracticed eye more or less unhelpful.[56]

But Engels is not to be stymied by the indescribable, and he takes us out of this set from an earlier version of *The Cabinet of Dr. Caligari* and into some other courts that branch off Long Millgate and are reached by covered passages that run down toward the banks of the Irk. On reaching these courts, he finds himself met with an assault of "dirt and revolting filth, the like of which is not to be found . . . [and] without qualification the most horrible dwellings I have until now beheld." He is going to say this more than once; he has run out of superlatives before he has barely begun; the language itself is giving out on him. In none of which inadequacies was he alone; indeed, one of the saving functions of language honestly used is that it should collapse before such realities, that it should refuse to domesticate these actualities with syntax and imagery, that it should compel writer and reader to at least a momentary extralinguistic confrontation with such unspeakable man-made terrors, from which our man-made speech ordinarily protects us. In such a predicament, however, what is a writer to do? There is one course open, and Engels promptly takes it. He begins to specify.

In one of these courts, right at the entrance where the covered passage ends is a privy without a door. This privy is so dirty that the inhabitants

---

[56] In *A Child of the Jago* (London, 1896), Arthur Morrison tried to do the same thing for a small section of the East End, with relatively greater success—as far as the map is concerned.

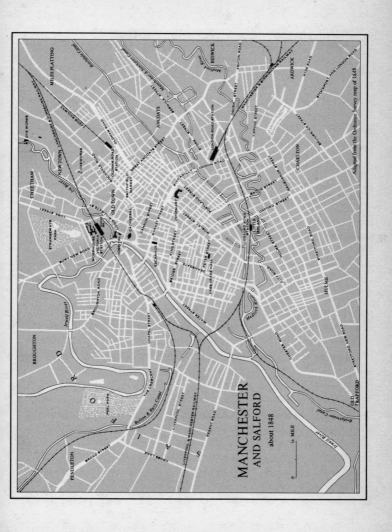

MANCHESTER
AND SALFORD
about 1848

0   ¼ MILE

Adapted from the Ordnance Survey map of 1848

can only enter or leave the court by wading through puddles of stale urine and excrement. (58)

This is the first of many such passages, and it will have to do service for almost all the others. It is at the same time difficult to know how and at what pitch of discourse literary criticism enters into such a scene. This difficulty has to do in the first place with what the intelligent student of literature can be expected to know. He may be expected to know something about Swift and about Freud; he may have heard of Norman O. Brown's excremental vision, and will probably have read *Our Mutual Friend*; if he is a hard-working graduate student he will recall a scene in chapter six of *Mary Barton* that vividly, if gingerly, rehearses this material. That is, I believe, about it. The difficulty is further compounded by certain limitations that may be inherent in the historical imagination. How in fact does one reconstruct and apprehend the existential quality of such a situation? It may not be possible to do so. Or perhaps we ought to alter our terms, and recall Wallace Stevens' remark that "In the presence of extraordinary actuality, consciousness takes the place of imagination." [57]

What seems to have happened is that at about this moment in history, advanced middle-class consciousness—in which consciousness Engels may be regarded as representing the radical wing—began to undergo one of its characteristic changes. This consciousness was abruptly disturbed by the realization that millions of English men, women and children were virtually living in shit. The immediate question seems to have been whether they weren't drowning in it. The catastrophe was worst in the great industrial towns where density and overcrowding went hand in hand with the interests of speculative builders, medieval administrative procedures and regulations—where they in fact existed—and produced a situation in which millions of

[57] *Opus Posthumous*, ed. Samuel Morse French (New York, 1957), p. 165.

grown people and their children were compelled to live in houses
and neighborhoods that were without drains and often without
sewers—and where sewers existed they took the runoff of street
water and not waste from houses—without running water—
sometimes not even in an entire neighborhood—and with one
privy shared by who knows how many people: in some parts of
Manchester over two hundred people shared a single privy. Such
privies filled up rapidly and were cleaned out on an average of
once every two years or so, which was as good as not at all.
Streets were often unpaved, and where they were paved no
provision often existed for their cleansing. And large numbers of
people lived in cellars, below the level of the street and below the
water line. Thus generations of human beings, out of whose lives
the wealth of England was produced, were compelled to live in
wealth's symbolic, negative counterpart. And that substance
which suffused their lives was also a virtual objectification of their
social condition, their place in society: that was what they were.
We must recall that this was no Freudian obsessive neurosis or
anxiety dream; but it is as if the contents of such a neurosis had
been produced on a wholesale scale in the real world. We can,
then, understand rather better how those main street palisades
were functioning—they were defensive-adaptive measures of
confinement and control. And we can understand what they
were concealing: plenty.[58]

Engels tells the reader exactly where this court is, in case he is
interested in confirming the truth of this account, and then takes
him out of there and up onto Ducie Bridge, which spans the Irk at
this point. Here he pauses to take a view, and composes a formal
landscape in a style one may call authentic urban picturesque.

The view from this bridge—mercifully concealed from smaller
mortals by a parapet as high as a man—is quite characteristic of the

---

[58] The *locus classicus* for this subject is of course Edwin Chadwick's *Report on the
Sanitary Condition of the Labouring Population of Great Britain* (1842); two secondary
works of interest and importance might be mentioned: S. E. Finer, *The Life and Times of
Sir Edwin Chadwick* (London, 1952); and R. A. Lewis, *Edwin Chadwick and the Public
Health Movement, 1832–1848* (London, 1952).

entire district. At the bottom the Irk flows, or rather stagnates. It is a narrow, coal-black stinking river full of filth and garbage which it deposits on the lower-lying bank. In dry weather, an extended series of the most revolting blackish green pools of slime remain standing on this bank, out of whose depths bubbles of miasmatic gases constantly rise and give forth a stench that is unbearable even on the bridge forty or fifty feet above the level of the water. . . . Above Ducie Bridge there are tall tannery buildings, and further up are dye-works, bone mills and gasworks. The total entirety of the liquid wastes and solid offscourings of these works finds its way into the River Irk, which receives as well the contents of the adjacent sewers and privies. One can therefore imagine what kind of residues the stream deposits. Below Ducie Bridge, on the left, one looks into piles of rubbish, the refuse, filth and decaying matter of the courts on the steep left bank of the river. Here one house is packed very closely upon another, and because of the steep pitch of the bank a part of every house is visible. All of them are blackened with smoke, crumbling, old, with broken window panes and window frames. The background is formed by old factory buildings, which resemble barracks. —On the right, low-lying bank stands a long row of houses and factories. The second house is a roofless ruin, filled with rubble, and the third stands in such a low situation that the ground floor is uninhabitable and is as a result without windows and doors. The background here is formed by the paupers' cemetery and the stations of the railways to Liverpool and Leeds. Behind these is the workhouse, Manchester's "Poor Law Bastille." It is built on a hill, like a citadel, and from behind its high walls and battlements looks down threateningly upon the working-class quarter that lies below. (60)

It is Tintern Abbey forty-five years hence, with the further exception that the ruins are densely inhabited.[59] Right up to the

[59] After Engels had visited Ireland in 1856, he wrote to Marx that ruins were characteristic of Ireland, "the oldest dating from the fifth and sixth centuries, the latest from the nineteenth, with every intervening period included." *Werke*, XXIX, 56. Beginning in the eighteenth century, when artificial ruins were first constructed for taste and pleasure, civilization moved on in the nineteenth century to create instant, modern ruins—of which Ireland is a rural and Manchester an urban instance. The twentieth century has, in America at least, kept up the record.

end, the representation is unusually telling. It sticks unwaveringly
to the point, and in the presence of catastrophe, consciousness,
observation, *becomes* imagination. The juxtaposition of the paupers' cemetery and the railway stations is very good; but it should
be added, the work of synthesis is being selectively noted by
Engels—it is already there. There is no evidence, insofar as I am
aware, that Engels knew anything of Pugin, but this is *Contrasts*
and more, and by a much more complex and civilized mind.[60]
With the workhouse, Engels introduces some imagery and along
with it a note of equivocation. The description of its situation and
architectural style is accurate, and, insofar as it is, communicates
its own symbolic weight. But the representation is a trifle too
"medieval" in its suggestive associations and tones, and these do
not really work well with the idea of the Poor Law Bastille. The
current power of the phrase was contained in the threat implied,
and that threat is the reverse of the one indicated by Engels.
What the phrase brought to mind in these years of turmoil,
protest and crisis was less how the Bastille functioned in
seventeenth- and eighteenth-century France than it was the fate
it met in 1789. Still, on any reading, this is a minor falling-off on
Engels' part.[61]

---

[60] *Contrasts; or, A Parallel between the Noble Edifices of the Fourteenth and Fifteenth
Centuries, and Similar Buildings of the Present Day; Shewing the Present Decay of Taste:
Accompanied by Appropriate Text*, by A. W. N. Pugin, was first published in 1836.
Among the plates illustrating the contrasts is one that represents two poorhouses, one a
medieval cloister or college, the other a modern jail-like structure, with high walls and
blind enclosures. In the ancient poorhouse we see a poor brother being lowered into his
grave, while his fellows stand about in reverent and prayerful attitudes; in the modern
institution we see the corpse of a pauper being carted away for dissection. The master of
the medieval institution is a benign abbot; the modern workhouse master holds handcuffs
in one hand and a whip in the other.

Engels, for his part, has in some measure introduced the cemetery and the railway
stations in order to use them again, and to considerable effect, later on.

[61] This does not of course mean that people did not feel threatened by the New Poor
Law. They did in overwhelming numbers, even and particularly in places like Manchester
where its most odious provisions were irrelevant and could not be enforced. For an
account of how it was resisted in the North, see Cecil Driver, *Tory Radical: The Life of
Richard Oastler* (New York, 1946), pp. 331–377.

He moves back into Long Millgate and up along the Irk. If one turns left off the street here, he writes, "he is lost. He wanders from one court to another. He turns countless corners, through innumerable narrow, befouled pockets and passageways, until after only a few minutes he has lost all direction and does not know which way to turn." (61) This is certainly a sufficiently familiar report; to which we may add that it is also Todgers'—the comic boardinghouse in the center of London that no one can find, in *Martin Chuzzlewit*—but without the fun and games.[62] Wherever one turns, Engels continues, there is filth—"heaps of rubbish, garbage, and offal." Instead of gutters, there are stagnating pools, and the entire region is pervaded with "a stench that would alone make it unbearable for any human being who was in some degree civilized to live in such a district." The ambiguity pivots evenly and is going to take considerable working out. Either those who live there are uncivilized, or those who live there do so under conditions which cannot be borne. If it is the latter, then a further series of contradictory alternatives come into play.[63] Engels does not pursue these at this point. Instead, he continues to produce these large analytical observations.

The recently constructed extension of the Leeds railway which crosses the Irk at this point has swept away some of these courts and alleys, laying others in turn, and for the first time, completely open to view. Thus, immediately under the railway bridge there exists a court that in point of filth and horror far surpasses all the others—just because it was

[62] See also *Oliver Twist*, ch. 50, for Dickens' similar description of Jacob's Island.

[63] Reflecting on the significance of these early exposures of the actual condition of the urban industrial working population to public view, G. M. Young remarked that "there was no reason to suppose that Manchester was any worse than other towns, and the inevitable conclusion was that an increasing portion of the population of England was living under conditions which were not only a negation of civilized existence, but a menace to civilized society." "Portrait of an Age," *Early Victorian England* (London, 1934), II, 435.

formerly so shut up, so hidden and secluded that it could not be reached without considerable difficulty. I thought I knew this entire district thoroughly, but even I would never have found it myself without the breach made here by the railway viaduct.

One is reminded of the epic passages in *Dombey and Son* (1846–1848) to which this condensed and miniaturized passage has useful applications. Great projects like the railways led, among their many other inadvertent effects, to large-scale slum removal and clearance.[64] In addition, if one follows Engels in thinking of the city as a systematic, dynamic whole, the inherent course of its development brings that which has been pressed away and hidden into sight; it exposes itself by its own movement, the exposure being understood in a double sense. And the disarming, self-confident admission is in no way extraneous to the systematic effort of mind: self-moving intellect, self-realizing intention of will could never have made these discoveries by themselves. They are not victories of the study, wrested by rigor of method from the philosopher's teeming brain. Nor are they immediately victories of language, since social reality, on this side, expresses itself first in the concrete language of the nose, the eyes and the feet. It is this developing group of signs that the young investigator must meet and follow and transform into the language of conceptualization. These are axioms of philosophy being proved upon the pulses, and elsewhere. It only remains to add what Engels could not then have known: that each of these

[64] Further along, Engels notes that the Liverpool railway has led to such a result in Salford. (74) In *Dombey and Son*, the pertinent subpassage in ch. 20 reads:
> Everything around is blackened. There are dark pools of water, muddy lanes, and miserable habitations far below. There are jagged walls and falling houses close at hand, and through the battered roofs and broken windows, wretched rooms are seen, where want and fever hide themselves in many distorted chimneys, and deformity of brick and mortar penning up deformity of mind and body, choke the murky distance. As Mr. Dombey looks out of his carriage window, it is never in his thoughts that the monster who has brought him there has let the light of day in on these things: not made or caused them. It was the journey's fitting end, and might have been the end of everything; it was so ruinous and dreary.

new railway lines became itself the source of new divisions and demarcations; that for every slum destroyed in their construction a new one came into existence around them; that they became the new dialect lines of social distinction, having each of them a right and wrong side, and serving in their finished state to restrict and confine as much as in their building they cleared out and exposed.[65] Indeed the poor of such central urban districts who were displaced by eviction and demolition to make room for the railways, did not move off into new housing or out into the suburbs. They largely were shifted into adjacent streets and courts, thereby increasing the already suffocating density . of numbers in such quarters, ensuring their further rapid dilapidation, and paying higher rents into the bargain. Paradoxically, then, the railways which opened things up simultaneously acted as forces of compression; the promise of liberation went along hand in hand with deepening degradation.[66]

Engels thereupon leads the reader into this microsection of previously inaccessible slum.

Passing along a rough path on the river bank, in between posts and washing lines, one penetrates into this chaos of little one-storied, one-roomed huts. Most of them have earth floors; cooking, living and sleeping all take place in one room. In such a hole, barely six feet long and five feet wide, I saw two beds—and what beds and bedding—that filled the room, except for the doorstep and fireplace. In several others I

[65] It was just such an experience that proved momentous in the career of Dickens' brother-in-law, Henry Austin. While working at surveying for the construction of the new Blackwall railroad, Austin first caught sight of what it was that the railway was clearing away and building through. The effect on him was to turn his interests permanently toward working for the alleviation of the living conditions of the laboring classes. See K. J. Fielding and A. W. Brice, "Bleak House and the Graveyard," in *Dickens the Craftsman*, ed. R. B. Partlow (Carbondale, Ill., 1970), pp. 115–139, 196–200.

[66] See H. J. Dyos, "Railways and Housing in Victorian London," *Journal of Transport History*, II (1955), 11–21, 90–100; "Some Social Costs of Railway Building in London," *Journal of Transport History*, III (1957), 23–29; John R. Kellett, *The Impact of Railways on Victorian Cities* (London, 1969), pp. 1–122, 150–174, 287–382.

found *absolutely nothing*, although the door was wide open and the inhabitants were leaning against it. Everywhere in front of the doors were rubbish and refuse, it was impossible to see whether any sort of pavement lay under this, but here and there I felt it out with my feet. This whole pile of cattle-sheds inhabited by human beings was surrounded on two sides by houses and a factory and on a third side by the river . . . a narrow gateway led out of it into an almost equally miserably-built and miserably-kept labyrinth of dwellings. (63)[67]

He has gotten almost to the center and the bottom, and what he finds there is that something has happened to the species. Men have gone back to living in holes (those thousands who dwelled in cellars were literally doing so). These nests or dens are virtual emptinesses, whose evacuated spaces are the counterpart of the densely packed humanity with which such absences are filled. The transformation may be taken one step further. Just as the pavement has disappeared beneath the accumulated wastes of the natural social life of the species, so too is man himself tending to vanish. He has taken to living in cattle-sheds, or, what is the same thing, in shelters that cannot be told apart from them. It is quite impossible to know whether this is an image or a reality; that is its point.

The filth inside these hovels is in keeping with what is outside them. Engels describes the condition of these interiors, which can only be compared to the pigsties that were frequently to be found in such quarters. Indeed, he remarks, it is impossible to keep such places clean or to keep oneself clean in them. The facilities for getting rid of wastes have already been mentioned; the only water available was from the Irk itself, in which washing would only be a further form of pollution. It is at some such point in this account that the modern reader begins to realize that what Engels is embarked upon is a description of what has been called the

---

[67] The reader will recollect to what use Dickens put such properties of poor urban life as the posts and washing lines of the opening sentence. In *Little Dorrit* they became part of John Chivery's pastoral "groves."

Culture of Poverty, and that this is historically the first full-scale attempt at the representation.[68] Engels himself seems to have been struck by this awareness, and by the immensity and difficulty of the task he had undertaken. After conducting the reader through a number of other subsections of the Old Town, he brings his account of this quarter to a close and then turns to address the reader.

This then is the Old Town of Manchester. On rereading my description once more, I must admit that, instead of being exaggerated, it is by far not nearly strong enough. It is not strong enough to convey vividly the filth, ruination and uninhabitableness, the defiance of every consideration of cleanliness, ventilation, and health that characterise the construction of this district, which contains at least twenty to thirty thousand inhabitants. And such a district exists in the very center of the second city of England, the most important factory town in the world. (63)

Of all the characteristic utterances that issue from the humane consciousness of the middle classes—whether this consciousness be beleaguered, on the attack, or simply thunderstruck—during the decades around the middle of the century, this remains among the most poignant, the most authentic and the most recognizably modern. One could compose an anthology of some decent size of such remarks and exclamations, whose authors represented every variety of political opinion and every substratum of middle-class life. Manchester itself, as we have seen, was often the source of such comments, but in this it was only hypertypical. The occasions were legion; among them were conditions that prevailed in all kinds of industrial work, in child labor, in agriculture, and everywhere in Ireland from 1846 onward. And of course the twentieth century has been prodigal in the creation of such mind-stunning spectacles, mass events of such inhuman extremity

[68] See Oscar Lewis, *La Vida* (New York, 1968), pp. xlii–lii for a summary discussion.

that the only response to them is no response.[69] Out of all the responses from the earlier period, we can select only one more to represent the rest. After Lord Normanby accompanied Dr. Southwood Smith on a tour through Bethnal Green, he wrote: "So far from any exaggeration having crept into the descriptions which have been given, they had not conveyed to my mind an adequate idea of the truth." [70]

In confessing that he was unable to represent the phenomenological character of this reality, Engels was in effect coming very close to revealing its inner form. It was the dissolved and negated analogue of the unexampled transformation wrought by the industrial middle class upon the world. "The bourgeoisie . . . has been the first to show what man's activity can bring about. It has accomplished wonders far surpassing Egyptian pyramids, Roman aqueducts, and Gothic cathedrals; it has conducted expeditions that put in the shade all former Exoduses of nations and crusades. . . . The bourgeoisie, during its rule of scarce one hundred years, has created more massive and more colossal productive forces than have all preceding generations together." [71] Another part of that hegemony was revealed in the location of these working-class districts. They were at the very center of things yet out of sight. To say that they were at once central and peripheral is to describe their contradictory existence in the structure of social consciousness of the time. It is also to define them in a rigorous

[69] The literature on this subject is enormous. One may, however, point to the work of Robert J. Lifton, who has made a special study of responses to extremity. See in particular *Death in Life* (New York, 1967). The discussion of the relation of changing consciousness to such events is exceptionally tricky. It is certain that natural and social catastrophes on a mass scale existed before the nineteenth century; it is also certain that consciousness responded to these catastrophes differently before that time than after it. Something happened to consciousness, but something was happening to society as well, to stimulate that consciousness and legitimize it. The tracing out of such intricately connected reciprocal developments is a study in itself.

[70] Quoted in S. E. Finer, *The Life and Times of Sir Edwin Chadwick*, p. 161.

[71] *The Communist Manifesto* (Penguin, 1967), pp. 82–85.

and classical way as the hidden ground of things, a substructure. Nevertheless, to be at once central and peripheral is to occupy a place in society that is ordinarily relegated to crime and its attendant institutions; criminal sections, prisons, police courts and stations. The wealth of contradictions implied in such relations did not escape Engels or other writers at the time.[72] We shall briefly return to them later.

Engels proceeds to conduct the reader on a methodical survey of the other working-class sections. Beginning with the New Town, which is adjacent on the south and east to the Old Town, and then moving on around the compass to Ancoats and the area south of it, he analyzes the structural composition of each of the districts. These areas were built up later than the Old Town, and as he describes each section, Engels also describes the three different kinds of working-class cottages (all of them built in connected blocks or rows) that were to be found. Each style of building came into existence at a certain point in the Industrial Revolution and the expansion of Manchester, so that although sometimes the different methods of construction exist side by side, they are usually located in different parts of town and make it possible to "distinguish the relative age" (67) of each district. That is to say, even these working-class districts have their history, their industrial archaeology, their discernible meaning.[73]

---

[72] See J. J. Tobias, *Crime and Industrial Society in the Nineteenth Century*, for an extensive discussion of this subject.

[73] J. H. Plumb has observed that the social purpose of certain kinds of public monuments and of certain practices such as the keeping of king-lists and elaborate genealogies is "to enhance the authority of the present by linking it visibly with the grandeur of the past. For the same reasons English gentlemen in the eighteenth century built palaces which they called Palladian and referred to themselves as Augustans. Whatever is built for the working class, however, is usually strictly contemporary." *The Death of the Past* (New York, 1970), p. 29n.

The prevalent contemporary style of urban working-class housing featured cottages built back-to-back. These formed the core of many a nineteenth-century urban-industrial slum, and large numbers of them survived in Manchester (and elsewhere) into the twentieth century. One of the gravest defects of such housing was that it was impossible—because of the lack of space—to add onto it privies or water toilets.

Conditions in these districts are pretty much on a par with those already described. Some of the reasons for this have already been given, and include the want of public facilities for drainage and cleansing. Others have to do with methods of building and terms of land-holding and tenure, into all of which Engels goes in considerable detail. The outcome of this number of converging circumstances has been the building of working-class houses that last for about forty years: the houses themselves have their own life cycle, which is on average only slightly longer than that of the industrial working people who inhabit them. This is another signifying part of the structural composition of Manchester—and not of Manchester or nineteenth-century cities alone.

As he systematically passes along this great circle, Engels drops pertinent observations about the ecological relations of the various parts of the district to the rivers, streams and flats amid which they are situated, to the factories that surrounded them, and to the middle-class residential districts that begin at their outskirts. He takes us south of Great Ancoats Street, along the area crossed by the Birmingham railway and through which the Medlock twists and turns. He then stops to represent in some detail the enclave of Little Ireland that lies in a bend of the Medlock.[74] This slum was described by Kay (later Kay-Shuttleworth) in 1831, and Engels remarks that in 1844 it is in a virtually unaltered state. It is surrounded by factories and embankments and is below the level of the river. Four thousand people live in it, most of them Irish; or, rather, they wallow in it, along with the pigs that thrive upon the garbage and offal in the streets. Large numbers live in porous cellars, and the density of habitation is ten persons per room.[75] He

[74] By this juncture, however, not quite willingly. "If I were to describe all these separate parts in detail," he conceded, "I would never get to the end." (71)

[75] Almost thirty years later Engels returned to his description of this infamous district. In 1872–1873 he wrote a series of articles on the "housing question," and in the course of a discussion of the "Haussmann method" of urban renewal found the relevant occasion to revert to his earlier work.

In *The Condition of the Working Class in England* I gave a picture of Manchester as

moves on next to Hulme, to Deansgate and its rookeries, and
finally to Salford, which faces Manchester in a bend in the Irwell.
Conditions here in this district of some 80,000 people resemble
those in the Old Town again, and Engels closes his discussion of
this district and his entire survey of the belt of working-class
quarters with the following observation.

It was here that I found a man, who appeared to be about sixty years of
age, living in a cow-shed. He had constructed a sort of chimney for his
square-shaped pen, which had no flooring, no plaster on the walls, and
no windows. He had brought in a bed, and here he lived, although the
rain came through the miserable ruined roof. The man was too old and
too weak for regular work, and sustained himself by removing dung,
etc. with his handcart. Puddles of excrement lay close about his stable.
(75)

---

it looked in 1843 and 1844. Since then the construction of railways through the
centre of the city, the laying out of new streets and the erection of great public and
private buildings have broken through, laid bare and improved some of the worst
districts described there, others have been abolished altogether; although, apart from
the fact that sanitary-police inspection has since become stricter, many of them are
still in the same state or in an even worse state of dilapidation than they were then.
On the other hand, thanks to the enormous extension of the town, whose population
has since increased by more than half, districts which were at that time still airy and
clean are now just as overbuilt, just as dirty and congested as the most ill-famed parts
of the town formerly were. Here is but one example: On page 80 et seq. of my book I
described a group of houses situated in the valley bottom of the Medlock River,
which under the name of Little Ireland was for years the disgrace of Manchester.
Little Ireland has long ago disappeared and on its site there now stands a railway
station built on a high foundation. The bourgeoisie pointed with pride to the happy
and final abolition of Little Ireland as to a great triumph. Now last summer a great
inundation took place, as in general the rivers embanked in our big cities cause more
and more extensive floods year after year for reasons that can be easily explained.
And it was then revealed that Little Ireland had not been abolished at all, but had
simply been shifted from the south side of Oxford Road to the north side, and that it
still continues to flourish.
He then cites a long passage from the Manchester Weekly Times, which does indeed
support his contentions, and moves to his own "triumph" and conclusion.
    This is a striking example of how the bourgeoisie settles the housing question in
practice. The breeding places of disease, the infamous holes and cellars in which the
capitalist mode of production confines our workers night after night, are not

We have at length reached the bottom, the bottom of the heap. The image has been actualized and become the literal reality— that is to say, in such an actualization the structure is openly disclosed. It is *Our Mutual Friend* without the Golden Dustman. And it is our urban pastoral again, but it also catches up another side of the microstructure. The old man has been productively

---

abolished; they are merely *shifted elsewhere*! The same economic necessity which produced them in the first place produces them in the next place also. As long as the capitalist mode of production continues to exist it is folly to hope for an isolated settlement of the housing question or of any other social question affecting the lot of the workers.

This final passage reveals some of the changes in tone that distinguish the young from the mature Engels. See *Zur Wohnungsfrage, Werke*, XVIII, 260–263; trans. *The Housing Question* (Moscow, 1955), pp. 116–122.

Little Ireland was only one of the more notorious of the Irish slums that characterized nineteenth-century English urban existence. In 1841, there were more than 400,000 Irish-born people living in Great Britain; more than 100,000 of these were located in Lancashire (constituting over 6 percent of the population), and almost 50,000 out of that number were in Manchester; almost 40,000 were concentrated in Glasgow; and almost 60,000 in the county of Middlesex, including London. Such figures omit an equal or greater number of second-generation Irish who were born in England and who were often as discriminably Irish as their parents. By 1851, after the famine, the number of Irish-born residents had gone beyond 700,000. As Marx was to write soon after: "Ireland has revenged herself upon England, *socially*—by bestowing an *Irish quarter* on every English industrial, maritime, or commercial town of any size. . . ." "Irlands Rache" [1855], *Werke*, XI, 117.

On the other side, certain modern studies on the structure of immigrant ethnic communities should be noted. In *The Urban Villagers* (Cambridge, Mass., 1960), Herbert Gans demonstrates how Boston's West End slum served as an agent for the transformation—over a period of three generations—of immigrant villagers into city dwellers. Along similar lines Nathan Glazer and Daniel Moynihan, *Beyond the Melting Pot* (Cambridge, Mass., 1963), describe how in an urban setting large ethnic groups retain their ethnic identity for several generations. Studies of urbanization in modern Africa suggest how neighborhoods in towns reproduce or maintain certain institutions and structures of the rural tribes who have migrated there. See W. B. Schwab, *Urbanization in Newly Developing Countries* (Fort Lee, New Jersey, 1966); H. Kuper, ed., *Urbanization and Migration in Western Africa* (Berkeley, 1965). There is also some evidence that argues a strong persistence of rural kinship and communal structures for a number of generations among working-class families in Preston. See Michael Anderson, *Family Structure in Nineteenth Century Lancashire* (Cambridge, 1972). Whether and in what degree such persistences could have been inferred in such slums as Little Ireland is another question again.

used up and discarded as refuse; accordingly in his old age he sustains himself from refuse. Yet he too is part of the life of the city and his life has a meaning, although the terms in which that meaning may be assessed will give comfort and peace of mind to almost no one.[76]

Engels has completed his first examination of what lies behind and between the network of main streets. It is Manchester itself in its negated and estranged existence. But this chaos of alleys, courts, hovels, filth—and human beings—is not a chaos as well. Every fragment of disarray, every inconvenience, every scrap of human suffering has a meaning. Each of these is inversely and ineradicably related to the life led by the middle classes, to the work performed in the factories, and to the structure of the city as a whole. The twenty-four-year-old Engels has achieved a tour de force. I know of no representation of an industrial city before this that achieves such an intimate, creative hold upon its living subject. For anything that stands with it or surpasses it, one has to go to the later Dickens, to *Bleak House, Hard Times, Little Dorrit* and *Our Mutual Friend*.[77] But even to mention *The Condition of the Working Class* in the same sentence with such masterpieces suggests the quality of critical neglect it has suffered and the misuses to which it has been put. And, one may add, in this last

---

[76] One makes wide exception for such sociological theorists as Edward Shils, in whose way of thinking such phenomena are part of the positive functioning of any society, and serve to accentuate its blessings. "The humanitarian element in Marxism—its alleged concern for the poor—" he feelingly observes, "can have no appeal when there are still many very poor people in Communist countries and the poor in capitalist countries can now be seen not to be poor, not to be miserable, not to be noble—but to be as comfortable and as vulgar as, if not more vulgar than, the middle classes." And again, "Every society has its outcasts, its wretched, and its damned, who cannot fit into the routine requirements of social life at any level of authority and achievement. . . . Those who are constricted, who find life as it is lived too hard, are prone to the acceptance of the ideological outlook on life." Where would we be without such wisdom? "Ideology and Civility: on the Politics of the Intellectuals," *Sewanee Review*, LXVI (1958), 450–480.

[77] Mrs. Gaskell's representations of Manchester in *Mary Barton* and *North and South* are very good—and, as has been mentioned earlier, are in accord with Engels'—but they do not have the generalizing and organizing power of Engels' account.

section it has *not* been Hegel's system that has been primarily instrumental in the creative achievement, but the courage and intelligence of a young foreign intellectual—and a businessman at that—who during his first stay of twenty months in Manchester opened himself to its great and terrible realities and was not afraid of what they might do to him or where they might take him.

The Condition of the
Working Class (2)

No society can surely be flourishing and happy, of which
the far greater part of the members are poor and miserable.
It is but equity, besides, that they who feed, cloath and
lodge the whole body of the people, should have such a share
of the produce of their own labour as to be themselves
tolerably well fed, cloathed and lodged.
> —Adam Smith, *The Wealth of Nations*,
> Book I, chapter 8

IN THE remaining two thirds of *The Condition of the Working Class* Engels attempts to create a comprehensive representation of the conditions of existence in general and of work in particular that prevailed among the working class in the industrial England of his time. This representation is in the first place a vision of demoralization and alienation, of the most profound social and personal distress. In part it is the Culture of Poverty again, but it is much more as well.

Engels begins with a chapter that he entitled "Competition." The justice of this choice becomes evident if we reflect that it enables him to discuss a social model that precedes and includes industrial capitalism—the model of the market economy, and of a society whose values and relations are refractions of those that might be found if an ideal-type of a free market existed. It enables him, moreover, to resume overtly a theme that he had in the urgency of his personal testimony about Manchester allowed temporarily to lapse. Competition, he writes, "is the most perfect expression of that war of all against all that dominates modern middle class society. This war, a war for life, for existence, for everything—and in extreme instances a [literal] life and death struggle—is waged not only between the different classes of society but also between the individual members of these classes." (88) This struggle for existence is to be found in interclass and intraclass relations. And at every point the working classes are at a disadvantage. In its pure form, each individual person is regarded as a single, equal unit; in reality of course no single workingman was the equal of a single large employer. Hence the efforts of the industrial workers to combine in unions, and hence the resistance of the members of the middle classes directly concerned against such projects, whose aim on the part of the workers was to nullify and transcend [aufzuheben] this intraclass antagonism. (89) Such resistance is founded in the interests of the middle classes, who do need the working class as well, not indeed as a source of immediate sustenance but in the sense that one needs and uses "an article of commerce or a beast of burden," as a source of profit or means of enrichment. (91) The process that Marx would describe as "objectification" is touched upon here; in part it involves the "commoditization" of human beings, and Engels goes on to quote with approval a relevant passage from Adam Smith: "the demand for men, like that for any other commodity, necessarily regulates the production of men; quickens it when it goes on too slowly, and stops it when it advances too fast." (93) Behind this standard of measurement lies another, the ultimate quantifying demonstration of profit. Yet this demonstration, which is both motive and end as well, gives rise in its execution to a further series of irreconcilables. In the modern world, Engels writes, "production and the division of the means of subsistence are [wholly] unregulated." Both of these are undertaken "not for the immediate satisfaction of needs" but solely for profit. "In such a system, in which everyone works on his own and with an eye to his own profits, disturbances and blockages [*Stockung*] break out continually." (95) Engels is saying that in a system in which profit is both the end and the rule of conduct, certain human needs are bound to be neglected. There is no question that Engels, like Marx, understood the test of profitability to be a relatively new and more advanced form of rational economic behavior. But there is equally no question that he, like Carlyle and others at the time, also understood that this rationality brought with it new irrationalities as well. He was in fact describing in one of its first appearances the irrational rationality that has become increasingly significant in modern society. It was to the further exploration of this obfuscated nexus that Max Weber was to give the central part of his career, and, latterly, that Herbert Marcuse has given a major part of his.[1]

The demonstration of this assertion is that even on its own terms the system doesn't work well enough, and Engels then goes on to discuss such currently pertinent problems as depressions and trade cycles, the question of the "reserve army of labour," the theoretical problem of surplus labor, and the actual existence of surplus laborers, largely in the form of an immense pool of casual laborers in the cities and beneath them of an almost as large group of unemployed and unemployable members of the proletariat. He is describing a number of the chief consequences of the gigantic social dislocation and reorganization that attended the Industrial Revolution. All these working together produced a prevailing circumstantial atmosphere and emotional tone of "insecurity,"

[1] This is to suggest only the dissident theoretical tradition. By far the largest majority of theoretical commentators from Engels' time to the present have persisted in regarding the social realities in question as essentially and increasingly rational, without the paradoxes and contradictions, and as essentially and increasingly benign, without even the Weberian ambiguity and finally despair. "Literary" evidence, such as novelists, poets, philosophers and critics, does not of course "count" in these latter terms of discourse, although by the same token it figures heavily in the account rendered by the dissident tradition.

whose effect upon working people, Engels writes, "is far more demoralizing than poverty." [2] Among the many other blessings that accompanied the transition from a society based primarily upon status to one based primarily on contract was the creation for the working class of a continuously dissolving world. Compelled now to live solely upon wages, and "from hand to mouth," the English industrial worker had become insecure in his very "place in life." [*Lebensstellung*] (131) He had, in other words, been precipitated into a thoroughly contingent world. This world had been anticipated in the daring, dazzling and bewildering epistemologies of Hume and Kant, but it was in the collective life of the English industrial working class that the epistemologies were realized as massive existential entities. [3] It was a life in which the present was unstable and the future without grounds or guarantee. It was in short a world that almost no one would choose—not even modern middle-class intellectuals, who often seek to cultivate a philosophical consciousness of contingency, in some measure, at least, because our real insecurity is in fact mental and philosophical, the larger circumstances of our existence being so assured. [4]

[2] No disagreement has arisen on this question; Asa Briggs, for example, typically affirms: "Social insecurity was at the heart of the industrial and consequently the urban system." *Victorian Cities*, p. 273. Or there is this, taken from another context: "the sense of insecurity . . . proved to be the main solvent of the old social order." David Williams, *The Rebecca Riots* (Cardiff, 1955), p. 67; also see E. P. Thompson, pp. 248, 261, and *passim*.

[3] The experience of Heinrich von Kleist may be pointed to as the *locus classicus* for the observation of how Kant's philosophy worked as a solvent to unstick the world of traditional, ordinary experience. See *Sämtliche Werke und Briefe* (Munich, 1953), II, 651–655.

[4] This subject is connected with the large-scale loss of active religious faith among the English working class, and the equally large-scale retention of some kind of religious commitment among them, largely in the form of conversion or allegiance to some species of dissenting sect. The question is much too elaborate to go into here, but it seems clear that the extreme conditions of working-class urban existence were likely either to severely damage the possibility of continued religious belief, or to stimulate an intense and

After appending a short chapter on Irish immigration, which acts as a footnote to and additional confirmation of the arguments advanced in the chapter on competition, Engels goes on to compose a systematic accounting of the effects of industrialization on the bodies, minds and moral existence of those who have undergone such extremities of experience. He undertakes to describe further that "impossible" world. The terms in which he frames this description are, first, that of a formal charge in a court of law: he accuses the English middle classes of mass murder, genocide, as we would say today.[5] But since no actual or legally recognizable murder has been committed, his evidence is in the nature of the case circumstantial or inferential—he must, like a novelist, discover realities in discrepant appearances.[6] Hence, he reasons, thousands of English workers find themselves existing under conditions "in which they meet a premature and unnatural death," in which they are "deprived of the necessaries of life." They find themselves "placed in a situation in which they cannot live." When they perish they are the victims of murder. Yet it is a very odd kind of murder, and this on several counts: "no one can defend himself against it"; indeed, "it does not appear to be a murder" at all, "since the murderer is not to be seen." Moreover,

---

relatively aberrant experience of belief. See E. P. Thompson, pp. 350–400; Owen Chadwick, *The Victorian Church* (London, 1966), pp. 325–440; K. S. Inglis, *Churches and the Working Classes in Victorian England* (London, 1963), pp. 1–20 and *passim*.

[5] In his letter to Marx of November 19, 1844, he mentioned that this was exactly what he was doing at that moment.

[6] According to Karl Mannheim, the impulses to "unmask" or "debunk" constitute historically the form in which "the discovery of the social-situational roots of thought" first finds expression. "Political discussion is, from the very first, more than theoretical argumentation; it is the tearing off of disguises—the unmasking of those unconscious motives which bind the group existence to its cultural aspirations and its theoretical arguments. To the extent . . . that modern politics fought its battles with theoretical weapons, the process of unmasking penetrated to the social roots of theory." This analysis could be applied with equal cogency to Engels' critical account of Manchester dealt with in the preceding chapter. See *Ideology and Utopia*, trans. Louis Wirth and Edward A. Shils (New York, 1936), pp. 34–38.

"everyone and yet no one is responsible for the murder," while at the same time "it appears as if the victim had died from natural causes." On top of all this, "the offense is less one of commission than omission." And yet, Engels affirms, "it is murder all the same." [*Aber es bleibt Mord.*] In order to argue his case with conviction, Engels is going to have to demonstrate that English society—by which he means the group or groups that possess at the moment legitimate political and social authority, and therefore, to his way of thinking, responsibility—has materially created and placed the working class in this impossible world. And he is going to have to demonstrate as well that they *"know"* about this, that they are conscious of the consequences upon life of such a world, and that they have done actually nothing to improve the situation. The charge then is not manslaughter but murder, "social murder." (108f.)

He returns to the great towns, the centers of concentration, and begins to describe the conditions of health that are to be found there. From this point onward, although he continues to draw upon his own experience when he can, he is relying for the most part upon printed evidence, much of it compiled by members of the middle classes for the middle classes—a paradox which he tends to ignore. In the great towns, diseases of every kind flourished. Lung disease and various grades of fever, all generally classified at the time as tuberculosis and typhus, were endemic, and epidemic contagious diseases had returned after an absence of some generations.[7] After discussing in detail the frightful incidence of these virulent afflictions, Engels moves on to a preliminary summary of diseases connected both directly and in a secondary way with diet deficiency, such as scrofula, rickets, and a variety of alimentary troubles.[8] What ought to have been

---

[7] See E. J. Hobsbawn, *The Age of Revolution* (New York, 1964), pp. 241f.

[8] John Burnett, *Plenty and Want* (London, 1966), p. 89, discusses the virtually universal adulteration of food at the time and remarks that poisonous metallic substances were frequently used as adulterants: "Often the quantity of poisons used was not sufficient to produce immediate symptoms, but many of them were cumulative, and would leave trace

included in this category but was not because of the state of
medical knowledge at the time, was the legion of ailments and
dysfunctions in the sexual and reproductive systems, particularly
among working-class women. Engels includes a discussion of
these in a later section. (181ff.) He mentions as well the absence
of provisions for medical attention for the poor and the working
class, a deprivation that we now know was not as serious as it
then seemed, but which was none the less a deprivation of care.[9]
He does not overlook the nostrums and patent medicines to
which the working class resorted in huge numbers, then as now,
or the widespread use of a multiplicity of opiates, such as
Godfrey's Cordial.[10] (109–119) Engels then goes on to cite the
absolute and comparative death rates for the large industrial
towns. Even at this remote interval of time, the simple familiar
statistics are enough to make one tremble. The annual death rate
for England and Wales was 1 in 45; for Manchester, including
Salford and Chorlton, 1 in 32.72; excluding them, 1 in 30.75. For
Edinburgh as a whole, from 1838 to 1839, it was 1 in 29; in the

---

elements of lead, copper, mercury and arsenic to build up in the system over the course of
time. Here again, we may well have a cause of the chronic gastritis which was one of the
commonest diseases of urban populations in the early nineteenth century."

[9] It has been estimated that before 1900 one's chances of recovering from any serious
illness were equal whether one was provided with medical attention or not. This does not
mean, however, that the chances remained equal if one was deprived of the most basic
comforts, attention and care.

[10] In 1822 Thomas De Quincey reported that "some years ago, on passing through
Manchester, I was informed by several cotton manufacturers that their work people were
rapidly getting into the practice of opium-eating, so much so that on a Saturday afternoon
the counter of the druggists were strewed with pills of one, two, or three grains, in
preparation for the known demand of the evening. The immediate occasion of this
practice was the lowness of wages, which, at that time, would not allow them to indulge in
ale or spirits. . . ." Confessions of an English Opium-Eater, "From the Author to the
Reader." The widespread use of opiates in Lancashire (and elsewhere) was repeatedly
confirmed. See Mary Barton; also Alethea Hayter, Opium and the Romantic Imagination
(Berkeley, 1968), pp. 32f., 346f.; W. L. Burns, The Age of Equipoise (London, 1964), pp.
28f., 53. In 1861, Beeton's Book of Household Management, p. 1024, went out of its way to
warn the mistress of the house and new mother against the epidemic use by wet nurses of
Godfrey's Cordial and other opiates.

Old Town, in 1831, 1 in 22. Life expectancy in 1840 in Liverpool among the "gentry and professional persons" was thirty-five years; among tradesmen and their families, twenty-two years; among "labourers, mechanics and servants," fifteen years. In Manchester, nearly 54 percent of the children born into working-class families died before they reached the age of five. (119ff.)[11] The distribution of these incidences among the different classes was as regular and symmetrical then as it is today.[12] T. S. Eliot's Sweeney seems to have been right. That's all there is to it, but mostly death.

Engels concludes this section with the following synoptic statement.

The consequence of all these influences among the workers is a general weakening of the body. There are few strong, well-built and healthy people among them—at least among the industrial workers who generally work in closed rooms and with whom we are here concerned. They are almost all weakly, gaunt and pale. Their bone structure is angular but not powerful. Their muscles are flabby from fever, with the exception of those especially exercised in their work. Almost all suffer from digestive troubles, and they are therefore more or less hypochondriacal and of a troubled, gloomy and irritable disposition. Their weakened bodies are unable to withstand illness and are therefore seized by it on every occasion. This is why they age early and die young. (118f.)

[11] In London, "in Church Lane, St. Giles's, within the Irish rookery, 310 out of every 1,000 children born in the 1840's died before reaching the age of one, and of every 1,000 children aged one, 457 died before reaching the age of two." Francis Sheppard, *London 1808–1870: The Infernal Wen*, p. 17.

[12] "In Ancoats, out of 100 children born, only 40 or sometimes 35, reached their fifth year: in the healthy quarter of Market Street, 60 survived. But in Manchester, where a sixth of the labouring population was Irish, one family in ten lived in a cellar. In Liverpool, incredible as it sounds, the figure was one in five." R. H. Mottram, "Town Life," *Early Victorian England*, I, 167. For figures in series on crude death rates and infant mortality, see Brian R. Mitchell and P. Deane, *Abstract of British Historical Statistics* (Cambridge, 1962), pp. 36ff.

The general physical debility is in turn connected with something that other observers also noted—a kind of sub-epidemic mental depression that generally bears the same kind of relation to the classical depression as, in Freud's terminology, an actual neurosis bears to a psychoneurosis. There are a number of such representations in Victorian fiction, each of them the more authentic because the authors were only partially aware of what it was they were describing and because there did not yet exist an adequate vocabulary for such descriptions. One thinks of John Barton, Stephen Blackpool, and the protagonist of *The Ragged-Trousered Philanthropists* as immediately striking instances.[13]

Correlated with this depressed state at a variety of points—and dependent upon it and contributing further to it in a variety of ways—are a group of other circumstances and kinds of behavior which were then and still remain notorious as parts of the "legend" of the working class. First there is drunkenness, which is a symptom of this state, an effort to gain temporary release from it, and a further auxiliary cause in its worsening. Engels recognizes those multiple influences that worked toward disposing members of the industrial working classes of his time toward excessive drinking—including the absence of almost all facilities for sociability and recreation—and understands that this addiction is part of a larger system of symptoms.[14] Under such circumstances, he remarks, "drunkenness ceases to be a vice" in the sense that one cannot hold the person who commits it responsible

---

[13] Pertinent illustrations from the novels of Thomas Hardy and George Gissing are reserved from this account because of the sense one has of the overwhelming personal presence of the author in the depressed characters being represented.

[14] He does not, however, discuss the subject in historical terms, being apparently unaware of what English drinking habits were reported to have been in the eighteenth century. Some excellent observations on this subject are to be found in G. Kitson Clark, *The Making of Victorian England* (London, 1962), pp. 127f. For a general survey see Brian Harrison, *Drink and the Victorians* (London, 1971), especially pp. 392ff., where Harrison discusses Engels' account and conducts an elaborate quibble, disguised as an argument, with the passage in question.

of viciousness. It becomes instead, "a phenomenon, the necessary, inevitable consequence of certain conditions upon an object that, as over against at least these conditions, is without will." (116) Such an excuse does not deter Engels from describing a typical scene in a Manchester beer-house or gin-vault.

Quite apart from all the usual consequences of drunkenness, one must consider that in these places men and women of all ages, even children, often mothers with babies in their arms, meet with thieves, swindlers, and prostitutes, who are the most degraded victims of the bourgeois regime. When one reflects that some mothers give spirits to children in arms, the demoralizing effect of frequenting such drinking places can certainly not be denied. It is particularly on Saturday evenings that drunkenness can be seen in all its bestiality. Wages have been paid, the evening's enjoyment begins rather earlier than is usual on other days of the week, and the whole working class streams from its miserable slums into the main streets of the town. On such an evening I have rarely come out of Manchester without meeting many people staggering drunkenly about or lying helplessly drunk in the gutters. (143)[15]

What Engels has seen is that the counterpart of the depriva-tions, instabilities, degradations and depression of the working-class life he knows, is its tendency to be impulse-ridden. This has always been the classical diagnosis of the culture of poverty; it

[15] Against such a passage, one may juxtapose the following: "but still I must say, speaking from an extensive experience of the manufacturing districts, that the publicans in those districts, taken as a class, are not the heartless social vampires, gorging and fattening on the misery and ruin of mankind, which some teetotallers represent them to be. In such towns as Manchester and Birmingham there is no class of tradesmen which does more out-of-the-way trade for the working classes than publicans. In such towns as these, artisans and others are in the habit of taking their meals in public houses; and in times of dull trade it is a common practice with the proprietors of these houses to turn the remains of joints and other broken meat to account by making large quantities of soup, which they distribute, in conjunction with 'hunches' of bread, among the workmen's families in the neighbourhood; and I have known many families who, when their money-earning members have been out of employment, have derived no inconsiderable portion of their support from such sources." Thomas Wright [The Journeyman Engineer], *The Great Unwashed* (London, 1868), pp. 154–155.

remains so today.[16] It consists of behavior and attitudes that are
generally regarded as "nonadaptive." [17] In addition to drunkenness, Engels discusses the other classical components of this
syndrome: impulsive and promiscuous sexuality,[18] general im-
providence, lack of foresight, inability to plan for the future,
insufficient internalization of disciplines, regularities and normative controls, and adaptive inflexibilities. All these are, furthermore, connected with and reinforced by the low degree of
education, the widespread illiteracy, found among the working
class. (132; 124f., 128) The behavior in question is short-term
and consummatory, and Engels includes among it certain kinds of
theft (130) and even suicide. (130)[19] He is himself far too deeply
confirmed in middle-class culture to condone such conduct, but in
view of the circumstances of the working class, he finds that
conduct explicable and even pardonable. It is explicable because
in such circumstances members of the working class—no matter
what they do—can almost certainly expect no more than a

[16] See Oscar Lewis, *La Vida*, pp. xxviff.; also Lee Rainwater, *And the Poor Get Children*
(Chicago, 1960), a study of contraceptive practices among American working-class
families, written very much from this standpoint. It should be noted that the idea of the
culture of poverty is particularly associated by Lewis and others with the kinds of social
groups that Marx and Engels were later to speak of as the *Lumpenproletariat*, as distinct
from the classical industrial proletariat itself. At this early stage of development, however,
Engels has not sharply defined such subgroupings nor distinguished between the various
subcultures attaching to them.

[17] See, for instance, the modern sociological classic on this issue, Robert K. Merton,
"Social Structure and Anomie," *Social Theory and Social Structure* (New York, 1968,
enlarged ed.) pp. 185–214.

[18] Although Engels believes that, after drink, sexuality is the chief pleasure of the
working class and the poor, and that they are passionately addicted to sexuality and engage
in it to excess (144; 166), he does not juxtapose these assertions to those he cites from
medical reports that have to do with the unmistakable evidence of widespread sexual
malaise, particularly among working-class females. The entire matter remains obscured
because of the relative lack of certain kinds of information, particularly intimate personal
testimony, that for the period and the social group in question are extremely hard to come
by.

[19] Richard Hoggart's discussion of working-class suicide, *The Uses of Literacy* (New
York, 1957), pp. 76ff., is much to the point here.

microscopic share of the distributed social rewards; it is pardonable in large measure because of the unreal (that is, unstable and contingent) future that extends phantasmally before them.

Another related series of circumstances was to be found in what was taken at the time to be the virtually universal deterioration of family life. The stupendous social dislocation had affected this most fundamental of institutions, and if anything was calculated to alarm the middle classes into a consciousness of possible social disaster, it was the notion that the most stabilizing of social maintenance systems was imperiled.[20] These structural changes in family life were notoriously visible among the textile workers. Among them emigration from countryside to town along with transformations of the division of labor within the family had occurred earliest and with the greatest speed and thoroughness. The rapid shift from a mixed household economy to a wage-earning industrialized household had affected the relations of all the members of the family to one another. Child-rearing practices and traditions had been disrupted; with all the members of a household working in factories, the pattern of authority within the family was in the course of dissolution and uncertain reformation; with women and children often employed more steadily than men, the distribution of sexual roles had been upset if not reversed. Traditional skills on the part of both men and women had been undermined, neglected and lost. In

---

[20] See Neil J. Smelser, *Social Change in the Industrial Revolution*, pp. 180–312. Smelser's discussion is useful for its gathering of material and also because it is written altogether from the standpoint of the values and interests of the middle classes, although like many such discussions it fails to acknowledge its point of view and is therefore one more specimen of ideology—this time in its preferred late-middle-twentieth-century form, sociological structural-functional analysis.

It may be noted that a similar phenomenon occurred in America in the 1960's when it was suddenly "discovered" that the *"real"* social problem among Negroes was their deteriorated family structure. Those familiar with the course run by such arguments do not need to be convinced again that, however substantial and accurate such reports and analyses were, there was something transparently diversionary in their emphases as well.

particular the regular performance of household duties had come apart; children were increasingly left to their own devices (when they weren't at work, that is), and large numbers of women even seem—if contemporary evidence is to be trusted—to have forgotten how to cook, if they had ever learned. Into all these circumstances, and others, Engels enters with unsparing detail. (145ff.; 157ff.)[21]

Then there is the problem of work itself. Rebel against his family's pietist culture though he may be, Engels is a bearer of its values; and like his masters, Hegel, Carlyle and Marx, believes unwaveringly in the gospel of work. "Man knows no higher pleasure," he writes, "than that derived from productive work undertaken voluntarily." By the same token, however, there is "no crueler or more degrading torment than forced labour." Nothing is more terrible than to be constrained to labor "every day from morning to night against one's will at work that one abhors. And the more of a human being the worker feels himself to be, the more hateful must such work be to him, because he can feel for himself the compulsion and aimlessness for him that lies

---

[21] If I may offer a hypothesis in this connection, one gauge of the depth of rapid social change might be its influence on a group's cookery. England is an almost made-to-order case in point. The culture to undergo the earliest, most drastic of industrial transformations (not to speak of the earlier Puritan revolution), it emerged at the end with the worst cookery in Western Europe. Contemporary British observers from at least as early as Cobbett onward recorded what they took to be such a decline. But this is only a hypothesis with, as I have said, a ready-made conclusion awaiting it; the work of specific demonstration is much more difficult—although the instructively contrasting instances of France and Italy tempt one onward, while Germany divides itself into sections, each of which when regarded in relation to industrialization confirms at first glance this speculation. To which it may be added that the Culture of Poverty thesis, argued in concrete detail, supports this notion as well, as Lewis does in *La Vida*.

For a first-hand account of working-class food habits in Manchester some fifty years later, see Robert Roberts, *The Classic Slum: Salford Life in the First Quarter of the Century* (Manchester, 1971), pp. 78–100. The author spent his childhood close to the spot where Engels had found the old man living in a cow-shed; by 1900 the cow-shed was gone, "but much that was vile remained." (p. 2) Further material on dietary topics is to be found in T. C. Barker, et al., eds., *Our Changing Fare* (London, 1966); John Burnett, *Plenty and Want* (London, 1966).

inherent in that work." Indeed, he does not work out of any pleasure in performing a task or out of some "natural impulse or drive." He works only because he must and for money, "for something that has nothing whatever to do with the work that he performs." Moreover, his hours of work are endlessly long and of "an uninterrupted monotony." The increasing mechanization of the division of labor has only intensified these circumstances. In most branches of industry, "the activity of the worker is limited to some insignificant and purely mechanical [repetitive] manipulation, repeated minute after minute, remaining year in and year out the same. How much human feeling or capacities can a man of thirty expect to retain if since childhood he has spent twelve hours or more every day making pin heads or filing cogwheels, and has in addition lived amid [all the other] circumstances of the English proletariat." (133f.)

At a later point, Engels returns to this problem of the quality of industrial work. He has been discussing some early examples of factory legislation, and the tendency of his argument leads him to remark that there are certain evils connected with the factory system that are not amenable to legislative provisions. To tend machinery, for example, the continual "tying of broken threads, is not the kind of activity that can engross the thinking powers of a worker. At the same time, however, it is a kind of activity that prevents him from occupying his mind with anything else." Further, it is typically work that for the most part is without the accessory compensations of providing the occasions for physical exercise or muscular activity. It is actually thus "no work at all, but pure boredom, of the most deadening and exhausting imaginable kind. The factory operative is condemned to allow his physical and mental powers to atrophy and perish. From the age of eight he has the mission [den Beruf] of boring himself all day long. Moreover, he has not a moment's respite from it: the steam engine works ceaselessly; the wheels, belts and spindles hum and rattle without pause in his ears. If he thinks of snatching even a moment's rest, there at once behind him is the overlooker with his fine-book. This condemnation to being buried alive in the factory, in the continual service of tireless machines, is experienced by the workers as torture of the severest kind. The effect is, in the highest degree, stunting to both the body and mind." (199f.)

Engels has taken the argument beyond the point to which Carlyle had carried it.[22] He has of course anticipated a number of the great passages in Ruskin's "On the Nature of Gothic" and Marx's "The Working Day." The work in question is not of a self-moving, self-fulfilling kind.[23] Since the time of Engels' writing many kinds of work have become more like the typical machine-tending duty in the textile mill than less. Typists, key-punch operators and computer programmers, bank clerks— the watchers and tenders of the new electronic technology—and not merely assembly-line operators, all confront a working life whose quality is to say the least problematical. The matter therefore remains of central concern to anyone who has a serious, humane interest in the future of culture and society. The researches of industrial sociologists have in this respect often served to darken counsel. And as for those social theoreticians who have written at length about how leisure activities are in the near future going to take the place in life that work once

[22] Several reasons may be suggested for Carlyle's having stopped where he did. First, he was significantly enough older than Engels to be not entirely aware of what the new kind of work entailed. Second, he was writing in the midst of the deepest depression in trade, and work itself was the pressing question rather than its quality. Third, he was more puritanical than Engels and did not really believe that suffering could be avoided or work made less onerous. Fourth, he was aware of the problem at hand, but preferred to refer to it obliquely, as in his statement that in the motto "A fair day's wages for a fair day's work" the workers had discovered the truth, but that in interpreting it strictly in terms of money they had only begun to approximate the larger truths concealed within that phrase. *Past and Present*, Bk. I, ch. 3.

[23] Marx's coinage for work that is self-moving is *"Selbständigkeit"*: self-activity. For a formulation of this problem in psychoanalytic theoretical terms, see Phyllis Greenacre, "Youth, Growth, and Violence," *The Psychoanalytic Study of the Child*, XXV (1970), 354f.

occupied—what work? what place? and for whom?—one is inclined after consideration to conclude that they are in ideological orbit, whistling bravely in the dark vacuums of inner space. One moment in this passage bears directly upon this point. Engels states that the machine-tending work of the spinning operative is a kind of activity that prevents him from occupying his mind with anything else. This assertion, true enough about spinning, has been demonstrated to be incorrect about other kinds of tending work. Experiments have indicated that persons employed at work of this general order do indeed tend to think about other things. They think about what they are going to do when they get off from work, how they are going to spend their holidays; they characteristically spend a good deal of their time in sexual reverie and fantasy, and wile away their hours, when they can, telling jokes to one another. From this data, the researchers concluded that these human beings were satisfied with their work. There is no need to enter here into an examination of their conception of either human beings or their satisfaction, both of which, one suspects, would have been worthy of Andrew Ure.[24]

[24] See Harvey Swados, "The Myth of the Happy Worker," *Identity and Anxiety*, eds. Maurice Stein, Arthur Vidich and David M. White (New York, 1960). Also Robert Blauner, *Alienation and Freedom* (Chicago, 1964), from which the following extract has been taken:

> Many industrial commentators feel that most modern jobs cannot be intrinsically involving and the best solution would be to make them so completely automatic that a worker would be free to daydream and talk to his workmates. Evidently, we are still far from this outcome, since the Roper survey, based on a representative sample of 3,000 factory workers, found that only 43 per cent could do their work and keep their minds on other things most of the time. . . . The most unsatisfactory situations seem to be the job which is not intrinsically interesting and yet requires rather constant attention.
>
> Still such work does not necessarily result in intense or even mild dissatisfaction. The capacity of people to adapt to routine repetitive work is remarkable. It is quite likely that the majority of industrial workers are self-estranged in the sense that their work is not particularly involving and is seen chiefly as a means of livelihood. Yet research in job satisfaction suggests that the majority of workers, possibly from 75 to 90 per cent, are reasonably satisfied with such jobs. Thus, the typical worker in modern industrial society is probably satisfied *and* self-estranged.

The insolubilities of work and its discontents—to use Daniel Bell's adaptation of Freud—remain with us. As should the awareness that it was at this period in history that men's consciousness of work veered radically in the direction of the problematical.[25]

Finally, there is one further encompassing circumstance which serves as a test for the historical imagination. This has to do with what today is called child labor, what the nineteenth century called the employment of children. We have to try to imagine reconstructively what it was concretely like, say, in Manchester during Engels' time, where 54 percent of working-class children did not reach the age of five; of the surviving 46 percent virtually *all* would be at work within the next few years, and most of them would enter the textile factories at the age of nine.[26] And that, for the most part, would be that. Some might die before their statistical number was up; some might emigrate; some, under the pressure of technological unemployment, might find other work, sometimes worse, sometimes better; some might through talent and energy be promoted or even start small enterprises of their

---

Self-estranged workers are dissatisfied only when they have developed *needs* for control, initiative, and meaning in work. (p. 29)

Further intelligent accounts of this inexhaustible subject are to be found in Joachim Israel, *Alienation: from Marx to Modern Sociology* (Boston, 1971); and Schlomo Avineri, *The Social and Political Thought of Karl Marx* (Cambridge, 1968), pp. 1–124; see also Richard Schacht, *Alienation* (New York, 1970).

[25] See Hannah Arendt, *The Human Condition* (New York, 1959), pp. 71–153, for some interesting speculations in this connection; also István Mészáros, *Marx's Theory of Alienation* (London, 1970), pp. 261ff. and *passim* for vigorous disagreements with Arendt's theses.

Marx's and Engels' brief joint attempt at Utopia foundered upon just this ragged problematical edge. To be a hunter in the morning, a fisherman in the afternoon, and a critical critic after dinner is to contemplate a life which is incommensurate with the seriousness and urgency that has induced its original imagination. The same discrepancy is to be found in some of Herbert Marcuse's more recent remarks about a "liberated" future.

[26] The age was set by the provisions of the Factory Act of 1833, which applied to the textile industries. In other industries not covered by the act, children still began industrial labor—as they previously did in textiles—at yet earlier ages.

own. Still when we speak of the nineteenth-century industrial working class, or of a single adult member of it, we have to try to recall that we are speaking of a group in whose individual members the consciousness of existence, of life itself, was virtually coterminous or identical with the consciousness of labor. The term "working class" had a more than literal sense to it. No one of these conditions was in itself altogether new, certainly not that of small children working. What was qualitatively different was the massive numbers of people involved, the character and conditions of industrial work, often in an exclusively urban setting, and the consciousness which beheld and responded to all these in their numberless variety of forms.[27]

Engels represents one branch of this consciousness, and naturally a radical one. It is not, however, a Continental or later Marxian radicalism that is at this moment in question, but a radical moral attitude that he shares with such native figures as Blake and Dickens. It is, he says, simply and unpardonably wrong for children to be treated like this. It is "inexcusable under any circumstances to sacrifice that period of children's lives which should be devoted to bodily and mental development to the greed of the unfeeling middle classes. It is unpardonable to take children from school and the fresh air, in order to exploit them for the benefit of the manufacturers." (169) [*um sie zum Vorteil der Herren Fabrikanten auszubeuten*] This uncompromising judgment has withstood the test of history. It is, in fact, about the only kind of judgment elicited by this context that has proved to be of trans-historical power and value—which is in part why Blake and Dickens are relevant to it. Those qualities derive in the first place from an intelligence and courage that impel one to deliver such judgments in a certain form. That form, typically, is *not*, "Our society, for all its imperfections. . . ." but rather "This society in which we live has something profoundly wrong with it. . . ."

[27] See R. K. Webb, *Modern England* (New York, 1968), pp. 111f. By 1835, children under fourteen made up about 13 percent of the labor force in cotton.

It is not a question of an easy fashionable radicalism, of a moral superiority that is its own end or that is justified by the distance it establishes between itself and the objects of its contempt and indignation; it is a question of bearing one's witness in social and historical circumstances that are intolerable to almost everything one has learned about the decent possibilities of human life. And it is not a question of having a blueprint for the future all worked out; it is quite enough to know that means do exist for the amelioration of present injustices and suffering, that one is not protesting against laws of nature or dealing with a preindustrial economy with no margins for sizable alternatives. If the history of all subsequent legislative encroachments and limitations on the practices of industry proves nothing else, it proves this. And even in 1845 the employment of children was a flagrant human abuse. The best way of convincing oneself of the soundness of this assertion is to read the defenses and justifications offered at the time for the continuation of such practices. They still make one blush for the spiritual condition—for the very souls—of those who honestly held such beliefs.

Engels spends many pages setting down in full detail what the conditions of life and work were like for children in the textile and other industries; what extraordinary bodily and mental effects they produced on both the children themselves and on those that survived into maturity. We cannot go into these here, but can recommend to the reader either Engels' account or those to be found in his sources, particularly the various reports of the Commissioners and Inspectors. What these experiences at their most intense could issue in were individual and collective states of being for which words like "aberrant" or "demoralized" cease to carry meaning, and whose existential quality is only displaced and muffled by terms such as "psychotic" or "quasi-psychotic." Here, for example, is Engels' quite accurate summary of the report of one of the members of the Children's Employment Commission on conditions in one of the districts in the Black Country.

Commissioner Horne [R. H. Horne, of the Children's Employment Commission] stated that in Willenhall no moral sense at all is to be found among the workers, and he gives ample evidence to support this assertion. In general he found that the children recognized no obligations toward their parents, nor felt any affection for them. These children were so blunted, so stupid, so animally ignorant, that they were almost altogether incapable of reflecting upon what they said. They often asserted that they were well treated and that things were going splendidly for them, although in fact they had to work from twelve to fourteen hours, were dressed in rags, were not given enough to eat and were beaten to the degree that they felt the effects for several days afterwards. They simply knew nothing of any other way of life than to slave from morning till night until someone gave them permission to stop. They had never before been asked whether they were tired, and did not know the meaning of the question. (229)

The extremeness and exceptionality of these children's fate suggest its typicality as well. Yet what is one to think of a response to conditions of existence that is so wildly aberrant? One might have supposed that this bird-brained, grotesquely merry anarchy would have ideally filled the bill of the profit-bent industrial middle class and their outriders. In fact such reports brought forth widespread exclamations of horror (along of course with general denials from certain expectable quarters). Which suggests that the middle classes had a notion not merely of certain relative social-historical norms, but of certain human limits as well, of boundaries beyond which something happened to the species itself—and that in the industrial and urban revolutions they were apparently coming close to overstepping that fatal mark.[28]

Yet what did all these myriad circumstances of oppression lead to for the working class as a whole? The question put in this form is of course unanswerable, since there were so many different kinds of responses and formations to so many combinations of hardships and grievances among so many different working-class

[28] One general circumstance that Engels significantly omits to mention or take into account is the compunction, guilt and fear that began effectively to alter middle-class attitudes and behavior during this period.

groups and communities. Engels does, however, try to find a coordinated range of discriminable, characteristic responses. First, there are those that are beaten down and either perish, or drop out of the proletariat into the urban underclasses and their subgroupings, or who rub along in demoralized misery without hope yet without active despair. These may all be included within the description of the culture of poverty that I have referred to before. Then there are those who acquiesce in the openly declared values of society at large and try to live according to them; sometimes they are rewarded for this allegiance, some-times—in Engels' view more often than not—they get no reward at all.[29] In addition to these there are a further series of responses that sociologists like to class as deviant—among which, naturally, those responses which go into making up the culture of poverty are included—and that Engels gives special place to. First among these is crime.

Engels distinguished among various kinds and degrees of crime. The simplest is that which is induced by want, distress or necessity. Faced on the one hand with religious and civil law, and with the notion of the sacredness of property, and on the other with their own exigencies and irreducible needs, working people recognize that Mammon is the god of this world, turn "practical atheist," and commit crimes against property rather than starve slowly, or persist in unbearable deprivation. (130) Thefts of this kind are by far the most common—and probably remain so—are the easiest to remedy, and for Engels the least important. He touches upon crime and criminals of another sort in the course of one of his vivid discussions of the urban underclasses, the "surplus population" of casual workers, street-sweepers, beggars, prosti-tutes, and peddlers in petty miscellaneous articles, street-sellers and odd-job men of every description. (98ff.) Toward the bottom of this collection are the army of beggars, and Engels describes at

---

[29] In this connection Engels gives very short—indeed inadequate—shrift to the role of religion among members of working-class communities and subcommunities.

length how they frequent the working-class districts of Manchester, appealing, with their families, to the charity of the workers, either by singing doleful songs, or by reciting an account of their misfortunes, or merely by standing mutely still on street corners, they and their families silent testimonies to their sufferings.[30] They do not appeal to the middle classes, but only to their former fellows; they are continually at war with the police, and their activities are particularly visible on Saturday nights, when the "secrets" of life of the working-class districts are revealed on the Manchester streets, the middle classes having at such times withdrawn from those districts that the working classes come out into and "pollute." It is from this "surplus population," including the beggars, that Engels sees the second kind of criminal emerging. He is a man who has been provoked by his intense distress, and who has the "courage and passion to revolt openly against society. He wages *open* warfare against the middle classes, and thus answers the *concealed* warfare they have waged against him, and goes forth to steal and rob and murder." (100)[31]

This notion of the criminal as rebel owes much of course to the romantic Byronic cultural tradition. And insofar as there is some truth to the Hobbesian conception of society, or to that conception which regards conflict as its moving, generating force, there is some truth in this conception as well.[32] What Engels has failed to take into account here is that for every Byronic Corsair there is an old Lambro; or that, to return to solid earth, for every

[30] For a full account of the elaborate ritual performances and astonishing variety of roles and dramas enacted by the "professional" street-beggars, see Henry Mayhew, *London Labour and the London Poor*, IV (London, 1862), 404–438.

[31] On another occasion, Engels called the uprooted, propertyless proletarian himself "a free outlaw." [*los und ledig* vogelfreien *Proletarier*] *Werke*, XVIII, 219; trans. *The Housing Question, p. 38.*

[32] It is also in accord with the theory of alienation or estrangement. In these terms, such crime is estranged labor coming to perverse life, endeavoring immediately to cancel its frozen and "objectified" existence and behave in accordance with its deformed conception of a free human being.

Bill Sikes there is a Fagin. That is to say, the structure of crime reproduces the structure of existing social arrangements fully as much as it protests against them. At other moments, Engels recognizes the intricate character of this question, remarking at one point, for example, that if the brutalizing and demoralizing influences acting upon the workingman are particularly concentrated and powerful, then he loses all will, all command over himself, and turns to crime as inevitably as if he were some natural phenomenon obeying immutable laws of nature. (145f.) This kind of assertion is in flat contradiction to the earlier, essentially volitional account of how criminals are made, although a more modulated statement of determination would not be. At a later juncture, he does offer such a statement. It occurs at the opening of the chapter on working-class movements, and is part of Engels' historical explanation of how resistance and hostility to the world in which they lived came to organized existence among the working class.

Criminal activities were the first, the crudest and the least fruitful form of this rebellious resistance. [*dieser Empörung*] The working-man lived in poverty and want [*Elend*] and saw that other people were better off than he. His understanding was unable to make it intelligible why it was that he, who contributed more to society than the idle rich, should be the one to suffer under these conditions. Want and necessity overcame his traditional respect for private property—he stole. [And as we have already] seen crime has increased as industry has expanded. . . .

The workers, however, soon realized the crime did not help their cause. The criminals, through their thefts, could protest only singly and as individuals against the existing order of society. The entire power of society hurled itself against each individual law-breaker and crushed him beneath its enormous overwhelming force. In addition, theft was the most unformed and least conscious [*ungebildetste, bewusstloseste*] form of protest, and for that very reason it never became the general expression of the collective overt opinion of the workers, however much they might as individuals approve of it in private. (242f.)[33]

There is thus a series of developmental stages. Crime is a primitive form of insurrection, driven by need and deprivations, an incomplete but not altogether mistaken response to a bad situation, and coming into active existence only by overcoming the resistance of inherited values and internalized sanctions. It is by no means necessarily or exclusively what is thought of among certain social theorists as anomic or deviant behavior. It is in the first place much too intimately connected with the values and norms it violates to be considered as simply anomic in respect to them; and secondly, no behavior that is both an inversion and a parody of another can be properly or fully understood as a deviant form of the latter. Nevertheless, an inescapable part of the meaning of crime is its essential failure. It is insufficiently rational and excessively, or too purely, symbolic and symptomatic.[34] Most of all, in it the criminal remains socially untransformed: he is still an isolated individual pursuing activities in an underground and alternate marketplace; if he is successful, he is a small-time entrepreneur; at best, he is the member or leader of a gang. In no instance is he capable of organizing a movement to withstand the

---

[33] These theoretical remarks on crime have been assembled from distinct and separated passages of the text. They are not, however, scattered or casual observations; each of them occurs within the context of several general, extended and very intelligent discussions of the subject of crime and its relation to the larger concerns of the work. The critical juxtaposition and examination of these remarks, as a result, does not wrench them out of context, but brings into connection a series of passages that because of his method of exposition Engels has had to distribute among different discussions in the book. It may also be useful to note once again how here, as elsewhere, Engels makes observations and offers insights whose originality at the time is obscured to us because they anticipated so much of what has become commonly accepted.

[34] The axial distinctions for crime, then as now, were class (and/or education) and age. Even the unreliable statistics of the nineteenth century were overwhelmingly clear on these essential stratifications: crime was committed in the main by juvenile offenders; and most offenders came from lower income groups and were at the lowest level of educational attainment, if such a euphemism is permissible. See J. J. Tobias, *Crime and Industrial Society in the Nineteenth Century*.

institutional forces that are arrayed against him. He lives in a parallel and parasitic world whose horizon is bounded and obscured by the larger society upon which it depends.

Part of the importance of crime to Engels, then, is to be found in its transitional character. The criminal is an unconscious and premature social rebel.[35] For what Engels is interested in theoretically discovering is the motive power, the springs of action, that can begin to lead the working class at large out of the demoralization that he has represented.[36] For him the large alternatives are two drastically opposed extremes. In their present circumstances, he writes, "it is not surprising that workers who are treated like beasts actually become beasts." It is either that or this: "they are able to preserve the consciousness and sense of their humanity only through the most burning hatred, through a continual inner rising up in outraged indignation [*Empörung*] against the powerful middle-classes. The workers retain their humanity only so long as they feel anger against the dominating class. They become animals as soon as they submit patiently to the yoke, and merely strive to make life endurable beneath it without attempting to break free." (129) Allowance has to be made for Engels' hyperbole, and for his overlooking in this formulation all the possibilities intermediate between the extremes (elsewhere he does not). When this has been done, something remains to be said in support of his contention, however unwelcome this may be. The working class has been universally negated and is universal negation; its members can discover their power and the present state of their humanity only in what they are, in negation itself, and in its corrosive emotions and passions. But it may be useful to recall that "we may then affirm without qualification that *nothing great in the world* has

[35] See E. J. Hobsbawm, *Primitive Rebels* (New York, 1959).

[36] That there was an abundance of such resources is one of the principal burdens of E. P. Thompson's work.

been accomplished without passion." [37] Adapting the imperial paradigm of Hegel to his own uses, Engels regards the position of the worker as at the outset structurally akin to that of the Bondsman. He is essentially "the passive object [*das willenlose Objekt*] of every possible combination of [unfortunate] circumstances, and must count himself fortunate when he has saved his bare existence for even a short time. . . . He may struggle to keep himself up in this whirlpool; he may seek the deliverance of his humanity. This he can do only by rebellious resistance against the middle classes, who exploit him so ruthlessly and then abandon him to a fate that compels him to live in a way unworthy of a human being." (131) It is the grand account of the history of the idea of freedom again, this time written upon actual human flesh and in real human blood. And again it may be appropriate to recollect that freedom comes about only through constraint and oppression, only through unfreedom, and proceeds and develops only through its own absence.[38] Indeed, he goes so far as to assert—overlooking what he has observed about the general circumstances of urban life—that it is only by means of this outraged indignation and rebellious resistance that the factory operatives have been saved from the stupefaction that their work might be expected to produce in them. If in spite of this the factory operatives "have rescued their intelligence, and developed and sharpened it more than any other group of working-men," it is because they have steadily maintained this inward and active negativity—"the sole subject on which under every circumstance they can think and feel while at their work." (200) We are—understandably, I believe—in the presence of a personal projection; certainly this is the consciousness of Friedrich Engels ideally reconstructing his own twenty months in Manchester.

[37] G. W. F. Hegel, *Reason in History*, p. 29.
[38] Thus, "constraint is part of the process through which is first produced the consciousness of and the desire for freedom in its true, that is, its rational and ideal form. . . . [Indeed] such limitation is the very condition leading to liberation; and society and the state are the very conditions in which freedom is realized." *Ibid.*, pp. 54f.

But it is not all displacement and wish-fulfillment, and along with this notion there goes another that is of less questionable and schematic character. Engulfed in this murderous and dehumanized world, he writes, "the workers must themselves strive to escape from this brutalizing [*vertierenden*] condition. They must try to achieve for themselves a better and more human place in life. They can do this only by attacking the interests of the middle classes, which exist precisely in the exploitation of the workers. . . . As soon as the workingman determines to work himself free from [or to alter] the present state of things, the bourgeoisie becomes his open enemy." (241) The interest of these assertions is in the idea that a working-class or labor movement—revolutionary, socialist or other—will have to be essentially the activity of the working class itself. It represents one of the earliest acknowledgments by a socialist writer of any theoretical standing of this critical historical circumstance, and distinguishes in advance the kind of socialism that Marx and Engels were to develop theoretically from the socialism of their immediate predecessors, the Owenites, Saint-Simonians, and Fourierists and the socialists in Germany. It is a socialism in which the notions of class cooperation and collaboration are sunk within the notions of class conflict and class consciousness. It implies that whatever socialism may ultimately be, it will not do anything *for* the working class, since it will be their active exertions that bring it into being, and they will be their own agents in this undertaking. It is an argument to be put with striking force and clarity in the *Manifesto*.[39]

Thus the feelings of outrage and anger that Engels singles out do not remain abstract or undeveloped passionate impulses. They are incorporated into new states of consciousness and the

---

[39] "The workers declare that they need no assistance from other classes in society. They demand the Charter so that they can secure the *power to help themselves*." (316) And Marx never tired of insisting that the emancipation of the working class must be the work of the working class itself.

beginnings of new kinds of activity. And it is here that the great urban centers, the home of modern industry, return as part of the argument. For the cities in their concentration further both the increase of middle-class wealth and power and an accelerated complementary development among the working class. The concentration of working people under these new conditions is accompanied by a new awareness of their increased separation and division from their superiors. This awareness leads in turn to further reflections on their pernicious conditions of existence, to the beginnings of a common or class consciousness and to the first organizations in the working-class interest—the trade-union movement, Chartism and socialism all had their origins in the towns. As always in this mode of analysis, loss, separation and division are the necessary preconditions for the advance of consciousness and the advent of self-consciousness.

In the patriarchal relation [of the past and in the countryside] that deceitfully concealed the slavery of the worker, he had to remain spiritually dead, entirely unknowing of his own interests and a mere private, isolated being. Only when the worker became estranged [*entfremdet*] from his master [*Brotherrn:* also, employer] did matters change. Only then did it become manifest that he was connected with his employer solely through private interest, solely through the cash nexus. Then the ostensible bond of affection between them proved unable to bear the slightest test and fell entirely away. And it was only then that the worker began to recognize his position in this relationship and to develop independently. Only now did he also cease to be the slave of the middle classes in his thoughts, feelings and acts of will. (137–138)

The urban-industrial experience is the inevitable scene, the forcing house, of this momentous transformation. And Engels never ceases to keep his double-sided argument before the reader: that the working class is both worse and better off under their present circumstances. Worse off for all the reasons already offered at such length; better off because this unexampled mass experience of suffering and degradation has become, as he believes, the historical grounds of a new and fuller humanity.[40] In this rich and open ambivalence toward the central experience of his epoch, Engels takes his place with the other great Victorians.

This ambivalence is given additional expression in Engels' projected observations about the immediate future. At frequent intervals throughout the book he utters dire predictions about what is in the offing for English society—and we should never forget that he was certainly not alone in this apprehension of imminent disaster. England is suffering from a social disease; like any physical disease, it runs a regular course of crises, "the last and most violent of which determines the fate of the patient." But since a nation, unlike a person, "cannot succumb to such a final crisis, but must go forth from it again, renewed and reborn, we must welcome any circumstances that bring the disease to its climax." (139) Again, severe commercial crises are to be periodically expected. Before the next one occurs, the English people will have had enough. "If before that time the English middle class do not pause to reflect—and every appearance indicates that they certainly will not do so—a revolution will follow with which none ever known until now can be compared." Even if some part of the middle classes went over to the party of the working class, "even a general reform on the part of the middle classes would not help matters." All these are "inferences that may be drawn with the greatest certainty. . . . The revolution *must* come. It is already too late to bring about a peaceful solution to the affair. . . ." (334f.) In part these

---

[40] In another long and acutely reasoned passage—which again takes part of its origin in Carlyle—Engels compares in detail the condition of a bound serf of the twelfth century with that of a modern industrial worker. The circumstances and status of the serf had, he concludes, much to recommend them. But there is also this difference. "The deceitful, concealed servitude [of the present] recognizes the right to freedom, at least in outward and apparent form. It submits to a public opinion that cherishes the principles of freedom. And herein lies the historic advance over the old slavery—that at least the *principle* of freedom has succeeded in being affirmed. The oppressed will one day see to it that the principle is also carried into effect." (207f.)

doom-laden avowals are wishful thinking on the part of a young and heated revolutionary; in part they are the only conclusions—social, moral, experiential, logical and even aesthetic—that his material allowed to be drawn; in part they were presentiments that were shared by others, not all of them by any description insurrectionary youths. In any event they are not to be confused or equated with certain recent contemporary impulses whose radicalism seems to have been defined by crying "Fascist pig!" and heaving a rock at a policeman's head—behavior that is more reminiscent of B. Wooster gone sour in his cups than F. Engels even at his most fanciful.[41]

In considerable measure, however, these conclusions depend on Engels' conception of the middle classes. Toward them he expresses the kind of exasperation and despair that one can properly feel only about one's own social group or family. Compared to the liberal and open-minded workingman, the typical member of the middle classes is without hope. "He sits," Engels writes, "buried up to his ears in his class prejudices, in those principles that have been drummed into him from youth. There is nothing to be done with such a person. He is essentially conservative, even when he is liberal. His interests are bound up with those of the property-holding class. He is dead to all

[41] One partial exception requires notation. At certain moments in his exposition, Engels applies the idea of the social war with literal force. It has been openly declared in England, he affirms, and working-class violence serves only to "lay bare the true state of things, to destroy the hypocrisy" of peaceful social existence preached by the middle classes. (242) In this connection he describes activities such as strikes as "skirmishes" in the social war; "they decide nothing, it is true, but they are conclusive proof that the decisive battle between bourgeoisie and proletariat is approaching. These stoppages are the military school for the industrial proletariat, in which they prepare themselves for the great battle that draws inevitably nearer. . . . As schools of war, trades unions are unexcelled." (254) Without impugning Engels' motives, it is not difficult to observe how much of Georges Sorel—and Sorellian manipulation—might be extracted from the implicit tendencies of such remarks. It is one of the infrequent moments in the text at which Engels reveals a middle-class superiority of mind, although it should be added that, put back into context, it does not appear so drastic a departure in tone, and that Engels does go on to make modifying statements on the same topic.

movement." (141) Even more, in contrast to the uneducated and passionately unrestrained member of the working class, the English middle-class male is a regular Dombey: "Among the middle classes the cultivation of the reasoning powers has most significantly developed their self-seeking predisposition. It has made selfishness the ruling passion. It has concentrated all powers of feeling upon the sole concern of greed for money." At this point the young revolutionary no longer stands alone. There is hardly an English writer of importance from the period who did not agree—including Jeremy Bentham, who thought that such a concern was just fine. It was not a new perception but it could now be made with newly heightened awareness. The development of reason in English culture and society had largely taken the direction of the development of the powers of rational calculation. The cultivation of the rules and methods of rational acquisition had become an uncontrollable, irrational obsessive activity. Moreover, the logic of profitability was not an adequate definition of reason, although it might in certain contexts be part of a negative definition.[42] And, as we have seen, self-seeking might in fact become the negative form of self-realization. A social class and its culture were involved in this inversion and

[42] In an analogous recent context Hannah Arendt has referred to certain professional problem-solvers who "were drawn into government from the universities and the various think tanks, some of them equipped with game theories and systems analyses, thus prepared, as they thought, to solve all the 'problems' of foreign policy. . . . they were not just intelligent, but prided themselves on being 'rational' and they were indeed to a rather frightening degree above 'sentimentality' and in love with 'theory.' . . . They were eager to find formulas, preferably expressed in a pseudo-mathematical language, that would unify the most disparate phenomena with which reality presented them; that is, they were eager to discover laws by which to explain and predict political and historical facts as though they were as necessary, and thus as reliable, as the physicists once believed natural phenomena to be. . . . The problem-solvers did not *judge;* they calculated. Their self-confidence did not even need self-deception to be sustained in the midst of so many misjudgments, for it relied on the evidence of mathematical, purely rational truth." "Lying in Politics," *Crises of the Republic* (New York, 1972), pp. 9–11, 37. There is thus a vital distinction to be maintained between logicality and rationality, or to use the categories of Max Weber, between formal rationality and value rationality.

perversion of values and proportions. This is, one suspects, something like the kind of development that T. S. Eliot had in mind when he referred to a dissociation of sensibility beginning sometime in the seventeenth century, although it is no doubt incorrect to think of what came later as an aberrant departure from some preexisting norm. What commentators at this time tended widely to agree upon was that middle-class culture in its era of domination and self-conscious success was at the same time hounded by a fearful apprehension of inner constraint and limitation, by a sense of spiritual and human starvation—even though those dreads might be apparent to and were acknowledged almost exclusively by those members of the middle classes who were the commentators upon them.

Engels is aware that this concentration and distortion of energies were requisite accompaniments to the heroic phases of the middle class's economic and social transformation of the modern world—without such focusing and constraint nothing on a grand scale could have been accomplished.[43] But he also argues that the heroic age of this class has passed, that it must now pay the price that such an achievement immutably exacts. It is this conviction that allows him to make the following astonishing statement—he is talking particularly, he notes, about the liberal, manufacturing middle class.

I have never seen a social class so deeply demoralized as the English middle classes. I have never seen a class so incurably corrupted by egoistic self-seeking, so inwardly corroded, or rendered so incapable of progress. . . . For it nothing exists in the world that does not solely exist for the sake of money—itself not excepted—for it lives for nothing except making money. It knows no happiness [*Seligkeit:* also, bliss] except quick profit. It knows no pain except monetary loss. In the

---

[43] He touches here upon the general thematic concern of another one of those young men who attended Schelling's lectures in Berlin. Jacob Burckhardt's *The Civilization of the Renaissance in Italy* (1st ed. 1860) is in some measure a historical testing out of this and related hypotheses.

presence of such avarice and avid greed of gain, it is not possible for a single human quality to remain untainted. (311)

He adds a footnote to this passage acknowledging his debt in it to *Past and Present*, and referring his German readers to the sections that he had the year before translated. And he goes on pointedly to remark that he is not in this disquisition talking about the members of the middle classes as private individuals, many of whom he has found to be perfectly respectable, decent and upstanding men. Indeed he much prefers them in their capacities as men of business to their Lilliputian German counterparts; they are much more authentic in the social roles they profess. He is, however, talking about their behavior as a group, as a class pursuing certain interests.

What is remarkable about this description is not its youthful sweep, false universalization, or polemical excess—its tendency to mythologize the middle classes as a whole, just as at those moments in which he feels impelled to make predictions he tends to mythologize the working class.[44] The striking thing about it is that Engels applies the same term to the middle classes that he has used in his analysis of the working class—they are demoralized. This is not to be taken as a careless slip of the pen. On the contrary, the demoralization that he ascribes to the middle classes is the structural counterpart of that suffered by the working class, just as in Manchester the anatomy of the city revealed that the isolated and divided classes were in fact parts of a total whole. They too are estranged; they too have lost their real human existence and can recognize it only in "objectified" entities; they too have undertaken to appropriate a world through means which

[44] What is implied here is that Engels' analysis of the present condition of the working class is not mythologized—or sentimentalized or overdramatized for that matter. The testimony of other contemporary witnesses supports almost all his major descriptive and analytical claims. As we have seen, he mythologized the preindustrial past, largely but not entirely out of ignorance. His mythologization of the future is an extremely complex matter and requires a separate study in itself.

render it permanently alien to them. They possess and yet they do not. It is once again a Hegelian notion in origin that Engels and his colleague had already assimilated to their own developing synthesis.

> The possessing class and the class of the proletariat represent the same human self-estrangement. But the former is comfortable in this self-estrangement and finds therein its own confirmation, knows that this self-estrangement is *its own power,* and possesses in it the *semblance* of a human existence. The latter feels itself annihilated in this self-estrangement, sees in it its impotence and the reality of an inhuman existence.[45]

This formulation does not in the least minimize or overlook the immense material differences between the parties concerned, any more than the diagnosis of the middle class's demoralization and estrangement implies a softening of critical attack. The demonstration is presented forcefully to our minds that these two "nations" are really parts of one; that they are connected not by

[45] *Werke,* II, 37; *The Holy Family,* ch. 4. There is something owing to Feuerbach as well in this passage. See W. Schuffenhauer, *Feuerbach und der junge Marx* (Berlin, 1965); David McLellan, *The Young Hegelians and Karl Marx* (London, 1969).

The lucidity of all this is immediately succeeded by the following verbal cataclysm:

> *Sie ist, um einen Ausdruck von Hegel zu gebrauchen, in der Verworfenheit die Empörung, über diese Verworfenheit, eine Empörung, zu der sie notwendig durch den Widerspruch ihrer menschlichen Natur mit ihrer Lebenssituation, welche die offenherzige, entschiedene, umfassende Verneinung dieser Natur ist, getrieben wird.*

> It is, to use an expression of Hegel's, in its abjectness [lit., cast-away-ness] the rebelliousness against this abjectness, a rebellion to which by necessity it is driven by the contradiction between its human essence and its life situation—which is the candid, decisive and comprehensive negation of this essence.

Marx is referring to and attempting to secularize some murderous passages in the section "Spirit in Self-estrangement" in the *Phenomenology.* See *Phänomenologie des Geistes,* ed. J. Hoffmeister (Hamburg, 1952), pp. 368–370; *Phenomenology of Mind,* trans. J. Baillie [1910] (New York, 1964), pp. 538–540. The point of this note is to demonstrate once again how at this moment in their developments Marx and Engels oscillated regularly between or among several different idioms of conceptualization—which was their way of attaining or coming to their own.

proximity and in material exchanges alone, but inwardly and spiritually as well; that they are members of each other and one another's fate.

Engels does not of course confine his demonstration to its theoretical assertion. In his chapter on "The Attitude of the Bourgeoisie towards the Proletariat" he brings forward material —including that having to do with language that I mentioned earlier—that is calculated to convince the reader by its concreteness. Two of these illustrations are of outstanding interest and immediate pertinence; and both have to do with his experiences in Manchester. Here is the first.

One day I walked with one of these [liberal, manufacturing] middle-class gentlemen into Manchester. I spoke to him of the miserable, unhealthy method of building that is to be found in the working-class districts and of the atrocious, disgraceful condition of those districts. I declared to him that never in my life had I seen so badly built a town. He listened to all of this patiently and quietly, and at the corner of the street at which we parted he remarked: "And yet there is a great deal of money made here. Good morning, Sir." (312)

This gruesome little vignette merits its historic notoriety. It stands by the side of those other celebrated Victorian flashes of penetration and revelation: with Matthew Arnold's "Wragg is in custody"; with Ruskin's Britannia of the Market; with Carlyle's Edinburgh Irish widow; with Jo's "I don't know nothink" in *Bleak House*. It is the bland indifference, the indifferent hardness of this upstanding and respectable Victorian gentleman that remains capable of speaking to the modern reader across the gap of more than a century. He is—he has made himself into—a walking political economy, with hands and feet and mouth. He is a caricature of Josiah Bounderby, who as everyone knows is a caricature and never could have existed. His existence is as externalized and objectified as that of the most hapless and unconscious handloom weaver. And as his language persuasively reveals, he is truly de-moralized.[46]

The second illustration comes toward the end of this final chapter and is the ultimate illustration in Engels' discussion of the New Poor Law of 1834, which he quite properly discusses as a piece of class legislation. It was the first important piece of Victorian social legislation, and the most unguarded and extreme. The widespread public response that it induced among the lower

[46] In the original text, Engels first gives the English and then his German translation, which is itself an interpretation of the statement: *"und doch wird hier enorm viel Geld verdient."* In Germany money is "made" at the mint or by a counterfeiter. There is no precise equivalent for our making money through daily work. Although one ought not to take such cross-linguistic comparisons to excessive length, the example does suggest that in English, at any rate, the experience referred to seems to have been abridged, condensed and so thoroughly assimilated that all the intermediate steps can be dropped, and that someone who is making cotton yarn at a spinning machine is in point of fact really making money.

One must, to be sure, look at the passage as a whole in historical perspective and concede that progress of a sort had occurred since the time of Peterloo. At that period, Francis Place wrote:

These Manchester yeomen and magistrates are a greater set of brutes than you form a conception of. They have always treated the working people in a most abominable manner. I know one of these fellows who swears "Damn his eyes, seven shillings a week is plenty for them"; that when he goes round to see how much work his weavers have in their looms, he takes a well-fed dog with him, almost, if not entirely, for the purpose of, insulting them by the contrast. He said some time ago that "The sons of bitches had eaten up all the stinging nettles for ten miles round Manchester, and now they had no greens to their broth." Upon my expressing indignation, he said, "Damn their eyes, what need you care about them? How could I sell you goods so cheap if I cared anything about them." (Graham Wallas, *The Life of Francis Place* [London, 1898], p. 141)

Although such characterizations are commonly taken to apply, almost stereotypically, to the self-made, parvenu, dissenting middle-class Lancashire manufacturer or merchant, compare this by a recent historian: "For natural egoism, on the other hand, it would have been difficult to match, as a class, the English country gentlemen of the period. . . . Invulnerable in their independence, their rank, their property, they moved through life with a hard assurance that bespoke their restricted outlook and fixed prejudices. They concerned themselves for little in politics except rents, corn, and taxes: and if they deferred to anyone it was more likely to be a master of fox-hounds than a minister of state." *Mutatis mutandis,* or, so what else is new? Norman Gash, *Mr. Secretary Peel,* pp. 66f.

classes was in its revulsion, outrage and fury no more than commensurate with the aims of the new act. Some of its provisions, had they ever been carried through, would have struck at the human status itself of the indigent poor; and these provisions were widely interpreted in that sense. Under the new practices, the practical social definition of the pauper was to be transformed. Traditionally a member of the community destitute of all means of support, the pauper was reconceived as what we now understand to be the first unperson in modern history. And the purpose of this reconception was benign, "scientific," and in accord with the laws of nature that political economy had discovered: to create a self-acting market of free wage labor. Engels considers the act from this and other standpoints, but his final illustration includes something else. "In death as in life," he writes, "the poor are treated in an utterly feelingless way. They are flung into the earth like the carcasses of dead animals." He then returns one last time to his experience of twenty months.

In Manchester the pauper burial ground of the Old Town lies on the other side of the Irk. It, too, is a waste and desolate patch of ground. About two years ago a railway line was built that drove through the burial ground. Had it been a churchyard in which respectable people were buried, the middle classes and the clergy would have cried out in protest against the desecration. But it was a burial ground of the poor, it was the last resting place of paupers and other "superfluous" creatures, and so nobody troubled himself in the least about it. The trouble was not even gone to of taking up the half-decayed corpses and carrying them to the other side of the churchyard where they might be decently buried. The navvies dug holes where they pleased and piles were driven into fresh graves. Since this was marshy land, water laden with putrefying matter from these graves was driven up to the surface, and the whole district was filled with the most nauseating and dangerous gases. I cannot further describe in its details the disgusting brutality that was perpetrated here in broad daylight. (329f.)

The railroad has returned once again. In its first appearance in the text, it broke through the slums and revealed to the eye how the poor of Manchester were living hidden in sheds and stables like secret or forgotten livestock. In its second it drives through the graves of the poor, reveals how they are buried like livestock that have sickened and perished, and deprives their dead bodies of even this last resting place. In death as in life they have ceased to be regarded as members of the community, as belonging to that human world which defines itself as distinct from all other living worlds by conscious and deliberate preservation of its dead within it and as part of it.[47]

But Engels does not stop here. He stops only when he can go no further. What he has seen in this urban-industrial harrowing of hell is no Blakean proverb—"Drive your cart and your plow over the bones of the dead." He has had a glimpse into the distant future, a future it is safe to say that he was quite unable to imagine. It could not have occurred to him that what he had witnessed was a scene that was symbolic of the fate of millions to come, and not all of them paupers or worn-out and discarded workingmen. And if it could have occurred to him it would have made no more sense. He finds at the end of his long account that he is once again unable to bring himself to say what he had seen. There is more than reticence in this abstention from language.[48]

However powerful this account may be, and however just each concrete charge in the indictment brought forward against the middle classes, it is clear that Engels is unable to give them a fair shake (not that they especially needed one). His representation of the working class is distinguished for the largest part by a

[47] It was the chance glimpse of the pitiful corpse of a pauper, which fell out of a coffin that had been dropped on the ground, that turned the young Harrovian Anthony Ashley in the direction of his life's work. See J. Wesley Bready, *Lord Shaftesbury* (New York, 1927), pp. 18f.

[48] Another contemporary account of how the railway laborers behaved in the presence of the hallowed dead is to be found in Wordsworth's sonnet, "At Furness Abbey" (1845).

genuinely noble effort of disinterestedness—which does not mean that he isn't on their side. There they are, warts and all, weaknesses and demoralizations presented without palliation. Their virtues and qualities exist in the teeth of such overwhelming disabilities, coexist with them, emerge from and transcend them, and are almost never considered as separable from the mass suffering and living human sacrifice that are in Engels' view their necessary historical ground. By contrast the middle classes when they appear on these pages are colored villainously black. What is wrong with this unrelieved portrait is that it is both unnecessary and damaging to Engels' entire tendency and method of argument. One of the most deep-seated and far-reaching presuppositions in his thesis is that these unexampled inhumanities, this martyrdom of generations, are not the work of wicked or consciously malign men. Their gigantic horror is in considerable measure precisely found in the circumstances that those who can be held historically responsible for the perpetration of these unforgivable things are generally virtuous, hard-working, law-abiding and upright men of character and strength of purpose. This is the very nub of the Hegelian-Marxian mode of conceptualization. The cunning of reason has as its concrete content the crimes, follies and misfortunes of mankind that compose so much of the human historical record.[49] Like many another good writer, however, Engels himself provides internally all the evidence that is needed against him. One illustration will have to stand for all the others.

In his chapter on the "results" of industrialization, Engels has an extended account of the many causes of death among the working class, particularly among their infants and small children. One of these comes about because father, mother and older children in the working-class households generally have to be at work all day. When there are small children in the family, and no

---

[49] History, Hegel allowed, "is not the soil of happiness. The periods of happiness are blank pages in it." *Reason in History*, p. 33.

one is available to care for them during the working hours, they are perforce locked up at home, with the resulting, inevitable mishaps of drowning, burning, suffocating—the common run of household disasters. These occur with shocking frequency in industrial England, Engels reports, and he estimates that at least one such case per week is the average for Manchester and for London.[50] But, he continues, it "is rare for such matters to be reported in the press." He immediately makes a citation about such matters from the *Weekly Dispatch*, and a few lines later writes, "The middle classes read these things every day in the newspapers, and do nothing at all about it." (123) He cannot have the argument both ways, and this is simply one instance in the text that reveals with what childlike simplicity he is trying to work both sides of the street—he doesn't even have the guile to cover the contradiction or to separate the contradictory assertions by enough space of text so that the reader might not recall the first assertion when the second is made.

The reasons behind such critical malpractice are in the nature of the case manifold. Some of them are so transparent that they do not need to be mentioned; some have been referred to already. There is one, however, that merits separate discussion. It is Engels' ambivalence about the working class that in part compels him to be so monolithic and inflexible in his critical dealings with the middle classes. More closely stated it is his ambivalence about both the immediate and intermediate future of the working class that prompts him to shore up his uncertainties with the excessive dogmatic remarks that characterize his treatment of the middle classes. And this brings us back to such assertions as "the revolution *must* come"; it is as "inevitable" as the laws of chemistry; compared to what is "inescapably" around the corner, '93 will have been as a tea party.

For there is another side to Engels' attitude that such assertions are, I think, unconsciously calculated to offset. This side is

---

[50] Almost certainly a low estimate.

evident in two excellent chapters: "Working-Class Movements," and "The Miners," particularly in the latter. For it is here, in the activities of the miners, that he finds the highest form of development that working-class consciousness had yet attained, as well as its most moving expression. Conditions in the mining industry, particularly in coal mining, had enjoyed a long-standing notoriety. The employment of women and children underground had provided material for one of the earliest of the great industrial public scandals. Conditions of work and long-term effects on health were what one knows; incidences of death and disabilities from accidents, falls, collapses and explosions were, relatively speaking, about what they remain today. The standard of living of the miners in general was reasonably good, at least in comparison with that of the agricultural workers and small tenant farmers who were their immediate neighbors. For this section of the working class still lived for the most part in remote and neglected parts of the countryside. This lesser accessibility, plus the fact that children had begun work at so "tender an age," had led to an almost universal neglect of even the most rudimentary education, religious as well as secular, in many of the mining districts. Their ignorance was phenomenal, and duly shocking, upon which Engels characteristically comments: "Only when they curse and swear do the miners show any acquaintance with the categories of religion." [*Die religiösen Kategorien sind ihnen nur aus den Fluchworten bekannt.*] It is a wry little existential actualization of negativity.[51]

The miners had in addition their own special set of grievances. Most of them were still exploited by the truck system; almost all

[51] "Miners and heavy metal workers," writes G. D. H. Cole, "were often looked on as a race of savages, set apart from the rest of society." *Studies in Class Structure* (London, 1955), p. 31; see also R. Page Arnot, *A History of the Scottish Miners from the Earliest Times* (London, 1955), ch. 1; J. L. and B. Hammond, *The Skilled Worker* (London, 1919), chs. 2 and 3.

By the time of Engels' writing the number of women and children at work underground was decreasing.

had to live in tied cottages; [52] penalties and fines at work were
exquisitely devised to filch the miner's pay from him after he had
already earned it. Moreover it was still customary in the northern
counties in particular for miners to sign yearly contracts, in
which they engaged to work at no other mine during that period
of time. But the mine owner did not in turn pledge himself
obliged to give the miners work. As a result a miner could be out
of work for extended periods of time, yet if he sought work
elsewhere could be brought to trial for breach of contract and
imprisoned for six weeks' hard labor working the treadmill. This
outcome was almost certainly ensured since the mine owners had
the Justices of the Peace in their pockets. In the mining districts
the JPs were normally either mine-owners themselves, or their
relatives or friends. In other words, the magistrates were "acting
as judges in their own cause." (286)[53]

Matters had continued in this way for a long time. By the time
of Engels' arrival in England, however, trade unions had started
up here and there among the miners, some strikes had occurred,
Chartist influence and consciousness was occasionally notable in
certain districts. And during 1843 the miners of the great
coalfield of Northumberland and Durham at last came in. They
undertook to establish a trade union which would unite all miners
in the country. They appointed W. P. Roberts, a solicitor who
had distinguished himself in court through his defense of
Chartists, as their "Attorney General." Organizing work was
undertaken, agents appointed, demonstrations were held. "When
the Union held its first conference at Manchester in January,

[52] The equivalent in England of company housing: the cottages were owned by the
mining company, and the laborer-tenants were restricted to work in the mines.

[53] A famous infringement, and the same weighty charge that Edmund Burke brought
against the makers of the French Revolution. See *Reflections on the Revolution in France*
(Penguin ed., 1968), p. 150.

For an extraordinary account of life in the mining districts, see D. H. Lawrence,
"Nottingham and the Mining Country" [1930], *Selected Essays* (Penguin, 1950), pp.
114–122.

1844, it had a membership of over 60,000 miners." Six months later it had already grown to over 100,000. The miners' contracts of service in Northumberland and Durham expired at the end of March 1844. On their united behalf, Roberts drew up a proposed new contract and presented it to the mine-owners. The latter replied that "as far as they were concerned the Union did not exist. They would deal only with single, individual workingmen only, and would never recognize the Union." They put forward their own, very different contract, which the union naturally rejected. On March 31, 1844, "forty thousand miners laid down their picks, and every mine in Northumberland and Durham stood empty." (288)

The miners had collected a strike fund large enough to assure each miner's family of strike pay of half a crown a week for several months. Roberts organized and directed the strike with "unexampled vigor." He traveled all over England and collected subscriptions for the miners. Everywhere he went, he advocated "non-violence and respect for the law." At the same time he waged an unprecedented legal "campaign against the despotic magistrates and 'truckmasters.'" Whenever a miner had been put into prison by a local magistrate, Roberts secured a writ of habeas corpus from the Court of Queen's Bench, brought his clients before the Court in London, "and always secured their freedom." Similar results attended his exertions against the truck, or company store, system. Meanwhile the strike persisted into the summer of 1844, under increasing difficulties and distress. The fund ran out, the miners had to resort to credit at ruinous rates from small shopkeepers, they had almost no allies among the English press or the middle classes.

Yet in spite of all this the miners stayed out. And what is more significant, they remained quiet and peaceful in the face of every hostility and provocation that the mine owners and their faithful servitors could devise. No act of vengeance occurred; no blackleg was molested; not a single theft was committed.

At this point—it was July 1844—the owners decided to increase the pressure by dispossessing the miners from the tied cottages that were the owners' property. There then occurred scenes that anticipated what was to occur on an even larger scale in Ireland in a few years.

In July, 1844, the strikers received notices to quit their cottages, and within a week all forty thousand of them had been put out into the street. This measure was carried out with revolting savagery. The sick, the infirm, the aged, the infants and even pregnant women were mercilessly kicked out of their beds into the street. . . . The justices of the peace, who were in charge of the evictions, would only have had to raise a hand for the large contingents of police and soldiers who were present to attack the strikers at the first sign of resistance. This too the working men endured without resistance . . . The homeless miners, remembering Roberts's warnings, remained unmoved. They silently set up their household goods in the moors or fields (from which the grain had been harvested) and held out. Some, who could find nowhere else to camp, settled down in ditches at the roadside. . . . And so they survived for another eight weeks and more under the open sky during the wet late summer of last year. They had no shelter for themselves or their children except for the cotton sheets and hangings from their beds. (290f.)

At last things came to an end. Their credit was rapidly running out, and further funds were nowhere to be gotten. The owners began to bring in large numbers of miners from Ireland and Wales, and this last step finished off the strike that had lasted for five uninterrupted months. The miners were forced to dissolve their union, dismiss Roberts, and return to work on the owners' terms.

Engels' final commentary on this is singularly revealing. This protracted action, he begins, was conducted "on the part of the oppressed with a persistence, courage, intelligence and discretion that demands from us the highest admiration." In 1842 the miners had been described in the Children's Employment Commission

Report as utterly crude and without moral sense. Yet "what a degree of genuine human culture, of inspired enthusiasm and strength of character does such a battle imply on the part of forty thousand men" who only two years earlier had been so described. "How severe must have been the oppression that brought these forty thousand miners to rise as one man, to fight as if they were an army not only disciplined, but inspired, moved by a single will, and to carry on the conflict in cold blood and without violence until the point had been reached when further resistance was utterly without sense. And what a struggle it was—not a fight against visible enemies who could be struck down, but a fight against hunger and want, destitute misery and homelessness —*against their own passions which had been provoked almost to madness by the brutality of wealth* [italics added]." Had the miners permitted themselves to give way to violence that would have been the end of them and their undertaking. They did not, they remained nonviolent and law-abiding, "not out of fear of the batons of the police," but as a result "of deliberate reflection" that nonviolence was a better policy than violence. This is, he concludes, "the best proof of the intelligence and self-control of the workers." (291f.)

This moving account of an even more moving event is of the utmost importance for Engels. The miners' nineteen-week experience has had the consequences of "breaking up forever the intellectual and spiritual death in which they had hitherto lain. They have ceased to slumber. They are awake to their own interests. They have entered the moving stream of modern civilization, in particular that part of it which is the working-class movement." (292) Part of the importance of this strike is that Engels represents it as an act of transcendence. In it the miners have transcended their passionate resentment of how they have been mistreated and have transformed those violent emotions into new forms of political behavior. And in doing so they have transformed themselves. And indeed, Engels goes on to subsequently acknowledge, "the fury of the proletariat against their oppressors is the most important stimulus to promote a working-class movement *in its early stages*." (335) But this fury, of which he has made so much beforehand, must also undergo its own inner negation, its own alteration and development in consciousness, control and action. It requires little perspicacity to see in these two-sided formulations a refraction of Engels' ambivalence toward his family and his father. But they are more than that even though they almost certainly have their origins in such emotions. For they are being applied with considerable insight and delicacy to a historical nexus that had, from all accounts, just such an uncertain, touch-and-go, perilously balanced character. It is this double-sidedness that in addition provides some of the closing chapters of the book with their singular and rewarding complexity.

This ambivalence is expressed once again in Engels' notion at this moment of communism and the approaching social cataclysm. It may be that the revolution is inevitable, that it *must* come, but if there were the possibility of a peaceful solution it would be owing to changes in the proletariat more than to changes in the middle classes—as the workers "absorb more and more Socialist and Communist elements, so the revolution will be less bloody, vengeful and savage." [54] This is because "Communism stands in principle over and above the schism between the bourgeoisie and proletariat." Communism recognizes "the historical significance of this cleavage only for the present. It does not regard this conflict as justified in the future. Indeed Communism wishes to cancel and transcend [*aufheben*] this conflict of classes." It understands the bitterness and rivalry that informs the relation of the classes at the present time, "but it rises above such enmity precisely because it is a cause of humanity and not of the working classes alone." And, he goes on, "the more the English workers accept Socialist doctrines the more superfluous will be their

[54] The verbal sense of most of these statements is conditional, uncertain, and frequently inconsistent and confused.

present embittered anger, which were it to continue as violently as it exists at present could accomplish nothing." Were the English working class to become thoroughly socialist in character, then its opposition to the bourgeoisie would be less brutal and savage. Were it possible to turn all the English workers into communists before the outbreak of the revolution, then the revolution itself "would be a peaceful one." But, he turns about once more, "that is not possible. It is too late." Still, he says yet again, communism stands above the strife between bourgeoisie and proletariat. With this and with one more final swing to the opposite side, a declaration that the conflict is now entering its penultimate revolutionary phase, he brings the work to its oddly divided close. (335f.)

He has tried to imagine a peaceful, or nearly peaceful, transcendence of this ghastly strife and suffering. And what he has come up with is something that in its own curious way is not so very different from Matthew Arnold's notion of Culture—a notion of an ideal allegiance that transcends conflict and class and interest, and binds humanity together in a society that has gone beyond politics. In later years Engels was at pains to disavow this view. In his Preface to the English edition of 1892, he discoursed upon it at length. It was, he wrote, part of the "embryonic development" of modern international socialism; it revealed the traces of its descent "from one of its ancestors, German philosophy." In particular, he singled out the great stress the work laid "upon the dictum that Communism is not a mere party doctrine of the working class, but a theory compassing the emancipation of society at large, including the capitalist class, from its present narrow conditions." This may be true enough in theory, he later wrote, but politically it is useless or less than useless. No doubt there is much to be said in favor of this judgment. Yet if this later rejected attitude reminds us of Culture, there is something to be recommended in a conception that reveals its common heritage with Arnold's notion. That heritage is of course the European humanist tradition, a tradition out of which the socialism of even the later Marx and Engels was to continue to draw rich reserves of strength.

In either direction, whether it hopefully announces the impending revolution or turns about to imagine a peaceful transcendence of our social conflicts in a new humanity, *The Condition of the Working Class in England* is a work that looks to the future and to a new phase of things. And in either direction its brilliant imaginative representations and predictions were fated to be disappointed, at least in Engels' lifetime. That, however, is another matter, exists in another range of meaning, and is the subject of another study than the present. And perhaps the best way of bringing this account of Engels' book to a close is to cite a comment upon it from his great colleague. In 1863 Marx had occasion to reread the work, and wrote to Engels, praising him for it and for how many of his analytical conclusions still held true. He then reflected:

Rereading your book has made me regretfully aware of our increasing age. How freshly and passionately, with what bold anticipations, and without learned and systematic, scholarly doubts, is the thing still dealt with here! And the very illusion that the result will leap into the daylight of history tomorrow or the day after gives the whole thing a warmth and vivacious humor—compared with which the later "gray in gray" makes a damned unpleasant contrast.[55]

What Marx has to say about *The Condition of the Working Class* and about Engels is true enough. But he says something about himself as well, something that certain admirers of the eleventh thesis on Feuerbach (itself a kind of riddle) have not cared to emphasize, any more than they have lined up to quote this passage.[56] For in it Marx is referring to his and Engels' old master, and to one of that mighty thinker's grim and powerful

---

[55] *Werke*, XXX, 343.
[56] The thesis in question reads: "The philosophers have only *interpreted* the world, in various ways; the point, however, is to *change* it."

passages. It comes at the end of the Preface to the *Philosophy of Right.*

One more word about giving instruction as to what the world ought to be. Philosophy in any case always comes on the scene too late to give it. As the thought of the world it appears only when actuality is already there cut and dried after its process of formation has been complete. . . . When philosophy paints its gray in gray, then has a shape of life grown old. By philosophy's gray in gray it cannot be rejuvenated but only understood. The owl of Minerva spreads its wings only with the falling of dusk.[57]

The author of the eleventh thesis on Feuerbach is applying the profound weight of those reflections to himself and to Engels, and to the accumulated, accumulating exertions of their joint life's work. It says something about the complexity and integrity of mind of both men at their best that they never could and never would wholly repudiate this great teacher of theirs, or the tradition that came down to them from him, even as they broke with that tradition and modified its nature and its history. *The Condition of the Working Class in England* is part of that tradition and that history as well.

[57] Hegel's *Philosophy of Right*, pp. 12–13.

In Place of a Conclusion

THE INVENTION OF FRIEDRICH ENGELS

On that first visit he paid to Manchester in November 1838, Charles Dickens was invited to dinner by Gilbert Winter, a Manchester solicitor. Among the other guests were two local manufacturers, the brothers William and Daniel Grant. Dickens was evidently so impressed by the pair that shortly thereafter they made their appearance as the Cheeryble brothers in *Nicholas Nickleby*, which had begun publication in April of that year.[1]

The Grant family had migrated south from Scotland in 1783, and had settled at Ramsbottom, about twelve miles north of Manchester, and four miles from Bury, where in 1770 Sir Robert Peel had begun his famous works. When they arrived in 1783, Peel and Yates were just beginning to build their printworks at Ramsbottom. Father and sons went to work at once, in a variety of capacities; Daniel, in fact, started for himself a notable career as an "outrider," or commercial traveler, one of the earliest of his kind. Imperfectly educated though they were, hard work and frugality paid off: the brothers prospered; in 1800 they went into partnership in calico printing in Manchester, and in 1806 they bought Sir Robert Peel's printworks at Ramsbottom. Their warehouse in Cannon Street, Manchester, soon became well known as a center of widely extending commercial dealings, and

[1] *The Letters of Charles Dickens*, ed. M. House and G. Storey, I, 471.

they were known to have "extensive foreign operations" and an extensive connection among foreign merchants and manufacturers. Their benevolent activities and projects were equally celebrated, and what appears to have struck Dickens about them was their combination of quaintness and goodness with wealth or commercial success.[2]

What Dickens does with them in *Nicholas Nickleby* is something else again. In the first place, he takes them to London. His purpose in this tactic is only in part explained by his need for compactness and unity in the novel's scene of action—considerable parts of it are, after all, set in Yorkshire and Portsmouth, without damaging results. His major purpose, in my judgment, is to get them out of Manchester. He sets them down in the City, makes over their warehouse and counting-house into a domestic economy and represents them as directing a kind of Communitarian miniverse in which doing business and doing good have become identical behaviors. The account-books and methods of bookkeeping are humanized, domesticated, animated; their older style of conducting business is connected with their old-fashioned quaintness of dress and manner. Their habit of living in the same building from which they direct their business operations is equally anachronistic; for them economic realities have not yet been segregated from human relations. It is almost as if Dickens had been doing homework in Max Weber on economy and society, and is an admirable bit of maneuvering and special pleading on his part.

Yet what do the Cheerybles do—apart from dispensing benefits—in their warehouse-in-the-square? Dickens tells us (or has Nicholas "suppose," so crablike is he in coming up to the question) that they are "German merchants." (ch. 35) The word or term does not appear in the OED, but there can be little doubt that it was in open, if limited circulation or Dickens would not

[2] W. Hume Elliot, *The Country and Church of the Cheeryble Brothers* (Selkirk, 1893); *The Story of the "Cheeryble" Grants* (Manchester, 1906).

have used it.[3] What it does, however, is to allow Dickens to treat
the Cheerybles as if they were in the import-export business, or
some sort of carrying trade in which they did nothing more to the
goods they dealt in than transport them from one place to
another, and their workingmen might be a tribe of dockside
Tony Wellers. And so he does treat them, until he happens to
introduce Fred Engels. He appears, of course, in the form of
Frank Cheeryble, nephew to the brothers, and double of that
youthful straw man and hero, Nicholas, who drops down out of
the sky in order to provide a husband for Kate Nickleby. Frank
does not put in his appearance until Chapter 43, and so Dickens
has to offer some account of how he has been recently passing the
time. And he does. Frank has been away for the last four and a
half years, and has now returned to London "to take a share in
the business here." For the first four of those years, he has been
"superintending it [the business] in Germany"; and "during the
last six months he ha[s] been engaged in establishing an agency in
the north of England." It is still logically possible, to be sure, that
these are purely commercial offices, but the web of connection is
being woven fairly tightly. Yet the cloth that was woven served
for Dickens as a camouflage netting, for only a few chapters later
he was able to write the following passage about the gipsy
children at Hampton race-course.

Even the sunburnt faces of gipsy children, halfnaked though they be,
suggest a drop of comfort. It is a pleasant thing to see that the sun has
been there; to know that the air and light are on them every day; to feel
that they *are* children, and lead children's lives; that if their pillows be
damp, it is with the dews of Heaven, and not with tears; that the limbs
of their girls are free, and that they are not crippled by distortions,
imposing an unnatural and horrible penance upon their sex; that their
lives are spent, from day to day, at least among the waving trees, and not

---

[3] He does the same with the word *gonif*, transcribing it as "gonoph" and putting it quite
appropriately in the mouth of the police constable who has collared Jo. *Bleak House*, ch. 19.
The OED lists this as the earliest appearance of the word in English print.

in the midst of dreadful engines which make young children old before
they know what childhood is, and give them the exhaustion and
infirmity of age, without, like age, the privilege to die. (ch. 50)

Confronted with this, the reader is entitled to ask: what business
is it that the Cheeryble-Grants are in?

What we have in Frank Cheeryble is a disinfected preview
(with reverse English on it) of the career of the young Friedrich
Engels. Dickens knew enough about the German-derived and
-directed commercial community in Manchester to grasp in
passing at the representative significance of such a figure. But the
point of this note is not to introduce one more tedious discussion
of how art anticipates nature. Dickens could imaginatively invent
or re-create the outward shape of such a life, but it is also true that
he could not imagine an Engels himself. Dickens had no way of
understanding the inner or mental life of someone like Engels.
Cultural differences impose their intractable limitations, to be
sure; but the limitations in question here are those of the
imagination. It is impossible, in my judgment, to conceive of
anyone imagining Engels, or for that matter Marx. They could
only have been created by reality, human, social, historical, a kind
of creating, when all is said and done, that is distinct from the
creating that is known as art, although it includes that creating
within itself.

THE TEXT AND THE MAN AGAIN

The historical reclamation of a piece of writing entails in one
sense or another the modernizing of it. In connection with *The
Condition of the Working Class in England* this project becomes
more than usually challenging because so many of the circumstances discussed in it—problems of the modern city, of industrial
work, of poverty, of alienation and attempts in consciousness and
action to overcome it—remain themselves the currency of

contemporary discussion. As I have said earlier, it is difficult to realize—and more difficult to demonstrate convincingly—that these subjects were ever new, that Engels and Marx, more than any of their contemporaries, were making many of the terms of the discussion up as they went along. This difficulty is compounded still further by two tendencies current today, both of them antihistorical. The first is ahistorical as well as antihistorical and consists in assertions about the absolutely unprecedented character, the uniqueness, the incomparability of what is happening in the present era (meaning usually the last five years) to anything that ever happened before. This historical amnesia is commonly accompanied by technocratic views and proposes technological "solutions" for the problems of our society, the globe and on occasion the cosmos itself—if the cosmos may be said to have a problem. The second is not so illiterate and puts forward its antihistorical point of view in the form of a historical argument. The structure of industrial society has so altered, it argues, that the underlying problems as between Engels' time and the present have themselves been utterly transformed. This is a much more plausible line of attack, and indeed no one in his senses would deny the epic character of social change in the last hundred years. At the same time it seems to me at least arguable to question whether in fact it is the "underlying problems" that have changed. And I suspect as well that there is in this connection a sharp difference in opinion about what the "underlying problems" actually are.

As for Manchester itself, it was the Detroit of the first phase of the Industrial Revolution, and the historical fate that befell a town that was committed overwhelmingly to a single industry is a cautionary tale in itself. The civic history of Manchester in the second half of the nineteenth century, its gradual rehabilitation of itself into a center of other activities besides those of industry and commerce, is a story that has often been told, and told with pride. Its heroic age had gone; but heroic ages of societies are likely to be tragic ages as well, and one need not mourn their passing.

What did not pass, however, are the problems and conflicts that seem organic to the conditions of masses of men living together in an urban-industrial world, under economic, social and cultural circumstances of inadequacy and deprivation. They have not passed with us, and they have not passed in those societies that have gone through revolutions made in the name of the theories put forward by Marx and Engels. And we may assume that the enduring vividness of Engels' work is in part connected with the intractable persistence of such difficulties and injustices.

Engels himself would not, I think, have been dismayed by the fact that such problems persisted—sometimes unremedied, sometimes in aggravated form—in societies that had undergone a "socialist" revolution. (Let us leave to one side the question of the degree to which the doctrines of Marx and Engels have been perverted in such societies.) The impulses that most saliently informed and organized his consciousness were revolutionary and not tragic in character. To him, in his situation, and in the social situation of his time as he conceived it, it was morally impossible not to support revolution. At the same time he was impervious to the tragic consciousness that it might in fact be impossible, for both material and psychological reasons, simultaneously to achieve through revolution the regeneration that would—alone, perhaps—justify it. Almost a century later, another of the leading insurrectionary figures of history addressed himself to this subject. Toward the end of his life Trotsky remarked that the abundance of tragic experience that had fallen to his lot "has not only not destroyed my faith in the clear, bright future of mankind, but, on the contrary, has given it an indestructible temper." And he went on to speak of "the revolutionary optimism which constitutes the fundamental element of my life." [4] This optimism is neither sappy nor sentimental, as the lives and writings of such figures as Engels or Trotsky amply demonstrate. It is certainly not a species

---

[4] *The Case of Leon Trotsky: Report of Hearing on the Charges Made Against Him in the Moscow Trials* (New York, 1937), pp. 584–585.

of intellectual software, as was the radical chic of the recent and unlamented past few years. This is not to judge it as a correct or even a justified attitude. What such an optimism does suggest, however, is a kind of constitutional fitting or integration of what is experienced as inner and outer realities, between the desires, judgments and commitments of the self and what one senses to be the larger movements of history. At the same time, I find it difficult to imagine any society in which Engels would not have impenitently taken up a critical attitude that was radical and revolutionary. For a revolutionary critic may be defined as someone whose project in life is to dramatize the extent to which society does not fulfill its ideals, who demands that the discrepancy between ideals and reality be abolished, and who develops a theory that both accounts for that discrepancy—for how it came about—and as a result sets a direction for possible change. This is to be sure not the only way of defining or describing such a person, and perhaps it may be useful to bring this account to a close by introducing a radically divergent perspective. We find such a view in Engels' great contemporary, Tocqueville. In discussing the social cataclysm of the French Revolution, Tocqueville remarks that as a result of the violent and wholesale dissolution of the essential institutions of religion and government, the minds of men were thrown into a state of profound confusion—they no longer knew what to hold on to or where to stop. As a concomitant of such extreme circumstances, men of a new kind began to appear.

Revolutionaries of a hitherto unknown breed came on the scene: men who carried audacity to the point of sheer insanity; who balked at no innovation and, unchecked by any scruples, acted with an unprecedented ruthlessness. Nor were these strange beings mere ephemera, born of a brief crisis and destined to pass away when it ended. They were, rather, the first of a new race of men who subsequently made good and proliferated in all parts of the civilized world, everywhere retaining the same characteristics. They were already here when we were born, and they are still with us.[5]

In this book I have tried to present a more friendly, modulated and inward account of the making—of the early life and work—of one of the most prominent of these new men. However much one may differ from Tocqueville's general estimation, and however much one may prefer him when he speaks in a more moderate tone, there is at least one sense in which he compels the modern reader's assent. Engels and what he represents are still with us; he is in significant measure our contemporary, as he was Tocqueville's. I have tried to demonstrate here how he was also in a number of fundamental ways a representative Victorian. That he could be both should come as no surprise.

[5] Alexis de Tocqueville, *The Old Régime and the French Revolution*, trans. Stuart Gilbert (Garden City, 1955), p. 157.

Bibliographical Note

It would be both impractical and presumptuous to attempt to add a formal or systematic bibliography to this study. Any effort in this direction would quickly become prohibitive in length; yet however long it might become, it would still fall short of comprehensiveness. Much of the bibliographical material used in this work is to be found in the footnotes, and in the specific works referred to in them, many of which contain extensive bibliographical listings, notes and discussions. There is no point in repeating them here. What this Note will attempt to do, therefore, is to direct the reader to a number of the more general bibliographical sources that are pertinent to the topics discussed in this study.

For Marx and Engels, see Maximilien Rubel, *Bibliographie des Oeuvres de Karl Marx: Avec en Appendice un Repertoire des Oeuvres de Friedrich Engels* (Paris, 1956). To this nearly three-hundred-page listing, a *"Supplément"* of more than seventy-five further pages was published in 1960. An extensive German guide is to be found in Manfred Kleim et al., *Marx, Engels—Verzeichnis: Werke, Schriften, Artikel* (Berlin, 1968). John Lachs, *Marxist Philosophy: A Bibliographical Guide* (Chapel Hill, 1967) is also useful.

The long section of Notes appended to George Lichtheim's *The Origins of Socialism* (New York, 1969) is not to be overlooked. The select bibliography in G. D. H. Cole, *History of Socialist Thought* (London, 1955–1960), 5 vols., is wide-ranging.

Out of the immense mass of bibliographical material concerning the social and economic history of Victorian Britain, two works may be singled out. Josef L. Altholz, *Victorian England, 1837–1901* (Cambridge, 1970) is an excellent, general, one-hundred-page list covering a large variety of subjects. See also, H. J. Habakkuk and M. Postan, eds., *Cambridge Economic History of Europe, Vol. VI: The Industrial Revolutions and After: Incomes, Population and Technological Change* (Cambridge, 1965). Part 2 of this volume consists of a comprehensive bibliography of all six volumes. In particular, see the bibliography for chapter 5 of volume VI.

The study of urban history has recently attained formidable bibliographical proportions. The *Urban History Newsletter* (Leicester, 1963ff.) contains an annually updated bibliography of books and periodicals on urban history in England. H. J. Dyos, ed., *The Study of Urban History* (London, 1968) includes an excellent bibliographical essay by the editor. Gideon Golany, *History of Human Settlement from the Early Ages to the End of the 19th Century* (Monticello, Ill., 1969) will be found generally useful. There is, as far as I have been able to gather, no single bibliography on Manchester itself; but some use may be made of the list included in W. H. Thomson, *History of Manchester to 1852* (Altrincham, 1967).

The bibliographies that cover various parts of Victorian literature and culture are far too numerous in themselves to be canvassed here. A general guide and source of information is to be found in Lionel Madden, *How to Find Out About the Victorian Period* (Oxford, 1970). T. H. Howard-Hill, *Bibliography of British Literary Bibliographies* (Oxford, 1969) extensively covers part of the ground and is intended to be the first part of a three-volume *Index of British Bibliography*. George Watson, ed., *New Cambridge Bibliography of English Literature,* vol. III [1800–1900] (Cambridge, 1969), revises vol. III of F. W. Bateson, ed., *Cambridge Bibliography of English Literature* (Cambridge, 1940), 4 vols. Among the many specialized listings one may note Lionel Stevenson, ed., *Victorian Fiction: A Guide to Research* (Cambridge, Mass., 1964). The annual "Victorian Bibliography" published since 1957 in *Victorian Studies* should also be noticed. All the bibliographies listed here contain further bibliographical soundings and send the reader out in a large number of directions—toward Victorian periodicals, journalism, popular culture, education and so on. The study of Victorian bibliography is in point of fact something of a discipline in itself.

Index

Wadsworth, A. P., 76
Wales, annual death rate, 206
Walker, Thomas, 12
Wallas, Graham, 235
Watt, James, 9, 95
Wealth of Nations, The (Smith), 200
Webb, R. K., 217
Weber, Max, ix, 68, 79, 159-61, 202, 230
Week on the Concord and Merrimack Rivers, A (Thoreau), 58
Weerth, Georg, 98
welfare system, beginning of, 16-17
Wellek, René, 102
Wellington, Duke of, 97
Wells, H. G., 67
Werke, xii, 46, 74, 75, 76, 79, 89, 90, 95, 97, 101, 111, 112, 113, 121, 145, 157, 186
White, David M., 215
Williams, David, 203
Wills, W. H., 41
Winckelmann, Johannes, 161
Wirtschaft und Gesellschaft (ed. Winckelmann), 161
Wischnewetzky, Florence Kelley, x-xii, 169
Wittich, Claus, 161
Wolff, Kurt H., 155
Wordsworth, William, 147-48, 152, 237
workhouses, 16
working class, the, 98-100, 131-248; absence of medical attention, 206; American, contraceptive practices, 210; Chartist movement, 19, 20-27; crime and criminals, 220-24; death rate, 206-7; deterioration of family life, 211; difference between identification with "the poor" and, 99-100; distance and polarization between middle class and, 143; distribution of sexual roles, 211-12; drunkenness, 208-10; dwellings and living conditions, 179-92, 194-98; emotional insecurity of, 202-3; future leisure activities and, 214-15; ghettoization of, 177-78; groupings of, 143; health conditions, 205-8, 240; historical beginning (eighteenth century), 142; *Lebensstellung*, 203; loss of religious faith among, 203-4; Manchester population (mid-1830's), 5; middle class exploitation of, 225, 226; miners, 240-44; preindustrial rural, 134-36, 137, 232; promiscuous sexuality, 210-11; radicalism, 14-15; religion and, 203-4, 220; sanitary conditions, 183-85, 191, 194; struggle for existence, 201; suicide rate, 210; types of cottages, 194; *Vertierenden* condition of, 226, work and, 212-16
"Working Day, The" (Marx), 214
Wright, Thomas, 209
Writings on the Paris Commune (Marx and Engels), 97
Writings of the Young Marx on Philosophy and Society (eds. Easton and Guddat), 111

Young, G. M., 109, 188
Young Germany (literary-democratic movement), 76
Young Hegelians, 80, 81, 86
Young Hegelians and Karl Marx, The (McLellan), 233

ABOUT THE AUTHOR

STEVEN MARCUS is Director of Planning for a National Humanities Center and professor of English and comparative literature at Columbia University. Among his numerous writings are *Dickens: From Pickwick to Dombey* (1965), and *The Other Victorians* (1966). He has also edited *The World of Fiction* (1967) and, with Lionel Trilling, Ernest Jones' *Life and Work of Sigmund Freud*. He is Associate Editor of *Partisan Review*.

From The College Department

RANDOM HOUSE/ALFRED·A·KNOPF, INC.

141 5187520 8885237

033175

138-01 1 V406 ENGELS MANCHESTER & 71406 2.95

FREE NO CHARGE

Please direct your
comments or requests
for additional
information to:

▶ PHILIP METCALF
243 CHESWOLD LANE
HAVERFORD, PA. 19041